CABIN FEVER

CABIN FEVER

THE SIZZLING SECRETS OF A
VIRGIN AIR HOSTESS

MANDY SMITH
WITH NICOLA STOW

This edition published in 2014 by:

Thistle Publishing
36 Great Smith Street
London
SW1P 3BU

www.thistlepublishing.co.uk

ISBN-13: 9781910198148

To my darling husband, Glenn,
you truly are my happy ending

Contents

CAN ANYBODY FLY A PLANE?

I t's not often the captain of a Boston-bound 747-400 collapses two hours before landing, but when he does, it causes one hell of a problem, especially when you're trying to serve afternoon tea to the tipsy Gin and Tonic Brigade in Premium Economy and maintain a pristine "nothing fazes me" cabin crew smile. He went down just outside the flight deck door – in full view of passengers sitting in the first few rows – clutching his chest, eyes rolling, bald head glazed with sweat as he crumpled to his knees then smashed facedown onto the floor.

Within seconds the cabin erupted into chaos, sparked by a half-cut woman in her thirties sporting cherry-red dyed hair, who started screaming, "Oh my God, the pilot's dead," before hyperventilating and waking up the man next to her, who'd managed to nod off after enduring almost six hours of her repetitive, drunken chat about her fear of flying and a "bastard" ex-boyfriend called Wayne.

She'd been necking red wine from the moment the seatbelt signs had gone out. I'd lost count of the number of times she'd come up to the galley asking for "just one more Merlot to settle my nerves" through magenta-stained lips and teeth. You always get one like her – citing nerves as a convenient excuse to get steamed with the free booze on board. The last glass she'd asked for was "to help with the landing", which was shortly about to happen ... with or without the captain, who it would appear had just had a heart attack in front of her.

Gasps and shrieks filled the cabin. People were clambering over seats and clogging the aisle, trying to have a good look at the captain, everybody talking over one another in panicked tones, some of them trying to help by suggesting various first-aid procedures that might work miracles and help the poorly pilot back to his feet. There were two of us working on the upper deck – me and my friend Felicity – and we swung into action at breakneck speed, flashing our bright-red MAC Ruby Woo smiles while assuring passengers, "Everything's fine."

On electronic route maps embedded in the backs of 452 passenger seats, blinking red dots edged closer to Boston. Time was of the essence. Felicity was closest to the flight deck, so she rushed to the captain's aid while I calmly, but rapidly, wheeled the trolley loaded with sandwiches, scones and rattling pots of tea and coffee back to the galley – a manoeuvre that got some passengers' backs up. "Hey, why are you taking the trolley away?" asked one bloke, who had so many miniatures lined up on his fold-down tray, it looked as though he was running a mini off-licence from his seat. "I'll have another G & T, please, love."

"I'm sorry, sir," I said, "The bar is now closed. If you wouldn't mind waiting a moment ... ?"

Premium Economy is renowned for its challenging passengers – people who can't quite afford Upper Class but feel they can click their fingers and demand the world, simply because they've paid a few hundred quid more than an Economy passenger for a little extra leg room and a slightly bigger seat. That's why we nicknamed them the Gin and Tonic Brigade: they believe they deserve as many freebies as they can get their hands on, which most often results in them drinking the complimentary bar service dry.

A gradual dragging sensation indicated that our descent had begun. A patch of turbulence was causing a bit of a bump and a bang, setting the woman with the cherry-red hair off on another breakdown. As Felicity attempted to revive our captain, I stowed the cart in the galley and used the intercom to make an emergency public address, using our special coded message. This signalled to the crew not present on the upper deck that we needed immediate assistance, including our defibrillator unit and emergency medical kits.

Seconds later our flight service manager, Jane, called on my intercom. "Defib is on its way to the upper deck," she said. "Is there anything else you need?"

"The pilot has collapsed," I said calmly. "Do we have anyone on board who can fly a plane?"

Not that we were about to start running *Airplane*-style up and down the aisles begging passengers to jump into the captain's chair, but we did have a list of off-duty crew on board whom we could surreptitiously approach in the hope that one of them might be a pilot. If not, the air hostesses would need to rely on their pilot-incapacitation training and step in to help with the checklists. Technically, the first officer could land the plane on autopilot, on his own. The danger was, however, if he ran into difficulty on approach, he would need another pair of hands at the controls in order to switch to manual operation.

I left the search for back-up to the guys downstairs, because at that moment my assistance was needed on the upper deck. Our captain was now shielded by a curtain so I had no idea how he was doing or how the first officer was coping without him. I straightened my neck scarf and strode confidently, with a slight bum wiggle, back up the aisle. I was fully aware that every single person in the cabin was scrutinising my demeanour with anxious eyes, making sure I was not wearing an expression that screamed, "We're going to crash." We know the score: watch the air hostesses, and if we're not panicking you know everything is okay. That's why we look so bloody cheerful all the time. Anyone who thinks being an air hostess is all about serving tea and coffee and looking pretty is kidding themselves. It takes stamina, patience, commitment ... and a whole load of acting talent.

As I was nearing the end of my aisle strut to assess my passengers' reactions, two of our more burly stewards came bounding up the staircase and slipped behind the curtain. At the same time, a sweet elderly woman sitting in one of the aisle seats reached up and lightly tapped my arm. "Excuse me, dear," she said. "How is that poor captain? Will he be okay? Is there anything we can do to help?"

I crouched down to speak to her. She smelled of Murray mints and Palmolive soap and was wearing powder-blue stretchy trousers teamed with a floral top – a typical "Nan abroad" outfit. Her eyes were rheumy and sincere. Thankfully, they're not all arrogant divas in Premium. Stored in the chair pouch in front of her, next to the laminated 747-400 safety instruction card and token sick bag, was a clear duty-free bag containing a cuddly toy and a giant bar of Toblerone. She was sitting inside an aluminium tube, hurtling towards New England. The plane was descending more rapidly now, bouncing through rainclouds. Very soon the seatbelt sign would illuminate, followed by the double ding bell instructing crew to prepare the cabin for landing. Downstairs, our colleagues were discreetly being asked, "Do you know how to fly a plane?"

I placed my hand on the woman's floral shoulder and said, "I'm sure he'll be fine. This kind of thing happens all the time – he probably got out of his seat too quickly. He'll just need a little break ... a cup of tea, maybe a little oxygen." I pointed at the teddy. "He's cute," I said, in an attempt to distract her from the ongoing crisis. "Who's that for?"

A proud smile lit up her face, instantly knocking a good ten years off her. "It's for my grandson," she said. "I'm going to see him for the first time. My son lives in Boston – he's got ever such a good job – very high up."

"Oh, how lovely," I said. "Now, you relax and enjoy the rest of your flight. I'm going to see the captain, so I'll tell him you were asking after him." *Christ, little does she know what we're dealing with here,* I thought, as I strode towards the flight deck. On a positive note, I noticed that the "nervous wreck" lush had slipped into an alcohol-induced slumber.

In the time it had taken me to park the trolley, make the call to Jane and calm the passengers, Felicity and the two stewards had managed to move the captain to the crew rest area within the flight deck. Felicity emerged from the flight deck just as I arrived at the recess.

"How is he?" I asked.

"Not good, Mandy," she said, closing the curtain behind us. "We've strapped him into one of the bunk beds, attached him to the defibrillator and given him oxygen. The cabin service supervisor is monitoring him now. He's drifting in and out of consciousness. I think he's had a bloody heart attack."

"Have you spoken to the first officer?"

"Yeah, he's fine. He's going to land on autopilot and he can use one of us to do his checklist with. I hope it's not me. Fingers crossed there won't be any complications. There's nothing else he can do really. He hasn't got a choice."

I gave Felicity a reassuring hug. "Jane's going through the crew list as we speak to see if we have any pilots on board," I said. And then the curtain swished behind us and our problem was solved. It was a junior crew member from Economy, dressed in his uniform tabard, head held high as he announced: "Hi, I'm Ben. I've come to help land this plane." It transpired that young Ben held a private pilot licence. And although he didn't have nearly enough flying hours under his belt to officially land a big jet, his knowledge was sufficient for him to assist the first officer better than we could.

"What took you so long?" joked Felicity, playfully slapping Ben's bum as he made for the flight deck door. Felicity was Miss Popularity of the airline. She had everything: looks, personality, a Jessica Rabbit figure and, above all, she was an outrageous flirt – far worse than me, and that's saying something.

"I'll tell you later, over a beer," said Ben, flashing Felicity a cheeky wink before disappearing into the cockpit.

With touchdown fast approaching, Felicity relayed the good news to our passengers. She kept the PA brief and light, explaining that the captain was "resting" but another pilot among our crew had taken over from him. It did the trick; her breezy announcement was greeted by a rousing cheer from the cabin. Even the wine monster, who had stirred from her booze coma, managed a half-smile. The double ding rang, the seatbelt signs were illuminated, tray tables were stowed and seats returned to their upward positions. And so began our final descent into Boston Logan International.

It wasn't the smoothest of landings; a powerful headwind made for a lumpy drop onto the tarmac. But we'd made it. As we taxied to the stand the weary travellers again cheered and clapped, clearly relieved to be back on terra firma. Their gratitude didn't last for long, though. Minutes later, many of them appeared to have forgotten about the mid-air drama as they leaped out of their seats and began the usual pushing and shoving to reach the overhead lockers, all desperate to exit the plane, even though the doors were still firmly locked. Some even had the audacity to moan and groan when told they wouldn't be going anywhere until medics had boarded the aircraft to tend to the captain.

"But I'm claustrophobic," slurred the lush as her fake Hermès tumbled from her lap, its contents – including a half-eaten, manky Pret A Manger sandwich, mini vibrator and a bottle of Coleen McLoughlin perfume – spilling onto the floor.

We helped the passengers off the plane as swiftly as possible, but Felicity and I remained on board for the best part of an hour, while paramedics stabilised the captain before carrying him off on a stretcher. We later found out he'd suffered a mild heart attack.

With the captain taken care of and a new pilot on his way for tomorrow's flight, it was time to relax. For the Virgin Atlantic cabin crew a trip to Boston beckoned, and I had a strong inkling it would be a messy one.

"Jeez," said Felicity, as we fell into our seats on the crew bus, "that was some flight."

"Tell me about it," I said. "Always a drama, eh."

"Here," said Felicity, delving into her flight bag and producing two vodka miniatures (courtesy of the lovely Sir Richard Branson), "Get this down your neck."

"Don't mind if I do," I giggled, grabbing one of the bottles. "Bottoms up."

There's nothing like a good stiff drink after a hard day at the office.

CHAPTER ONE

HELLO, DOLLY

When I cast my mind back to one summer night in 1999 – the night my then boyfriend, Neil, consumed with jealousy, booze and cocaine, beat me black and blue and left me lying in a bloody heap in a dingy stairwell – I think, *God, he did me a favour.*

Not that I enjoyed being battered: it was terrifying and humiliating. Nor do I condone domestic abuse, but it was the wake-up call I needed to turn my life around. Bizarrely, Neil knocking ten bells out of me was one of the main reasons I decided to fulfil my childhood dream of becoming an international "trolley dolly".

Back then, I wasn't the confident, take-no-prisoners Mandy I am today. I was naive, vulnerable and a hopeful romantic, with the heart on my sleeve throbbing for all to see. At the time I was working as a planning support officer in Virgin's engineering department in Crawley, West Sussex. I'd moved to the Horsham district not long after my parents, James and Sue, had relocated there from Hartlepool – where I was born and bred – for work. I'd recently graduated from the Hartlepool College of Further Education with a diploma in computer science, but there was little work available in the north-east and I wasn't sure what I wanted to do career-wise. I had no ties, so, on a whim, I accepted a six-month contract at Virgin, which is where I met Neil.

Neil was a charmer at first – the flirtatious IT consultant who found every excuse under the sun to fiddle with my computer. Tall and wiry, with Aegean-blue eyes, he had a chivalrous Milk Tray–man nature that I instantly warmed to. After several failed relationships, I thought Neil, with his gallant gestures, flowers and compliments, was a great catch. How could I not be beguiled by this seemingly decent, loving man? We dated for about five months. He was a sexual firecracker, and I swear my orgasmic yelps could be heard all over Crawley. Then, within the last few weeks of our relationship, he turned into a psychopath. The change in his demeanour was as though an ugly monster had taken over his soul; it was frightening. He became aggressive, possessive, accusatory, snapping at the tiniest thing, convinced that every other man fancied me. And I began to think I had a genetic defect, as if a warped part of my DNA had programmed me to reject all the good guys and let only the bad ones in. I actually thought I was to blame.

Neil's final outburst on that sweaty June night came after we left a Jamiroquai gig at the Brighton Centre ... and moments after I ended our relationship. I'd been looking forward to the concert for months, being a huge Jay Kay fan, but Neil vanished to buy drugs at the start of the gig, leaving me alone in the jostling throng of perspiring revellers. He reappeared near the end – halfway through "Virtual Insanity" – eyes black and vacuous, chewing his bottom lip and snaking his gangly arms around my waist. I tried to shrug him off, but there was no room for manoeuvring in the crowd, which was sweeping us from left to right, forwards and backwards. He was clinging onto me like a stranded swimmer to a buoy.

"Where the hell have you been?" I demanded, but my words were drowned by the throbbing music.

I confronted him again as we left the Brighton Centre and made our way to the NCP car park to meet Neil's mate, Darren, who was due to give us a lift home. Neil was clearly off his face, staggering and snarling at passers-by. He tried to force his hand into the back pocket of my jeans, and I flinched.

His voice was sour, cold. "What's the matter with you?"

I stopped walking. Neil carried on, muttering, "For fuck's sake," under his breath.

"I'll tell you exactly what the matter is, Neil."

He spun round, face tight with chemical rage, gnarly veins pulsating at his temples. I thought his shaven head was about to explode all over the pavement.

"Why did you bugger off and leave me? Are you that desperate for Charlie that you can't even stay and enjoy a concert with me?"

"I got lost going to the toilet. No big deal."

"What, for two-and-a-half hours? Face it, Neil, you don't want to spend any time with me lately unless it's in the bedroom." Neil's excuse was pathetic, laughable. I knew his routine; it wasn't the first time he'd done a disappearing act on me to feed his habit.

He rammed his fist into a nearby ornamental lamp post, shouting, "Fuck, fuck, fuck."

"It's over, Neil," I said. "I don't think we should see each other anymore. I can't handle your temper." Then I continued walking, my shadow bouncing before me on the pavement, tailed by Neil hollering obscenities. He followed me along Kings Road by the seafront, onto West Street and all the way down Russell Road and into the multi-storey car park where we'd arranged to meet Darren by his car on the third floor.

"What do you mean, 'It's over'?" said Neil, kicking the door open behind me. I ignored him and powered up the stairs, Neil's deranged yells echoing throughout the desolate building, scary and hollow. "Come back here, you bitch. I mean it, Mandy ..."

I continued climbing, taking two steps at a time, intermittently grasping the grimy handrail, heart banging. Neil was now bounding up the stairs, his heavy thuds chasing the staccato snaps and scrapes of my heels on the concrete until he was inches behind me. He grabbed the back of my leg. I clung to the handrail but my hand was so clammy I lost my grip.

It happened in a split second. Clamping my calf with both hands, Neil yanked my leg upwards then downwards with such force that I slammed face-down onto the steps. He dragged me all the way down the staircase, my face and body grazing against the concrete with every agonising bump. I screamed as loud as I could, but he wouldn't stop. At the bottom of the stairs, before I even had a chance to defend myself, he was on top of me, one hand clenched around my throat, the other balled into a fist, raining blows on my upper body. I was fighting for breath. My lungs felt as though they were being punctured, my head grinding into the grimy floor like a giant pestle against stone. Nothing felt or looked real. Beyond Neil's thrashing form, the door to the stairwell blurred in and out of focus, and a little voice in my head was chanting silent prayers: "Somebody, please save me."

I don't know what made Neil finally decide to end his attack. Maybe it was a sudden realisation that he actually might kill me if he continued. He released his grip. I gasped for air, tears streaming down my face. Neil knelt beside me, breathing hard through clenched teeth, wiping trickles of saliva from the corners of his mouth. Then he disappeared up the stairs and I was all alone, foetal on the floor in my jeans and Jamiroquai T-shirt, body rheumatic with pain, windpipe crushed.

A young couple found me and very kindly drove me to the nearest police station, where a sympathetic woman police constable with an agony aunt smile sat me down with a polystyrene cup of sweet tea and told me how she too had just come out of a violent relationship. "None of this is your fault. You do realise that, don't you?" she said.

I nodded, long locks of tangled brunette hair tumbling around my face, heavy with the scent of the car park stairwell: a dirty, antiseptic mix of stale urine, rubbish bins and Dettol.

After I'd given my statement – and agreed to press charges against Neil – the police officer asked me if there was anyone I could call to pick me up. "A relative, perhaps?"

It was gone two in the morning. I had no money. I'd paid for the concert tickets, and Neil had promised to settle up with me later in the evening. I should've known I'd never see the cash. I lived with my parents, so I had no flatmate to call upon. "I guess I'll have to call me dad," I said.

We drove home in silence. Dad was heartbroken. Even though I was twenty-five, I was still his little princess. We pulled up in the driveway. The house was in darkness. The engine hushed.

"Mam must be asleep," I said.

Dad cupped his hands over his face and dropped them to his lap with a groan. "I'll kill him, I'll kill him, Mandy ... I keep telling you: you're too soft. Tell me where he lives."

Once again I was crying. I couldn't think of anything else to say other than: "I'm sorry, Dad."

He turned to look at me, his huge brown eyes filled with pain. "Come here, pet," he said, pulling me towards him. I sobbed into his chest as he wrapped his comforting arms tightly around me, kissing the top of my refuse-stinking head.

"Don't cry, pet. I just can't bear the thought of anyone hurting you, that's all. We love you so much. There are good men out there, Mandy, men who will treat you well, how you deserve to be treated."

It broke my heart. "I love you, Dad," I choked.

He squeezed me tighter. "Me too, pet, me too."

I went to work as normal the next day. Despite the heat, I wore a polo-neck jumper to hide Neil's red handprint on my throat and plastered on the slap to conceal my black eye, busted lip, scrapes and grazes. Fortunately, there was no sign of Neil at the office. *Not so bloody tough now,* I thought.

That afternoon, as I stood at the photocopier, staring blankly at the jellyfish-shaped coffee stain on the wall, my mind flashed back to the previous night. What was I thinking? How on earth did I end up with somebody like Neil? And surely there had to be more to life than gawping at these dribbled tentacles. I was so lost in thought I wasn't even aware I had company.

"Hey Mands, how's it going?"

I spun round sharply, my nerves still shot. It was Jonathan, a design engineer who had just landed a job as a Virgin Atlantic steward – a career move he hoped would help him pursue his dream of becoming a pilot. He was tall, of Nordic descent with looks to match: blue eyes, soft and wavy blond hair, sparkling white teeth and the biggest feet I'd ever seen.

"Oh, Jonathan ... you made me jump."

"Sorry, Mands." He paused for a moment to observe my wounds. "Ouch, what happened to your face?" Jonathan was probably the nicest person in the office: caring, generous and so sincere – the kind of fella you could take home to your parents.

I looked at the floor, embarrassed. I was a walking advert for a campaign against domestic violence. I could hear the voice-over in my head: "Don't Suffer in Silence," accompanied by images of my mashed-up face. "It's nothing," I lied, turning my eyes back to the jellyfish.

Jonathan rested his hand on my shoulder. "C'mon, Mands, speak to me. I might be able to help."

I glanced up at his face, noticing how incredibly handsome he was. I'd never really looked at Jonathan this way before.

"I mean it, Mands, I'm here for you."

It was just what I needed to hear. The words avalanched from my mouth. And once I'd started, I couldn't stop. I told Jonathan the whole sorry story from start to finish, barely stopping for air.

"I just feel so stupid," I concluded. "And to make matters worse, I can't stay in this job now with him here."

Jonathan shook his head. "What a bastard."

"I can't believe I didn't see it coming."

"You know what?" said Jonathan. "Virgin is hiring stewardesses. You should apply. With your looks they'll snap you up. It'll get you out of this place and the perks are the same as here – plus free travel every week with your job, and lots of partying in five-star locations ... you'll have a blast."

"I might have to have some facial reconstruction first," I joked, retrieving my stack of papers from the tray. Secretly, however, I thought it was a great idea. I'd always wanted to be an air hostess, but Dad had done his utmost over the years to discourage me. "You don't want to be a trolley dolly, Mandy," he'd say. "Nothing but a glorified waitress in the sky, with men leering at you. You want to get yourself a proper job." I knew Dad was only being protective of me, but I felt like there was a whole world out there to explore and I longed to be set free.

A rose flush washed over Jonathan's dimpled cheeks. "Seriously, Mands, you're stunning. I've got a spare application form. You should go for it."

So I did – I actually went for it. Not that it took much more persuasion. I had one look at the application form Jonathan delivered to my desk and was immediately seduced by the bold text at the top of the page: "You'll work hard but party even harder." I can do that, I mused. After work, I headed straight home to fill out the form in the privacy of my bedroom, glass of wine in hand. By midnight it was in the post.

Life took a turn for the better over the next few weeks. Neil returned to work and was falling over himself to worm his way back into my life, apologising profusely for his behaviour, sending me notes and flowers and blaming his "little flare-up" on drugs. "I've never hit a woman before in my life, Mandy, honest," he said. As far as I was concerned, he could grovel until the bloody cows came home. My mind was firmly made up: no more bad guys for Mandy Smith. In fact, I'd told myself I'd steer clear of all men for a while. But there was one guy who was proving hard to resist: Jonathan.

It happened quickly, during Jonathan's final days at the office before he started his training course. Since I'd confided in him, he'd become my rock: I felt as though I could tell him anything. There wasn't a single aspect of his personality I disliked. He was the epitome of a gentleman. Attentive, caring and courtly, he made me feel good about myself – and wanted. At first the flirting was quite subtle: lots of accidental-on-purpose hand touching, coincidental yet convenient meetings in the stationery cupboard, a few sexual innuendos here and there. We got on spectacularly, even finishing each other's sentences. The build-up was electrifying. I'd gone right off my food, which allowed me to resurrect a slinky Miss Selfridge pencil skirt I'd bought months ago but never worn. I was wearing that skirt the night Jonathan first kissed me, in a cosy corner of a smoky bar down the Lanes in Brighton, as Tracy Chapman's "Baby Can I Hold You" played on the jukebox and life freeze-framed around us.

Once again I was in a relationship. Only this time, it felt solid, secure. It was impossible not to fall in love with Jonathan. He was adorable. I waited a while before I slept with him ... at least a couple of months. But, believe me, once we started, we couldn't stop. Location was a slight problem; Jonathan also lived with his parents, so our romps were confined to quickies in our bedrooms and contorted sex on the back seat of Jonathan's little silver S-reg Renault, normally with a seatbelt clip ramming my bum or a window winder nudging the back of my head.

Our first comfortable encounter happened in my bedroom while my parents were away on holiday. "I want to make love to you, Mands," Jonathan said, a hint of coyness creeping into his voice.

It was a Friday evening, after a scorcher of a day. Even then, as we lay on the bed by the open window, legs braided, kissing and pawing away at each other, I could feel the heat pouring in, bringing scents of lavender, cut grass and freshly lit barbeques.

I reached down to unzip Jonathan's trousers. *Make love?* That was an expression I hadn't heard in a long while. I wasn't quite sure how to respond. "Me too ... to you, I mean – not to myself."

He laughed. "Take off your dress."

We tore off our clothes and re-conjoined on the bed, skin warm and damp, pulses throbbing.

Jonathan rolled on top of me. "You're beautiful," he said, between urgent kisses.

I grabbed his bum and gave it a playful slap as he was grinding against me. "I want you inside me," I whispered.

Jonathan pulled away, slithered between my legs and sat back on his knees. "Not just yet," he said, parting my legs. He pulled me up onto his knees, pushing my thighs even further apart. "Beautiful," he repeated. "I want to make you come."

I closed my eyes, tilted my hips and revelled in the sensation of Jonathan's fingers, circling, tickling until my legs trembled and I came in ripples. That was most certainly one of Jonathan's finest talents: he was extremely good with his hands.

A proud smile spread across Jonathan's face. He reached over to the bedside table for a condom. "Did you enjoy that?" he said, rolling on the condom.

"God, yeah." I was still recovering.

He stretched out on top of me and eased into me, panting heavily as his strokes gained velocity and vigour. I came again, moaning loudly. Outside I could hear our neighbours' voices, which meant they could probably hear me, but I couldn't stop myself. Then, as the final wave crashed through me, Jonathan joined in, a crescendo of, "Ah, ah, ah," as he came in a series of mini convulsions.

We were so loved-up; I couldn't remember a time when I'd felt so happy. The following morning, after more sex, someone else put a smile on my face: the postman. It was the letter I'd been waiting for – from Virgin Atlantic. The interview letter.

I raced up the stairs squealing, clutching the piece of paper. "I've done it, I've done it – they want to meet me. They actually want to meet me."

I was dancing around the bedroom like a mad woman while Jonathan sat up in bed, laughing. I couldn't think straight for the excitement. *What shall I wear?* I thought, already rummaging in my wardrobe and sending a clothes storm in Jonathan's direction as I tossed various outfits over my shoulder.

"Come here, you gorgeous, funny thing."

I turned around to find Jonathan with a pair of my trousers draped over his head. I made for the bed. "Seriously, though, Jonathan. Do you think I have a chance? What if I mess it up and they don't pick me? This opportunity may never happen again and I'll be stuck in engineering with stalker boy for the rest of my life and ..."

Jonathan grabbed my hand and pulled me onto him. "Of course they'll pick you. They'd be crazy not to."

Bless him, he was so sweet; if I hadn't felt so shagged out I would have gone for round three. "Thanks, Jonathan," I said, curling up beside him.

"For what?"

"For being here for me."

I meant every word. At that moment, I felt like the luckiest girl in the world.

Despite doing my homework on the Virgin recruitment process, and receiving scores of valuable tips from Jonathan and other staff in the know, I still couldn't contain my nerves on the day of my interview. My legs were hollow, my palms were sweaty and I swear the entire cast of *Riverdance* was performing in my stomach. After much humming and hawing over what to wear, I'd settled on a smart black suit with a sensible just-below-the-knee skirt and black court shoes with a moderate heel. I didn't like wearing tights but I made an exception on this occasion, as I'd been warned by one seasoned hostie that Virgin Atlantic didn't like bare legs. My hair was folded up in a sophisticated French pleat, and my lips and nails painted crimson.

The first part of the interview – the group interview – was held in a basic training room at Virgin Atlantic's HR offices in Crawley town centre. I was among a crowd of about twenty girls who, like me, were all desperate to shine that day. Our interviewing panel consisted of three immaculately groomed, beautiful women – one petite and blonde, the other two willowy brunettes – all dressed in the iconic Virgin uniform. They were tough cookies alright.

"Not all of you will be successful today," said the blonde. "But try not to be too despondent if you're not chosen this time. It's not easy – some people attend several interviews."

"Take Jack, for example," added one of the brunettes, holding up a photograph of a jovial looking guy with heavily gelled black hair. "Jack was selected after his fifth interview. He was so determined."

She made it sound like we were auditioning for a talent show. I glanced around the room at my fellow interviewees, noting their expressions, their eager smiles and approving nods as Jack's story was relayed.

"He's doing brilliantly now," concluded the blonde.

Poor Jack. You have to wait six months after an unsuccessful interview before you can reapply, so he must have been attending interviews for years.

After the pep talk, it was over to us. One by one, we were asked to introduce ourselves to the group and explain why we wanted to become air hostesses for Virgin Atlantic. Some of the girls blurted out the wrong answer: "Because I want to travel the world." Of course they did – I did too, but I knew it definitely wasn't the response the panel was looking for. They didn't want to hire people who just wanted to go globetrotting on Virgin's budget. So I kept my reply to a short, sweet, "I love working in a customer-service based environment, with new challenges every day."

I also noticed that some of the girls had missed the point on the dress code. One of them, who introduced herself as Michelle from Croydon, was sporting a shiny polyester suit in the most luminous shade of turquoise, the skirt falling a good few inches above her bare knees. She wore a mask of bright orange foundation that clashed with the turquoise and ended in a sharp line around her jaw. She looked like a tropical cocktail. I did feel sorry for her though – she was so keen and bubbly.

Our next exercise was to form into small groups and compose a jingle for Virgin to the tune of a nursery rhyme. We were given newspaper articles from which we had to cut out sections of text to compile the lyrics, and each group was given a different tune. As we worked away the interviewers walked around the room, scribbling on notepads, scrutinising our behaviour. There were a few domineering characters; a girl in my group was trying to take over the task, but I adopted a more affable, helpful approach, since I knew they were looking for team players.

At lunchtime we learned our fate. The tension in the air was so thick I could almost hear a drum roll. The blonde woman delivered the news. "If I call out your name I'd like you to stay behind. Those whose names I don't call out, I'm sorry, but you haven't been successful this time."

She paused for effect – too long for my liking – hugging a clipboard to her perfect boobs. Meanwhile, I was convinced my name wasn't on that list and was already planning my journey home.

"Amanda Smith."

I was stunned. I'd made it through to the next round ... I was one of the four names called out. This was fucking fantastic. I watched the other interviewees leave the room, flashing faux smiles, no doubt asking themselves, "Will I be the next Jack?"

I gave it my best shot during the afternoon session. After two maths exams, incorporating questions on currency conversion and time zones, I was led into a small office for a one-to-one interview with one of the brunettes. This was actually a lot easier than the group interview, because I no longer had to worry about out-shining a room full of beautiful girls. Somehow, my nerves had become overshadowed by a sudden burst of confidence, positivity and determination. As far as I was concerned, that job was mine. I smiled, maintained eye contact and exuded a can-do attitude as I answered every question fired at me.

"Right then, Amanda," said the brunette at the end of the interview, "Let's get you weighed and measured." Back then we were also asked to submit two photographs with our application – a head-and-shoulders shot, and one full-length snap. Thankfully my height and weight matched the figures I'd stated on my application. A firm handshake and a "we'll be in touch" later, and I was out of there.

It was the most agonising, drawn-out two weeks of my life. Every morning when I heard the post arrive, I'd go charging down the stairs like a maniac, hoping to find the letter that would change my life. When it did eventually arrive I had to pinch myself when I read it, as it seemed so surreal: I'd been accepted. I was going to be a Virgin Atlantic air hostess. The letter I was holding in my trembling hand was my passport out of Horsham, a chance to escape from the dreary nine to five – and most importantly, I'd finally be away from Neil. He had still been skulking around at work, unable to accept that I was now with Jonathan. The police inquiry was no further advanced but, somehow, I wasn't too bothered anymore. My revenge was my happiness, my success, and whatever misery had come before was now securely filed away in a far recess of my mind.

It was a double celebration, since my good news coincided with Jonathan passing his cabin crew course – and his subsequent Wings Ceremony at Richard Branson's annual summer party. A weekend of sun, sex, alcohol and generally having the time of our lives was most definitely on the cards.

I'd met Richard Branson a few times in the past on his occasional visits to the engineering department. He was a good boss: fun, personable, fair and renowned for treating his staff well. His generosity knew no bounds; his summer party was, by far, the most lavish do I've ever been to. Held at his then home in the quaint Oxfordshire village of Kidlington, it was like entering a magic kingdom. No expense was spared, with activities such as quad biking, hot air ballooning, go karting and riverboating available. They even had an inflatable quasar arena. There were live bands on a huge centre stage and all the food and drink you could possibly imagine, from every corner of the globe.

Jonathan's Wings Ceremony took place outside Richard's sprawling mansion, on a small stage erected alongside his luxurious swimming pool. Watching Jonathan and his fellow new recruits receive their wings filled me with pride. They all looked so beautiful and polished in their uniforms. It was like being on a movie set. After the ceremony people were stripping off and diving into the pool. Richard was doing his habitual shake-and-spray-the-fancy-champagne-over-everyone routine, the girls pretending to be horrified that the spray had made their shirts see-through. There was a wild yet glamorous vibe among the crowd. Everyone was so sociable and cheery and confident. I was entering a whole new world – a world I knew I was just going to love.

I guzzled champagne and cocktails and numerous vodka Red-bulls. I whizzed around on the quad bikes like a crazy person and whipped Jonathan's arse at quasar. That night Richard joined us all for a singalong by the campfire. A bevy of gorgeous trolley dollies fawned over him as he attempted to play Oasis riffs on a guitar, consistently stopping and starting as his fingers struggled to find the right chords. It was amusing, in an endearing sense, to see a multi-billionaire business tycoon stumbling his way through a version of "Wonderwall". He was still entertaining his guests when Jonathan and I retired to our tent in the early hours, staggering like two drunks in a three-legged race.

Beneath the canvas we ripped off our clothes, limbs causing the tent walls to bulge as we tumbled around. I was in one of those take-me-now moods. Fortunately, so was Jonathan. No foreplay, just straight down to business. Admittedly a two-man tent isn't the ideal place for rough-and-ready sex, but we seemed to manage just fine, performing all kinds of acrobatics. Heavens knows what it must have looked – and sounded – like from the outside, though. At one point we were going for it with such vigour I thought the tent was going to uproot and collapse. It was one of those drunken romps, the kind that starts out with such enthusiasm and passion, and ends with you both crashing into semi-comas halfway through, because you were far too drunk.

The birds woke me up. It sounded as though they were having a good old gossip. Yes, I decided, I'm still pissed. The metal zip of the sleeping bag nibbled icily at my skin and, Christ almighty, I was really bursting for a wee. I nudged Jonathan. "Wake up," I urged.

He stirred, blinking awake with a sleepy moan. "Morning, beautiful."

I giggled, adding to my bladder agony. "Jonathan, I need a wee. I'm absolutely busting for a wee and I'm in a tent. Naked."

"Just go outside," he yawned, rolling onto his side.

It didn't even occur to me to put my clothes on. "Okay," I said, "come and help me." I unzipped the tent door and turned around to face Jonathan.

"What do you want me to do?" he said, wriggling free from the sleeping bag.

I crouched by the door. "Just hold my hands and don't let go."

So Jonathan held my hands while I stuck my bare bum out the tent door and urinated all over our little campfire. Anybody could have walked by and seen my naked arse sticking out the tent. But when you've got to go, you've got to go. And besides, I figured a bit of mooning would seem relatively tame to my uninhibited flying colleagues.

Who cares if they've seen my bum? I thought, as I fell back into the tent giggling. Although, in retrospect, I blame the vodka Redbulls.

CHAPTER TWO

AB INITIO

The noise was deafening: the sound of sheer terror in the face of death. People were screaming and sobbing and wheezing and choking. Some chanted desperate prayers. There were babies wailing, overhead lockers smashing open and items crashing around the cabin. Outside the air whined murderously past, ascending to an alarming pitch.

This was the sound of a Boeing 747, hurtling, like a missile, into the Atlantic Ocean.

The cabin was in darkness except for the strips of light on the gangway floor and the green glow from the emergency exit signs overhead. The only passengers vaguely visible were the ones sitting in the row facing me – a shaky line of deathly white faces searching my own for reassurance as we dropped from the sky. One woman hyperventilated and passed out in her seat. The man next to her shook uncontrollably, whimpering, "Please God, no." The aircraft shook and rattled furiously in the assault. Over the horrific noise the pilot announced: "Brace, brace," and even though I knew this meant we were thirty seconds from impact and the chances of survival were slim, I had to remain calm.

I pulled my seatbelt as tight and low as it would go, sat on my hands, pushed my head into the back of my seat, into the rear-facing brace position, and shouted my commands: "Heads down, feet back, heads down, feet back." There's a good reason for pushing your feet backwards: if you were to sit normally, your shin bones would shoot up through your knees on impact. I glanced across at my colleague

Angela, who was now also hollering, "Heads down, feet back," in synch with me.

The plane smacked violently into the sea, skidding and crashing through the waves. I could hear the water assailing the fuselage, ripping away the underside of the plane. The aircraft crashed across the sea for miles before coming to a shuddering halt. I unclipped my harness, grabbed the intercom and shouted over the PA: "This is an emergency, evacuate, evacuate."

Pandemonium spread through the cabin as passengers charged from their seats and fought their way to the emergency exit in the dark, screaming and tripping over one another. The woman in the front row, who had passed out but since recovered, fainted again as she tried to stand up, landing in a heap by my feet. The praying man was now on my shoulder, sobbing, "Please do something, you have to help us, please get us out of here." I shoved him to one side and peered out of the emergency exit porthole window. I couldn't see any flames. "Open the door," yelled the praying man.

I lifted the handle, swung open the door and immediately pulled the red tag to inflate the slide-raft. It was my job to get everyone onto the raft safely – and ensure no one had any sharp objects. Just one tiny stab of a heel would puncture the inflatable raft. People were climbing over me as I bent down to move the unconscious woman on the floor. I grabbed at the nearest passengers and shouted at two of them to take her with them. "You and you: grab her and take her to the end of the raft with you." One man cupped her shoulders with his arms and dragged her to the door, while the other grabbed her feet, pushing and shoving her as they shuffled along. *Better unconscious than dead,* I thought. In seconds the plane could break up or fill with water. We had precious little time. As Angela helped the remaining passengers off the plane, I carried out a final check of the cabin. Shining my torch down the aisle, I spotted an arm poking out from behind one of the aisle seats. "We've got a casualty," I shouted, making my way down the aisle, kicking bags and other debris aside. Angela followed. It was a woman, out for the count, still strapped into her seat. I unbuckled her.

"We'll have to carry her," I said, hooking my arms beneath the limp woman's armpits and heaving her upwards. "I'll get her legs," said Angela, pulling off the passenger's shoes. I could hear the ocean roaring and hammering against metal as we half-dragged, half-carried the woman to the emergency exit and eased her out onto the raft. Angela handed her to the passengers at the end of the raft, while I gathered all the provisions I could find – bottles of water, food, first-aid kit. Then, satisfied there was no one left on board, I could leave the aircraft. I threw the supplementary survival kit onto the chute and pulled the hooked knife from a pocket within the slide for my final task: cutting the raft free from the plane. Kneeling at the aircraft end of the raft, Angela and I unclipped the flap that was hiding the shoelace-woven rope keeping us attached to the sinking plane. I pulled at the cords as quickly as I could, my training kicking in and autopilot taking over – this was the hardest part, remembering which raft you were on – then at last we were separated. I could cut through the cord, and, just as the slide-raft detached itself, a monstrous yawning sound, followed by the creak of tearing metal, filled the air as the fuselage broke in half.

"So, how do you think Mandy did there?" said our Safety Emergency Procedure (SEP) instructor, Julie, as I took my position on the raft. The crowd replied with an animated round of applause.

Of course, this wasn't a real crash, but I had just passed the commands part of my SEP exam with flying colours. We were at the Rig – a makeshift plane in a warehouse at Gatwick Airport. The SEP exam is deliberately tough, to weed out any people who can't handle the pressure. Inside the Rig, sound effects are blasted through amps and footage is played on monitors behind the windows. It's very dramatic and you don't have a clue what kind of scenario is going to be thrown at you. Just before the ditching-in-water incident I'd also dealt with an engine fire. Smoke had filled the cabin, flames raged at the windows and I was responsible for getting everyone off the plane – even though the fire was blocking two of the exits. You have 4.3 minutes to evacuate in an aircraft fire, even when wearing a protective smoke hood. After that, it becomes an inferno. The plastic fixtures and fittings are also extremely toxic once they start burning, and you can die from inhalation alone.

I was one week into my Ab Initio training course, and already I felt overwhelmed by the information overload. There was so much to learn, and we were sitting exams nearly every day. As for the people I was meeting: I've never encountered so many drama queens in my life. The passengers on board my ditching exercise were all fellow students, and you won't find a more over-the-top group of actors than a classroom full of trainee Virgin cabin crew. There were some real divas. The first woman to faint during my crash scenario was Sarah, a stage-school graduate still waiting to see her name up in lights. Petite and proportionately curvy, with wavy blonde hair and American cheerleader looks, she demanded constant attention, her every gesture wildly theatrical. Then there was Ruth, the woman Angela and I had to carry off the plane, a part-time Posh Spice lookalike who had also been to drama school but was less vocal about it than Sarah. The third diva in the group – the praying man in the front row – was Scott, a flamboyant queen with greased-back black hair. Above all, he was a proper gobshite – always stirring and winding people up.

Angela was the person I really bonded with during the six-week course. Unlike the prima donnas, she was fairly timid for an air hostess in the making, but a good laugh all the same. She had a mane of glossy black hair, which she wore scraped back into a neat bun, and welcoming coffee-coloured eyes.

In addition to my new workmates, I'd also acquired some housemates. About ten days before my course started I moved into a house in Horley – literally a stone's throw away from the Flight Centre – with three other Virgin employees: Becky, an in-flight beauty therapist and bitch from hell; Jeremy, a senior air steward who spoke with a German accent even though he wasn't German and racked up huge phone bills calling boy bondage chat lines; and Karen, a Virgin Holidays brochure writer who was really sweet but rarely came out of her room.

Our house – a pebble-dashed semi – was like a seventies paradise inside, with woodchip wallpaper, Artex ceilings, garish patterned carpets and a strong avocado-green theme throughout. I was given a large room on the ground floor with patio doors leading out to a small weed-infested back garden. Most of the time I had the place to myself because everybody else was away on work trips. You sure knew about it if Becky was around, though. Territorial and possessive, she liked to think she was head of the household. I'll never forget her guided tour of my new abode.

"TV is mine, the remote control is mine, that coffee table and that magazine is mine. Lamp, candles, potpourri – and the bowl it's in – all mine," she'd said, gesturing at the items one by one with sharp jabs of a perfectly manicured hand. "I'm in charge of the bills and you'll pay me your share – by cash or cheque, your choice."

Becky was one of those girls who looked prettier than she actually was, because she knew every beauty trick in the book. Her make-up was always immaculate, eyebrows perfectly shaped and her red-brown hair styled in a sophisticated Meg Ryan-esque shaggy bob. Becky was also the proud owner of a spanking new red MX5 sports car. There were a number of dollies driving red MX5s at that time, the standing joke being they were post-coital thank-you presents from Richard Branson. We used to love winding Becky up over this.

I was surrounded by glamour. The Flight Centre was also used to coordinate staff travel and as a check-in point for Virgin crew flying out of Gatwick, so every day we'd see staff coming and going, looking so sleek in their uniforms, the girls gliding effortlessly in heels like models on a catwalk, impeccably made-up, not a hair out of place. Grooming rules were incredibly strict at Virgin, especially for the girls. As ambassadors of the brand we were expected to look spick and span at all times: in the air, on the ground, at the training centre ... basically, whenever we were in uniform. Long hair – any length below collar level – must always be worn up. Nails should be spotless and well-manicured. Neck scarves tied to the front, never on the side or at the back (although they are these days). Heels should be worn at all times while on the ground. A smart evening dress should be taken on every trip, just in case Richard Branson was in town and required you to attend a publicity function. And probably the most important rule on the list: never, ever be seen in uniform without sporting lashings of red lippy. This rule came with its own set of sub-rules. It couldn't be any red lipstick; there was a list of acceptable shades from top-of-the-range brands – all available in our own little duty-free shop at the Flight Centre, so there was absolutely no excuse for breaking this rule.

To help us look the part, we were given grooming lessons by two overly made-up, bitter-faced women in black suits, whom we nicknamed Bitch One and Bitch Two. They were harshly critical and mocking, constantly pointing out our faults, pulling us up for wearing the wrong make-up and making snide jokes about people's imperfections and blemishes. I'd been looking forward to grooming classes, excited about experimenting with make-up, trying out new hairstyles and being all girly and glamorous. Alas, it wasn't to be. During our very first lesson "the bitches" not only insulted me, but also reduced another poor girl to tears.

It was Bitch Two who had a pop at me, just after we'd taken our seats around the poisonous duo's sprawling make-up counter. The bottle blonde zoomed right in on me, narrowing her glacial eyes and forcing a tissue into my hand. Her voice was vinegary. "You've got the wrong lipstick on. Take it off."

"It's Clinique," I said, "It's on the list … it's allowed."

"That may well be the case, but it doesn't suit you. Off, wipe it off."

Bitch One nodded in assent. "You need a different tone of red."

I patted my lips with the tissue.

It got worse. As the class got underway, the bitch twins asked for a volunteer to be made up "Virgin-style". Sarah and Ruth's ears pricked up, and they both shifted in their seats, pushing their boobs out and flashing expectant looks that screamed "me, me, me" at the black-suited women.

"How about you," said Bitch One, pointing at Sabrina, a stunning girl with feline eyes and skin the colour of golden toffee.

Sabrina shrugged. "Okay." She made her way to the front of the room and sat on the stool by the make-up counter.

"So, we're going to start by taking the hair right back from the face," said Bitch One, aggressively scraping an Alice band over Sabrina's head.

"Indeed," said Bitch Two, squirting a generous blob of makeup remover onto a cotton wool pad, "We don't want to get foundation in her hair." Bitch Two removed Sabrina's make-up, tut-tutting under her breath while her lacquer-stiff mousey-haired partner in crime rummaged through the mountain of cosmetics.

The demonstration began, both women painting and drawing all over Sabrina's beautiful face while providing a running commentary of their work.

"A little problem area here beneath the eyes," said the mousey-haired artist, loading more and more foundation onto Sabrina's face. "Your complexion is very uneven … very, very uneven."

"Just a light dusting of blusher – less is more," added her colleague, colouring Sabrina's cheeks sunset orange. Poor Sabrina was being attacked from all angles.

"Blend, blend, blend," they nagged until they finally put down their tools and moved away from their model so we could all admire their work. My God, they'd made a mess of her. Sarah gasped, cupping her mouth. Bitch One handed Sabrina a mirror. "So this is the look we're aiming for, girls," she said.

Sabrina held the mirror up to her face and immediately burst into tears. Our so-called make-up artists had turned Sabrina's skin porcelain white. The foundation they'd used was clearly about ten shades too pale for her skin. Sabrina slammed the mirror down on the table, sending pots and tubes crashing onto the floor, and stormed out of the room sobbing.

The room fell silent. "What's the matter with her?" asked Bitch Two.

Bitch One shrugged her shoulders, her face swathed in a look of confusion. "Search me."

Understandably, Sabrina assumed the two women were deliberately being racist, although I'm sure this was more a case of *Dumb & Dumber*.

There was a drama almost every day. During our first SEP lesson, another instructor, Sophie, came a cropper while demonstrating how to use the emergency slide. Sophie was like a life-size Barbie doll: tall with slender limbs, perfectly sized pert boobs and a whittled-away waist you could comfortably fit your hands around. Her hair was ash blonde, swirled into a classic French pleat, and her huge swimming-pool blue eyes slanted upwards slightly at the outer corners. We all gathered round her on the Rig and watched as she placed her perfect bum onto the slide. "So, once your shoes are off you sit on the slide like so, arms crossed at your chest, and, staying in an upright position, you're ready to go down the slide." Sophie adjusted her weight forwards and she was away, her shiny French pleat getting smaller and smaller as she bobbed down the slide. Only, for some reason, Sophie seemed to be falling backwards instead of sitting upright as she'd instructed. She landed with a thud, her right foot crumpling and cracking beneath her. Sophie let out a little giggle. "That's how not to do it," she said. Then she rose to her feet and took a couple of steps before collapsing on the floor. Sophie had fractured her foot in three places and spent the next few months in plaster, hobbling around on crutches. But she had made no fuss when it happened. Sophie may have looked delicate and doll-like, but mentally, she was tough as old boots.

I was discovering that you have to be made of hard stuff to survive in this game. Ab Initio was highly intense – one minute I felt like I was at army boot camp; the next, a finishing school. It's extremely hard work and, quite often, people drop out within the first couple of weeks. Becoming an air hostess is not just a matter of learning how to look pretty. There's a lot of hard work that goes on behind the scenes, which people don't know about. The first two weeks are the toughest. That's when we do all our SEP training. In addition to this, we also had to sit through hour upon hour of air-crash investigation programmes, viewing reconstructions of some of the world's deadliest crashes in aviation history. The idea of this exercise was to see how and why accidents occur, and learn from any mistakes made in order to prevent them happening again. By the time we'd seen the twentieth video, we were all quite immune to the graphic images.

We also had to undergo fire safety training. The main perk about this was that our lessons were taught by a group of muscle-bound firemen from the local station. It's a wonder we learned anything; most of the girls – and some of the lads – were too busy swooning over them. One of our tasks was to find a dead body and rescue a baby – in this case a mannequin and a doll in a bassinet – from a mock-burning aircraft. Like the ditching exercise, it was terribly dramatic and very claustrophobic trying to navigate your way around the tight spaces in thick smoke while wearing a smoke hood.

Then there was the first-aid course, which involved learning how to help the on-board managers operate defibrillators. We were shown a video featuring an old man who had suffered a heart attack on board a Virgin flight. He was flanked by two gorgeous dollies who had saved his life by following our CPR procedures and shocking him with the defibrillator. "Virgin saved my life," he said with a false-teeth smile. I had no idea then that I'd end up using one myself one day – and, indeed, saving somebody's life.

We were also given SAS-style training – with ex-SAS officers and paratroopers – where we were taught how to spot sleeper terrorists, restrain people and deal with hostage situations. Obviously, for security reasons I cannot divulge these secrets.

Lessons in survival techniques entailed acting out every imaginable life-or-death scenario under the sun: how to survive in a snow storm, an avalanche, on a desert island, stranded at sea; hunter-gatherer techniques (eat your heart out Ray Mears); and bizarrely, how to fend off sharks – a good whack on the nose with an oar does the trick, apparently.

With so much to learn, I had no time for a social life. All my time at home was spent studying for exams. I was stressed out to the max and losing sleep because of Becky's annoying habits when she returned from trips. No matter what time it was – normally late at night or in the early hours of the morning – she would slam the front door, pour herself a huge G & T and vacuum the whole house from top to bottom – even if it was clean.

I was missing Jonathan like crazy. He was now flying all over the world as a Virgin steward and training for his commercial pilot's licence in his spare time. Every time that avocado-green phone trilled I'd race down the hallway, hoping it was him calling from America, or Johannesburg, or whatever far-flung destination he was in. Our phone calls were like extracts taken from Mills & Boon novels, I mean real gooey stuff – entire international calls filled with soppy lines such as, "No, you hang up first," "I can hear your heart beating," "I miss you so much my heart aches," "I love you to the stars and back," "I love you more," "No, I love you more." By the time we'd finished exchanging verbal love letters, his money would run out and we wouldn't have time to discuss anything else. Not all of the calls were gushy though – there were a few sexy ones thrown in ... full of explicit descriptions of what we'd like to do to each other.

There was a point – about two weeks into the course – when I thought I was having a nervous breakdown. I was plagued by anxiety dreams and the workload was humungous. Some days we'd be taught something new in the morning and sit an exam on the same subject that very afternoon – and be expected to achieve a grade of at least 90 per cent. There was also a pile of hefty manuals to memorise. I remember sitting on the bottom step of the hall stairs, sobbing down the avocado phone to Mum and Dad, anxiously twirling the coiled wire round my fingers.

"I can't do it – it's so difficult," I'd cry, gasping for air. "I can't cope. I'm never going to pass."

Mum was almost crying with me. "Oh baby, I hate to hear you so upset, but I know you can do this. You've worked so hard. We're so proud of you."

Dad never really offered the same level of encouragement, although he meant well. "They're not paying you enough for all this stress. Tell them it's too much. They're expecting you to do all this work for peanuts."

To which I'd reply: "Can you put Mum back on, please?" through more tears.

I didn't quit. Of course I didn't. And despite my mini panic attacks, I still managed to pass every exam with flying colours and make it through to week five. Although we still had a week's training left to go, it was a given at this stage that we'd passed the course and could now be fitted for our Virgin uniforms.

It's incredible how a red outfit can cause so much excitement. We were all high as kites on the day of our fittings. Before, everything had seemed like such a hard slog, the fear of failure overwhelming. Now, we could finally begin to look forward to life in the skies, adventures all over the world, wild parties and, of course, working our arses off.

The tailoress in the uniform department waited on me hand and foot. She was so complimentary and enthusiastic, I felt like I was in a posh changing room at Selfridges with my own personal shopper.

"Oh," she said when I walked into the vast dressing room, "What a beautiful figure." She clasped her hands to her chest, nodding her head. "Yes, this uniform is going to look amazing on you."

She pulled the tape measure from around her neck, circled it around my waist. "I think you've lost weight, Mandy."

She grabbed her clipboard from a nearby chair, scribbled my new measurements down alongside my previous ones. "Yes," she confirmed, "You've definitely lost weight."

I laughed. "I'm not surprised – it's been a stressful few weeks. Don't worry ... it's nothing a few pies and pasties won't cure."

I wasn't the easiest person to fit. Because I'm tall – just over five foot nine – with orangutan arms, I had to get a size-sixteen woollen overcoat for the shoulders and extend the sleeve length, then have it taken in every-where else. My size-ten skirt and size-twelve jacket and shirt, however, fitted beautifully.

I drew back the curtain and emerged from the cubicle. "How does this look?" I asked, walking towards the full-length mirror.

The kind tailoress's eyes met mine in the glass. "You look amazing, superb."

I twirled in front of the mirror, checking my reflection from all angles. "I love it, absolutely love it."

I was smiling so much I thought my face was going to explode. There was an air hostess staring back at me ... now all she needed was her wings.

CHAPTER THREE

WINGS

The spotlights were burning and blinding. I could feel the foundation melting on my face and the audience was a smudge of fidgety shapes through the haze. The woolly hum of chatter subsided to empty silence, punctuated by the occasional cough or exaggerated throat clearing. I felt giddy and sick – a combination of nerves and excitement ... or was it the five glasses of Asti Spumante I'd just necked kicking in? Stage fright, don't you just love it? However, the show must go on – and the opening bars of the Bee Gees' "Tragedy" pumping from the speakers signalled it was "tits and teeth" time.

This was the final hurdle – the show that would earn me my wings and launch me up above the clouds into the glamorous world of high flying. I couldn't afford to mess this up.

I was on stage with sixteen colleagues from my Ab Initio course. Collectively, we were known as Group 309. We'd completed our exams, made it through the rigorous training exercises, learned how to push a trolley and serve coffee (which, incidentally, is the last thing they teach you at Richard Branson's School for International Air Hostesses), survived the tears and tantrums, and now here we were, in uniform, dancing to "Tragedy" in front of Richard Branson himself.

We'd spent a week rehearsing for our Wings Ceremony cabaret show, holed up in our classroom at the Flight Centre for hours every night. We'd chosen the seventies-style Brit Awards as the theme for our performance, making up our own lyrics and dance routines to cheesy disco hits. It was supposed to be a team effort, but with resident divas Sarah and Ruth – and queen bitchiness himself, Scott – on board, it wasn't long before our group performance turned into a fierce battle of one-upmanship.

The rows were always instigated by Sarah, who, from day one, made it perfectly clear she was to be the star of the show, appointing herself group choreographer and flouncing round the room like Joan Collins.

"It makes sense that I choreograph the dances," she asserted, as we sat around an island of desks planning our show. "Because I'm the one who's been to stage school – Laine Theatre Arts College ... Posh Spice studied there too."

Ruth wasn't happy. After all, she was a qualified dancer – and she'd worked as a Posh Spice lookalike model. She shot her rival a sullen glare, lips twitching into an exaggerated "Posh" pout. The tension in the room was palpable; we all knew a bitch-fight was about to kick off.

"With all due respect, Sarah," said Ruth, still pouting, "if anyone's going to be in charge of choreography here, surely it should be me. You may have done a bit of acting, but I went to dance school. I'm proficient in ballet, tap, jazz, modern, ballroom ..."

"It's not just 'a bit of acting', Ruth," interrupted Sarah. "I went to a top drama school, studied alongside some of the country's most talented actors ..."

"Oh, really? Posh Spice isn't exactly clearing up at the BAFTAs, is she."

"Ha, that's rich coming from the girl who thinks she *is* Posh Spice."

Scott butted in. "I agree with Ruth. She should be choreographer. This isn't the fucking Sarah Show, darling."

And so the spat continued. There was lots of finger-wagging and nos-tril flaring and fists thumping desks, all three shouting over one another, insults flying, while the rest of us exchanged bemused glances. It was like being on the live set of a soap opera.

The matter was resolved ... eventually. Ruth was the one to surren-der. "Look, Sarah," she said, "we've only got a week to pull this number together. Why don't we both make up the dances – combine our talents?"

You could see the cogs turning in Sarah's prissy head. "I suppose we could do that," she said reluctantly.

Group 309 was back in business, and for a while there was harmony in our camp. Sarah and Ruth were doing a sterling job as co-choreographers and our show was shaping up beautifully. All was well until day three, when Sarah tried to create a solo spot for herself during a run-through of "Disco Inferno", which sparked yet another screaming match.

But despite the cat-fights, we were comrades – and we'd been trained to deal with far worse situations than this.

Flashbacks of our rehearsal rows whizzed round in my head as I danced on the mock stage at Virgin's head office. I could see Sarah at the front of the stage, wiggling her pert little bum and throwing some sexy new moves into our routine. I giggled to myself. *It's always going to be the Sarah Show,* I thought.

We made it through "Tragedy" without tragedy and, after another swift dose of fizzy wine backstage, my nerves all but vanished. As we performed our second number – "Night Fever" – I felt as though I was born to sing and dance. There I was, treading the boards, strutting up and down the stage like Bonnie bloody Langford, making love to the music with my angelic tones (although looking back at the video footage I realise I'd probably just had one too many Astis).

As my eyes adjusted to the blazing lights, I scanned the audience. The first person I noticed was Richard Branson, standing at the front of the crowd and cutting an avuncular figure in a navy jersey and pleated-front grey trousers. He looked as though he was having a whale of a time: clapping and grinning broadly through his trademark sandy beard, flashing his big pearly whites. He was flanked by a camera crew from an Australian news network who had jetted in to film our Wings Ceremony – another PR opportunity for Richard ahead of the glittering launch of his new service Down Under, Virgin Blue.

The music played on and Richard and his cameramen disappeared into a blur as I turned and marched in unison with my red-suited co-stars, Sarah's instructions playing in my head: "March, two three four, knee dip, finger click, knee dip, finger click … faces to the audience, big smiles – tits and teeth, girls, tits and teeth." And that's when I spotted the people I'd been longing to see all night: Mum and Dad, their two proud faces beaming back at me, Dad craning his head above an extraordinarily big-haired woman, Mum dabbing her eyes with a tissue. She was sitting between Dad and an extremely handsome young man I was sure I'd seen somewhere before. *Wow,* I thought, *he's a bit of alright.* Then, at a second glance through the searing lights, I realised I did know him ... it was Jonathan, my boyfriend.

I nearly messed up my knee dip, finger click routine. Jonathan wasn't supposed to be here – he'd told me he had "work commitments". I hadn't seen him since I'd started my Ab Initio course. What a lovely surprise. He looked so gorgeous, like a model from a Gillette advert: clean-shaven, chiselled, fresh-out-of-the-shower and manly. He gave me a little wave and mouthed, "I love you" – at least I think that's what he said. Then "Night Fever" slipped into "Ring My Bell".

How I made it through our finale of "Disco Inferno", I'll never know. Aside from trying to focus on counting, turning, clapping and shimmying – and remembering the new lyrics – my mind was also racing with saucy thoughts about Jonathan. Six weeks without sex. Six weeks and two days, to be accurate. Six weeks and two days of teasing phone calls. No wonder I felt so horny. "You won't be able to walk once I've finished with you," Jonathan had told me during our last conversation. "I'm gonna make up for lost time." *Let's hope he keeps that promise,* I thought, as I belted out "fly Virgin fly" for the final time.

The music faded and the audience rose to its feet, cheering, clapping and whistling. On stage we linked hands and bowed, dipping our immaculately coiffed heads to the wild applause. It was one of the proudest moments of my life – I was brimming with emotion. Group 309 had gone down a storm; we'd pulled it off without any tiffs or traumas. It was teamwork at its best, and we celebrated our efforts with a big group hug. Even Sarah and Ruth embraced, their differences now a distant memory.

The grand moment was upon us. We were about to receive our prized wings. But first it was time for a quick catch-up with our adoring audience.

Mum hugged me so tight I could feel my ribs cracking. "Oh, Mandy. Mandy, Mandy, Mandy. I'm so proud of you, baby," she choked, tears spilling from her velvety-brown eyes. "So, so proud. Ever so proud." Mum released her grip, tilted her head to one side and nudged Dad. "Look at our little girl, James. Hasn't she done us proud?"

Even with her tear-stained face Mum looked the epitome of elegance. She was in her late forties then, but could easily have passed for a woman in her mid thirties. Tall, slender and blessed with perfect bone structure and dazzling smile, she was by far the best looking mum in the room.

"She's been like this all night – cried through the whole performance," said Dad, enveloping me in his arms and kissing my head. "You were electrifying out there, Mandy – a star in the making. You really are talented."

I laughed. "I don't think I can afford to give up the day job just yet, Dad."

"I mean it, Mandy. I really think you could go a long way. I've always said it: our Mandy, she can sing." He glanced at Mum for encouragement. "Haven't I always said that, Sue: our Mandy can sing?"

Mum nodded, the glossy brown curls piled high on her head bobbing rhythmically. "You have, James, you have – I don't know where she gets it from."

"Any chance of a kiss?" piped up Jonathan, who'd been waiting patiently throughout my parents' rave reviews.

"Ah, come here you," I said, throwing my arms around his neck and planting a gooey lipstick kiss on his cheek. "I thought you were working. I didn't expect to see you here."

He grinned. "I swapped shifts. I wouldn't have missed this for the world. I wanted to surprise you." Then he pulled me towards him and whispered into my ear: "I can't wait to get you out of that uniform."

I was just about to respond with some dirty talk when the compere announced the start of our wings presentation.

"I'm needed back on stage," I said.

"Don't leave just yet," said Jonathan under his breath. "I've got a huge bloody hard-on."

I felt his cock twitch against my pelvis, springing to life like a pop-up toy. "I have to go," I giggled. "Take off your jacket and carry it in front of you."

I kissed Mum and Dad again and headed back to the stage. Jonathan limped to his seat, embarrassment concealed beneath his suit jacket. *He'll keep*, I thought.

Half an hour later I was awarded my wings. "Congratulations, Amanda," said Richard, pressing the silver badge into my palm and pecking me on the cheek. "Welcome to the world of flying."

"Thanks, Richard," I said. "I won't let you down."

I pinned my wings on my red blazer, held my bunned-head high and marched off the stage into the throng of over-enthusiastic engineers, who had also come along to see me off. I was flushed with pride and excitement ... and fizzy wine.

The celebrations continued at the bar and Richard, generous as ever, bought drinks for everyone. He's always enjoyed partying with crew. As the drink flowed, I found myself engaged in a rather embarrassing conversation with Richard (fortunately, Mum and Dad had left by this point). There I was, draped all over him like a drunken game show hostess, waving a glass of vodka in the air and cooing: "You're such a lovely boss, Richard."

Richard laughed and put his arm around my waist to steady me.

"Oh, and my nanna, Jeanie Mac – is your number one fan. She adores you. She's always saying, 'That Richard Branson, he's a smashing young man.' She'd love to meet you."

"Really?" said Richard. "She sounds like a character ... and where is Jeanie Mac tonight? I'd like to meet her, too."

"She couldn't make it – she lives in Hartlepool."

Then, in my inebriated state, I had a sudden brainwave. "I know," I squealed, delving into my handbag for my Virgin mobile phone (a recent Christmas present from Richard to all his staff), "Let's call her – she'd love to speak to you."

I handed the phone to Richard, insisting, "Ring me nanna, ring me nanna."

"I don't know her number, Mandy."

"Oh, give it here," I said, grabbing the handset. Squinting one eye I punched in Nanna's number, which I usually only called from my landline, but which was imprinted on my brain, even when drunk.

"Hello?" Nanna sounded surprised; she wasn't used to late night phone calls.

"Nanna, it's me, Mandy. Did I wake you?"

"Oh no, love, I was just putting me hair net on and getting ready to turn in. I've got me nightie on, poured a little tipple and ..."

"Nanna," I interrupted, "I've got someone here who'd like a word with you."

I passed the phone back to Richard.

"Hi Jeanie," he said, "Richard here, Richard Branson. I'm here with your granddaughter Mandy – she's been telling me all about you."

They chatted for at least five minutes. I didn't have a clue what Nanna was saying but Richard seemed amused.

"Thank you, that's very kind," he responded with an affectionate chuckle. "Yes, still got the beard ... yes, I promise I'll be careful up in those balloons. I'd love to pop in for a brew ... I'll pass you back to Mandy."

Bless Nanna. Any other person would have thought the call was a wind up ... anyone other than good old Jeanie Mac. She was over the moon. "Wait 'til I tell the girls at bingo tomorrow," she said.

Drinks at the bar progressed to even more refreshments at Ikon Diva – a tacky eighties-style nightclub in Crawley, popular among boozy hen and stag parties, mutton-dressed-as-lamb divorcees and sleazy married men whose wives don't understand them.

Richard was up for a night of clubbing but his PA wouldn't allow it. "You can't, you're flying to Antigua tomorrow," she warned him. So it was home to bed for Richard. Jonathan was driving, as he was due to fly to Orlando the following day. Not that he minded watching the rest of us getting hammered – he was just happy to be there.

The mood was vibrant, everyone still buzzing from the Wings Ceremony, recollecting amusing anecdotes from our Ab Initio course and chatting about the adventures ahead of us. We gathered at the bar, throwing back tequila slammers and declaring our love for one another after each toxic hit. Jonathan stood behind me, arms wrapped around my waist, nuzzling my neck, propping me up.

"Even if we never fly together, let's keep in touch," shouted Scott above the music. "Here's to Group 309."

We chinked glasses to out-of-synch slurs of "Group 309".

I was happy, euphoric. Finally, I was pursuing my dream career: Mandy Smith, international air hostess ... who would have thought it?

The club throbbed to the beat of Madness's "Night Boat to Cairo". I leaned into Jonathan's embrace and reached behind me to stroke his groin – that pop-up toy of his was rock-hard now.

"Shall we head home, big boy?" I teased.

Jonathan pulled me in closer, his erection straining against my hand, heart galloping in time with mine, pelting my back. "I thought you'd never ask," he said. "I might have to take off my jacket again."

I bade an emotional farewell to my colleagues, vowing to stay in touch – although the reality was I would never see some of them again.

It was raining heavily when we left the club. "Here, put this over your head," said Jonathan, handing me his jacket. We made a dash for his car, me slipping all over the shop in my heels (it had nothing to do with the drink, honest). Jonathan had parked his little Clio at Crawley Station next to Ikon Diva. The car park was dark and deserted, apart from a few drunken girls from a hens party who were staggering around aimlessly, dressed as St Trinian's schoolgirls, with flashing willy boppers on their heads.

"Back to your place?" asked Jonathan, wiping rain from his forehead as he started the ignition. He looked so cute: the orange glow from a street lamp warming his dewy face and casting droplet shadows on his cheeks through the rain-smeared windows. His shirt was soaked and vacuumed to his body, accentuating his finely-toned biceps. I couldn't wait until I got home ... I wanted him now.

"Not so fast, tiger," I said, slipping out of my jacket and unbuttoning my blouse. "Let's do it here."

An impish light danced in Jonathan's eyes. "What if we get caught?" he said, slipping a hand inside my bra, damp fingers lightly circling my boob, teasing my nipple. I let out a little gasp and reached for his leg, moving my hand slowly yet firmly up his thigh.

"No one will see us on the back seat," I husked. "Come on, let's get you out of those wet clothes."

Five minutes later we were at it like rabbits: horizontal, limbs contorted, skirt ruffled at my waist. Jonathan's little Clio rocked, rain hammering the roof, whipping the windows. It felt as though we were shagging inside a tin can. On the radio a world-weary American country warbler sang about his alcoholic father deserting his mother, who died of a broken heart.

"Blimey," I panted, as Jonathan was grinding away, "that poor bastard." And we both erupted into fits of giggles.

It was the perfect end to a perfect night.

Chapter Four

UPTOWN GIRL

I was so paranoid I'd forget something that I packed and repacked my bags about four times, double checking every item against my list: four bulky flight manuals; a set of ice tongs; ten pounds in change for my duty-free float; passport; Virgin ID; make-up and flat cabin shoes, all to be carried on board in my leather crew bag. In my hard Delsey suitcase: spare uniform for my return flight; undies; support tights; little black dress (in case Richard Branson's in town); casual yet sexy outfit for a night on the tiles; nightie (in case of emergency: never get caught naked if you have to evacuate the hotel in the middle of the night, advice which came in handy over the years) and toiletries.

I was ready far too early; I had at least four hours to spare until check-in, but I was so excited I wanted to get on my way as soon as possible. I was jetting off on my first flight as a Virgin Atlantic air hostess. My destination: New York City. How cool was this? I'd never been to the Big Apple before, so I was thrilled to discover my first roster included two New Yorks back to back.

I stood in front of the full-length mirror in my bedroom, admiring my reflection. I was a vision in red, immaculate and glamorous. My hair was scooped back into a neat bun, secured with enough hairspray to obliterate the ozone layer, and I'd paid meticulous attention to my make-up, ensuring I'd used all the correct colours in accordance with Virgin's strict palette. I almost didn't recognise myself.

A shrill voice blaring from the hallway interrupted my moment of self-appreciation: Becky. I grabbed my luggage and ventured into the warzone.

"One hundred and six fucking pounds, Jeremy. One hundred and six pounds, forty-two pence on gay bondage chat lines. Are you mad?"

Becky, wrapped in a white fluffy bathrobe nicked from some five-star luxury resort, was furiously waving our latest phone bill in Jeremy's face. A padded-satin pink eye-mask embroidered with the message "Do not disturb" was clamped to her forehead. Jeremy pushed past her, wheeling his case behind him. The poor soul had just returned from a Hong Kong trip. I turned to lock my bedroom door behind me, hoping not to get caught in the crossfire. Becky was a pain in the arse when it came to our bills – I always thought she'd make a great debt collector ... or loan shark. She was obsessively pedantic; we all had to go through the phone bill and highlight every single call we'd made.

"Don't you walk away from me." Becky was now screaming like a lunatic, stomping her fluffy slippered feet.

Jeremy's voice was light and lispy. "Nice ass, Mands."

I turned around. "Do I look okay?"

Jeremy fanned his face theatrically with his hands. "Oh my God. Talk about a cock tease. You look fantastic. *Wunderbar, wunderbar.*"

"What about this fucking bill?"

"What about the fucking bill? For heaven's sake, Bec, I'm just in the door."

"You owe me money ... for the bill ... for your pervy fucking phone calls."

"I don't know what you're talking about." Jeremy snatched the piece of paper from Becky's trembling hand and studied it for a brief moment before slamming it down on the chintzy phone table. "How do you know they're gay bondage chat numbers, anyway?"

Becky's face broke into a catty mock smile. "Because I *called* them ... every single one of them."

"Well then, sweetie," said Jeremy. "I do hope you're going to pay for those calls." Then he headed upstairs to his room, laughing.

Becky shot me a glare. "And you can wipe that smile off your face, too. Have you paid your share?"

I motioned towards the table with a saccharine smile. "Cheque's on there. Now if you'll excuse me, I've got a plane to catch." And with a new air of confidence I hooked my holdall in the crook of my arm, extended the handle of my case and breezed along the hallway, calling, "See ya."

I recognised only one person on the crew bus to Heathrow – Sian, one of the girls from my Ab Initio course. And although we hadn't got to know each other terribly well during training, we greeted each other like long-lost friends. We giggled and squealed and speed-talked at the tops of our voices all the way from the Flight Centre to Heathrow, full of beans, discussing our uniforms and destinations – Sian, I discovered, was off to LA – and anticipating our impending adventures down-route. No one else on the bus was as lively as us; most of the crew were sleeping. Why weren't they excited? Forty-eight hours later, after two gruelling transatlantic flights, I would discover why.

Our pre-flight briefing was held in a tiny room inside the Queen's Building at Heathrow, a dismal fifties-era construction eventually demolished in 2009. There were about twenty crew crammed into that room, all destined for Newark. Everyone appeared so chilled and confident. Realising I was the only newcomer (Sian was in a separate briefing elsewhere in the building), my excitement was suddenly eclipsed by a dragging sensation of fear deep in my chest. I found a vacant seat and tried to blend in amid the sea of red figures.

Our in-flight development supervisor, Martin, led the briefing. I warmed to him instantly. No taller than five foot six, with spindly arms and legs, he spoke in a boisterous Glaswegian accent that belied his tiny frame. His instructions were clear and to the point.

"I'm not going to beat around the bush," he said. "This is Mandy, she is new. You all remember what it's like to be new, so look after her. Here's how it works. We work hard on the flight out – look after the fuckers – feed them, water them ... whatever they want, we make 'em feel special, especially in Upper. Then we get them off the plane, have a fucking good party in New York, and do it all over again on the way back – all of you as fresh faced and beautiful as you are now, please. Anyone *not* understand?"

Next came the serious part – the moment I was dreading. Before boarding every flight each crew member must correctly answer a safety question each. Get it wrong and you're asked a further two questions. And if you fail on your third attempt, you're grounded, having to sit your SEP exams all over again before they let you fly. Fortunately, I didn't cock it up and, ten minutes later, I was strutting down the jetway and stepping into the aluminium tube that was to become my new home away from home.

My heart dropped when I met the colleague I'd been teamed up with. Her name was Leanne and she wasn't exactly the smiley, how-can-I-help-you air hostess type I'd anticipated. She was utterly miserable and angry. It was like working alongside someone who'd just bought a one-way coach ticket to Beachy Head. Not one positive word escaped her ghastly mouth, and she didn't paint an attractive picture of life in the sky. According to Leanne, the hours were shit, the passengers shit and everything was, well, "shit".

Leanne was tall and stocky – much heavier than your average hostie – with chunky wrists and ankles. She had one of those "Essex girl" facelifts, where the hair is tied into a ponytail so high and taut it actually stretches your face upwards. The first words she spoke to me will stay in my mind forever. I was all bright and breezy when I introduced myself to Leanne in galley two of Economy Class prior to take-off. "Hi, I'm Mandy. Lovely to meet you," I said.

Leanne frowned. *Wow,* I thought, *that's got to hurt with that ponytail facelift.*

"If you're going to fart, don't do it in here," she said.

I laughed. "I don't feel the need just now."

"If you are going to let off, do it out there," she added, jabbing the curtain with her thumb.

"Excuse me?"

"Oh, did they not explain the wind problems during training? Well, get used to it. Flying as many hours as we do makes your stomach swell up like a balloon. You'll be a walking cesspit, farting like a trooper. Never in the galley, though. Let it out down the aisles, over the passengers. It's called crop dusting. Your uniform will stink of farts – we call it Eau de Boeing."

"Nice," I said with a faint smile.

Leanne's jaded ramblings continued all through take-off and the meal service – it was relentless; she was like a psychic vampire, sucking every positive thought from my head. I felt slightly disillusioned, like all my initial enthusiasm and excitement had been zapped out of me by Leanne's stun-gun mouth. I had been so keen at the start of the flight, running around, sweating like mad, offering to help and attempting to put into practice everything I'd learned during training. But Leanne made no effort to welcome me, which made me question what I'd signed up for. And she broke all the rules. Once our dinner service cart was empty, she sat in the galley and wolfed down a portion of chicken korma meant for the passengers, which is strictly off-limits as the other crew were still in the aisles. Our crew meals were provided separately in the crew cart, so we usually only ate the passenger meals if there were any left over.

"You'd think doing this job as long as I have, I'd be a stick insect by now," she moaned, shovelling forkfuls of calorie-laden curry into her gob.

It was impossible to connect with Leanne. She obviously detested her job and simply didn't want to be there. My attempts to bond with other crew members didn't exactly go according to plan, either. Overhearing a conversation between two pretty, breathy-voiced Premium Economy dollies in the galley, I couldn't help but join in. One of them, a lofty blonde with supermodel looks, was gracefully displaying a dainty open-heart silver necklace.

"Oh. My. God," said her shorter, curvier friend. "That's stunning. Is it from ..."

"Yes, Tiffany's. He got it in New York."

"It's beautiful," I agreed, moving in to admire the shimmering heart. As all the girls started relaying trinkets of Gucci this and Prada that from admirers, they turned to me as I was the next in the show 'n' tell circle. "You know, my boyfriend gave me a *wonderful* pearl necklace recently – and I still can't get it out of my hair."

My joke was greeted with deathly silence, the two girls exchanging I-can't-believe-she-just-said-that glances. The awkward tumbleweed moment was broken by a piggy snort of laughter from Leanne, who was now tucking into her second passenger meal of bangers and mash. That was the first, and only, time I ever heard her laugh. The two girls breezed out of the galley arm in arm, the tall one glaring at me beneath half-closed smoky eyelids, hand protectively pressed over her gleaming piece of Tiffany's bling as though she was expecting me to rip it from her neck.

And I was left alone with bangers-and-mash face, wondering: will I ever fit in here?

My spirits lifted after touchdown. Even though I had the misfortune of sitting next to Leanne on the crew bus, nothing could tarnish my excitement at seeing New York for the first time. The Manhattan skyline took my breath away. It truly was spectacular: colossal monuments thumping into the sky, flirting with the apricot autumn light. The Empire State Building, Twin Towers, Grand Central Station, Macy's, yellow cabs ... it all actually existed. I was transfixed, emotionally overwhelmed. "Look," I said, nudging Leanne, nose pressed to the window, "Isn't it amazing?"

Leanne curled her upper lip on one side, shrugged a shoulder, "S'alright. Get bored of it after a while."

I should've known she'd say something like that.

"Any plans for tonight?" I asked her, as we pulled up outside the Lexington Hotel.

"Nah, Delsey Dining," she replied.

I didn't have a clue what she was on about, but I ended the conversation there.

I couldn't believe I was staying at the Lexington Hotel – in the very same street where the iconic scene from *The Seven Year Itch* was filmed – the one where Marilyn Monroe's standing over the air vent and you see her knickers as her dress blows up. I felt as though I'd walked straight onto a movie set, my depression from the flight now completely lifted, as I allowed Leanne to walk in ahead of me. I stood in the street taking it all in.

Things were about to improve. As I waited in the lobby for my room key along with the rest of the crew, I met my first proper work friend, Laura, who was standing next to me in the queue. The first thing that struck me about Laura was that her voice didn't match her features. Petite and slim – no larger than a UK size six – with alabaster skin, huge moss-green eyes and shiny brunette hair, she reminded me of one of the Corrs sisters. I was expecting her to speak with a cute little Irish accent, so I got rather a shock when I heard the familiar brash Geordieness I had grown up with.

"Eee, all this hanging around gets right on me tits," she said, looking up at me.

At last, I thought, *a normal, down-to-earth person.*

"Actually, this is my first trip," I said, almost apologetically.

"Ah yeah, I remember from the briefing. I'm Laura," she said, shaking my hand.

"Mandy ... am I relieved to meet you."

She laughed. "Man, if your first flight was anything like mine, you'll be wanting out of this game already."

"It wasn't great, but I love it here."

We reached the front of the queue and Laura requested adjoining rooms. "Stick with me babe," she said, winking as she slipped my room card into my hand, "Eee, we'll have a right giggle."

The atmosphere in the lobby was chaotic, everyone chatting and laughing loudly, exchanging room numbers, a few squeals here and there, cases sprawled across the marble floor, snippets of excitable conversation about where to go and what to do that night. I noticed a couple staring at us as they came in through the revolving doors. The woman couldn't take her eyes off us, swinging her head around to gawp further as they walked past. Everything was whirring around me, a muddle of red figures, voices over voices over voices. My head was spinning. Was I having an out-of-body experience? Or was it just jet lag catching up with me?

"C'mon," said Laura, pulling what appeared to be a genuine Chanel hand-bag out of her suitcase and over her shoulder. "Let's go crack open the vodka."

"Girl after my own heart," I replied.

As we attempted to leave, we were cornered by Martin at the lifts.

"Girls," he said, "We've been making some plans for tonight. W Bar seems to be the choice of venue – great place. Coming?"

He didn't have to persuade me.

"Yeah, I'm up for that."

"Absolutely," agreed Laura.

Martin rubbed his hands together. "Brilliant. Let's Foxtrot Oscar for three S's and see you down here in thirty."

"Okay," I enthused, although I had no idea what I'd agreed to.

I asked Laura to translate once we were in the elevator.

"Foxtrot Oscar means Fuck Off," she explained. "Three S's are: shit, shower and shave and thirty is half an hour. So, fuck off for a shit, shower and shave and meet in the lobby in half an hour."

"Oh I see." I said. "And do you know what Delsey Dining is? Is it a restaurant?"

Laura laughed. "No, it's literally eating out of your suitcase. We do it sometimes down-route when we want to save money – bring our own food, pocket the allowance and sit in our rooms eating packets of noodles and shit like that."

Gradually, I was learning the crew lingo, and the things they don't teach you in training. I had even discovered that as a thank-you for a hard day's work, Richard Branson let his crew each take two alcoholic miniatures from the drinks cart. I'd only found this out once I saw the rest of the crew start tucking into theirs on the crew bus, and I was the only one who had nothing to drink. I was given donations from other crew members and made a mental note not to forget this little bit of knowledge in future.

"I'll come through in twenty," said Laura, as we walked from the lift to our neighbouring rooms.

"Perfect," I replied, although secretly I thought I might struggle to get ready in twenty minutes – it would take that long to wash my hair. And I promised I'd call Jonathan, for which I'd need to buy an international calling card. Damn, why didn't I do that when I was in the lobby?

Jonathan and I were like ships – or, more aptly, planes – passing in the night. We hadn't seen each other in two weeks – since my Wings Ceremony – and he'd been all over the world in that time. Not that the distance was affecting our relationship; we were still madly loved-up and spoke on the phone nearly every day. And we'd discovered phone sex, which was what I was supposed to be doing now. Jonathan was currently in the UK before jetting off to Miami tomorrow morning. I'll call him later, I decided, throwing my luggage onto the super-king-size bed in my room. I'd have to put off the hair washing for now, too.

True to her word, Laura was banging on the door that linked our rooms exactly twenty minutes later. I'd had the quickest shower in history – over the gigantic bath – and was still doing my make-up when she knocked.

"It's open," I called, applying a slick of lip gloss.

Laura came sauntering into the room, vodka bottle in hand, wearing a sexy satin top in the same vivid green hue as her eyes, and black jeans with heels. Her glossy hair tumbled in mahogany waves over her shoulders and her skin looked so fresh – you would never have guessed she'd just stepped off an eight-hour flight.

I spoke to her reflection in the mirror. "Wow, you look fantastic."

"You too, hon," said Laura, already pouring generous measures of vodka. "It's party time."

"Diet Coke?" I said, opening the mini bar.

"Just a smidge."

We knocked back our drinks and headed down to the lobby, where the rest of the crew had congregated. The other girls looked breathtakingly beautiful, like celebrities on the red carpet – head to toe perfection. They all dressed chicly, smelt of posh perfume and cosmetics and all appeared to be clutching a Chanel, Louis Vuitton or Prada handbag. I glanced down at the beaded Topshop clutch in my hand and turned to Laura. "Looks like I'm the only one who doesn't possess a designer handbag here."

Laura laughed. "They're not real, like. They're knock-offs. You can get some in Chinatown – I'll take you there tomorrow if you like?"

I hooked my arm through hers. "Thanks babe," I said. "That'd be brilliant, I can't wait to hit the shops."

Miss My-boyfriend-bought-me-a-necklace-from-Tiffany's was there in the lobby, looking like Claudia Schiffer's doppelganger, face framed with long silky blonde locks, stylishly teased into gentle waves and not one split end in sight. She was wearing a classic, mid-thigh-length fitted black dress cut low at the back and sky-high glitzy sandals. Her willowy but toned limbs reminded me of honey-coloured fibreglass, like a mannequin's, and her eyes glittered like two Swarovski crystals. *No wonder he buys her gear from Tiffany's,* I thought.

The W Bar was also on Lexington Avenue, just a few blocks from our hotel – a short but thrilling walk. It was twilight and the skyscrapers were coming to life in dancing lights. I could hear horns tooting and the distant sound of sirens. A man in a suit whizzed past us on rollerblades, attaché case under his arm. I was awestruck by it all. I imagined that Laura and I were *Sex and the City* characters, strutting down the sidewalk in our heels, giggling. The show had only just hit our screens in the UK and I was hooked, hence my fascination with New York.

Everything inside the W Bar was white – white walls, white leather cubes for seats, swathes of white fabric hanging from the ceiling, white candles and tables. There were about fifteen of us altogether, taking over a corner of the room, making one hell of a noise.

"Right, you fuckers," shouted Martin, "Who's for cocktails? I say we start off with Manhattans."

No one disagreed.

We were huddled around a low frosted glass table. A couple of girls were perched on stewards' laps, sexual innuendos flying around the room. Everyone was chatting and laughing like they'd known each other for years. Martin and Tom, who I'd since learned was our first officer on the way out, returned from the bar with two trays full of Manhattans. "Time to get pished," Martin announced, handing out drinks. "Get 'em down yer."

I looked at Laura. "Do you know everybody here?" I asked.

"One or two," said Laura, between gulps of Manhattan. "Never met any of the others though. You rarely fly with people you know unless you put in a request. So, more often than not, you meet a whole new set of people on every trip. It's crazy, really; most people see the same faces every day at the office."

The more I spoke to Laura, the more I liked her. She was so stunning, yet she was not up herself in the slightest – and so funny and open. She told me she'd recently started dating a BA pilot called Dan, who was "proper tasty, like", and that she was a senior crew member working in Upper Class, serving all the "posh buggers".

I was beginning to lose the new girl feeling. Everyone was so friendly and lively, and even the Tiffany's girl, Sophie, was nice to me.

Manhattans turned into Cosmopolitans, which became an assortment of cocktails and spirits. Martin managed to burn the hair off his forearm during a Flaming Sambuca accident. The drinking games started and our rabble became rowdier. Outrageous stories were being told about other crew members – tales of hot-tub orgies in the Caribbean, Mile High Club capers and riotous room parties all around the world.

It was around 1am when we spilled, very noisily, back into the lobby of our hotel. "Right, who's up for a room party?" said Martin. For a man in his early fifties he had incredible stamina. I'd been up for twenty-four hours at this point and this was only a one night trip. The following evening we'd be heading home, and we were not allowed to drink eight hours prior to flying. As much as I wanted to join in the fun, I didn't want to spend my first and only day in New York sleeping off a hangover. Plus I still had to buy a calling card and phone Jonathan. It would be six in the morning at home. Jonathan would be getting up soon for his Miami flight. A sexy wake-up call from the Big Apple was most definitely on the cards.

I made my excuses to the rest of the crew and slipped away to buy a calling card from reception.

"Room 2204 if you change your mind, Mandy," called Martin, stumbling into the elevator.

The first thing I did when I got back to my room was to check under the bed and peek inside the wardrobes and bathroom – a routine we were advised to perform every single time we entered a hotel room, for safety purposes. Phew, it was all clear, no psychopaths lurking in the shadows. I kicked off my heels, sat on the edge of the bed, switched on the television and flicked through the channels, past CNN, *Frasier, Cheers, Die Hard 2* until I reached MTV, where Britney Spears was cavorting in a skimpy school uniform singing "Baby One More Time", which seemed an appropriate song to get me in the mood for my rampant phone call.

Ripping the cellophane packet off my phone card with my teeth, I ventured into the bathroom. I'd remembered there was a phone on the wall next to the giant tub. A luxurious bubble bath would be the ideal location for the business I had in mind. I was tipsy, but not drunk enough to drown during the act.

Singing along to Britney I spun on the taps, poured a generous amount of bath foam under the running water and headed back to the bedroom to undress. On the TV screen Britney had been replaced by Eminem, who was grabbing his crotch while asking the real Slim Shady to stand up. I took off my jeans, off-the-shoulder black top and underwear and draped them over a chair. Then I read the instructions on the back of the calling card and sat at the dressing table to remove my make-up. The digital clock on the TV screen indicated it was now 2am – 7am in the UK. *He'll definitely be up by now,* I thought.

Back in the bathroom I was greeted with a blanket of steam and a giant foam soufflé emerging from the tub. I giggled as the stiff peaks rose higher and higher. "Mmm, maybe too much bubble bath," I said out loud.

I turned off the taps and eased myself into the bath, enjoying the silky sensation of the water against my skin, caressing my aching feet, legs and back. I lay there for a while, relishing the moment of pure relaxation, then I reached up for the phone, grabbed my card resting on the lip of the bath and tapped in the ten-digit code followed by Jonathan's number.

He picked up on the third ring, his voice sounding a little deeper than usual. "Hello?"

I didn't hold back; phone sex is all about language – using sexy words and being downright filthy. "Hello gorgeous," I said in my best husky sex-goddess voice. "I'm naked, I want you ..."

"Is that you, Mandy?" Fuck, fuck and triple fuck. Bloody fuck, shit and bugger, it was Jonathan's dad, Stan.

I felt my face colouring, reaching a temperature greatly exceeding that of the bath water. I sat up sharply in the bath. What the fuck was I going to say? Blame jet lag for my mucky ramble? I couldn't exactly hang up – he knew it was me. I cleared my throat. "Yes, yes it's me," I said meekly. "I'm so sorry ... is Jonathan there?"

Stan laughed. "I'll get him for you, love."

At that point Jonathan picked up from the other extension in his bedroom. "Is it for me?"

"It's Mandy for you," Stan replied, then hung up.

Jonathan's opening line wasn't the most imaginative for an international sex call: "Got there okay, then?"

"Oh my God," I said, "I just started having phone sex with your dad. You said they were away."

Jonathan laughed. "You've probably made his day. Yeah, dad had to return early for work."

Embarrassed though I was, I decided to let it go – my minutes were precious.

"What are you up to?"

I'm naked," I said, "I'm all wet, bubbles everywhere. My pussy is aching for your throbbing Viking cock."

"Touch yourself and tell me how it feels," he ordered. Thank the Lord, *now* he was getting it.

Our smutty rapport went on for at least ten minutes, culminating in simultaneous orgasms on both sides of the pond. I writhed and convulsed as I touched myself beneath the foam, water heaving from the tub. And just after we'd expelled our final groans of ecstasy, my minutes ran out and the phone slipped from my hand and sprang against the wall with a crack. Definitely ten dollars well spent.

Later that morning I was woken by a phone call from Laura. "Ready to hit the mean streets of Manhattan?"

I lifted my head from the pillow. My hair was still damp from my raunchy bubble bath debut. "What time is it?" I asked.

"Nearly nine. Three S's and see you in thirty?"

"They don't call this the city that never sleeps for nothing, do they. I'd better get my arse in gear then."

Laura was the perfect tour guide – she left no stone unturned. After a much-needed feast of sesame bagels, cream cheese and tomato along with bottomless cups of coffee at the deli on Lexington, we headed up Forty-Second Street to Fifth Avenue and the Empire State Building. I was like a typical tourist, snapping away with my disposable camera (we didn't have camera phones in those days). The view from the observation deck was mesmerising – miles upon miles of silver buildings stretching into the mouth of the Hudson River, surrounding the huge green idyll of Central Park, so vast yet so miniature from such a height. I could imagine scooping the whole of Manhattan up into my palms.

From the Empire State we headed to Times Square, where I was introduced to the beauty mecca, Sephora, a huge store dedicated entirely to make-up and cosmetics.

"This is where we stock up," said Laura, snatching a tester bottle of Dune perfume from the shelf and spraying her neck. "They must make a fortune out of us."

I gazed longingly at the counters – Stila, Nars, Chanel, serums, fillers, lotions and potions. "Hold me back, Laura," I sighed, "I think I'm going to need a basket ... or a trolley." Seventy dollars each later we teetered out of the shop, arm in arm and swinging our glossy black bags full of goodies, into the buzzing energy of Times Square. A time-lapse film was playing around me – people whizzing past in hurried steps, the towering video screens flashing. I felt so lucky to be here – and so fortunate to have a pal to share it all with. Suddenly overcome with emotion, I gave Laura's arm a tight squeeze. "Thanks for showing me around – you've been amazing."

"Ah, don't be daft, babe," she said. "I'm having a blast – and it's not over yet. We've still got Chinatown to attack. You're gonna love Canal Street."

We packed so much into our day, including Canal Street, where I picked up a very authentic-looking pair of Dior sunglasses and a couple of pashmina scarves. On our way back I even got Laura to take a photo of me at the spot where Marilyn flashed her knickers on Lexington. We walked for miles and my feet were throbbing by the time we arrived back at the hotel, where, once again, we had a turnaround time of just thirty minutes to change into our uniforms and glam up before the crew bus rolled up.

Laura and I were inseparable. We sat together on the crew bus and talked non-stop en route to the airport, exchanging phone numbers and addresses. I was sad when we parted. "It's been emotional. You've gotta come to one of our house parties in Horley," said Laura as we boarded the plane. "They're legendary – I'll introduce you to some of the other girls, too. You'll love them – they're all PLU (People Like Us)."

"Absolutely, I'd love to," I said. Then she turned left and I turned right – back to Economy Class, and back to my po-faced pal Leanne.

The flight back to Heathrow was eventful. I figured at some stage of my career I would face some dramatic or traumatic circumstances, mentioned in training, but I wasn't expecting to be hit with such challenging episodes on my second sector.

The first drama happened as I was serving dinner. I was facing towards the rear of the plane pushing the trolley, Leanne on the opposite end. As I crouched down to grab a set of meals from the cart I felt someone grabbing at my skirt, it was a man bellowing and clicking his fingers behind me. "Hey, you, stewardess."

I looked over my shoulder to be confronted by the snarling features of a middle-aged man wearing a thatch of coarse grey hair. He was leaning over the side of his aisle seat, glaring at me.

"I need to speak to you, *now*," he demanded.

I flashed him a broad smile, the words "arrogant bastard" springing to mind. "One moment, sir."

I finished serving my passenger then headed back to his seat.

"How can I help you, sir?" I said, kneeling down to speak to him. Up close I noticed he had matching bristly grey nose hair, sprouting out of his nostrils like two paintbrushes. Next to him in the middle seat was a boy no older than nine or ten – presumably his son.

"What the hell do you call this?" asked the guy, pointing to the kid's meal.

"That's a chicken pizza, sir," I replied.

"I know it's a bloody pizza. It's a bloody pathetic, sloppy inedible pizza," he shouted, banging his fist on the boy's tray. "This is not what we ordered. My son can't eat this."

"Would you eat this?" he raged, grabbing the open carton containing the pizza and flinging it towards my face. The pizza leapt from its container, slapping cheese-side into my face before dropping to the floor with a splat. The other passengers were craning and twisting their heads round to see what all the shouting was about. His son shrank into his seat, eyes closed with embarrassment. I plucked a tissue from my tabard pocket, wiped the cheese and tomato from my face and leaned over the grey-haired man to speak to his son.

"Erm, that was actually an accident," said the pizza thrower.

"That may be so, sir," I said calmly. "But I think I'll speak to your son if you're going to act younger than him."

"What would you like to eat, honey?" I asked the lad. "You can have something special, if you don't like pizza. How about some nice chicken nuggets from the crew cart?"

The boy's face lit up. "Chicken nuggets, yes please."

When I returned with the nuggets the boy's father apologised for his outburst. I didn't bother explaining that this meant I would not be eating myself now, because at least it kept the peace.

"That's okay, sir, enjoy the rest of your flight," I said, smiling. I then strutted back to the waiting passengers I'd abandoned, wondering how he would react to having a pizza slung in his face.

The second incident happened about halfway through the flight, during a particularly rough patch of turbulence over the Atlantic. Leanne and I were sitting on empty bar boxes in the galley – our first chance for a rest since take-off – when the toilet alarm bell sounded. In training we were told the alarm signalled someone was in difficulty in one of the toilets at the front of the cabin.

Leanne rolled her eyes. "Probably some warped pervert with his knob hanging out ... it usually is. S'pose we'd better go and check it out. This might need two pairs of hands."

"Sure," I said, "let's go."

I followed Leanne to the toilet, situated in front of the middle row of seats. As we reached the door we heard a faint moaning sound coming from inside. I stood behind Leanne as she knocked but got no answer, so she unlocked the folding door from outside (we have a technique) and pushed it inwards. I nearly choked at the sight. Perched on the toilet, jeans and knickers around her ankles, was a woman in her late twenties, covered in blood, rocking back and forth, whimpering like an injured animal. Her face was smeared with blood, as were her arms and legs. There were bloody handprints on the cubicle walls and mirror, and the floor was also splattered. I had never seen anything so horrific.

The woman reached towards us with a quivering bloodstained hand. "My baby, my baby," she howled. "Please help me, please, please."

It then became clear to us what had happened – she'd suffered a miscarriage.

"We're going to help you, sweetheart," said Leanne, her voice soft and reassuring. We're here for you. What's your name?"

"Julia."

"Okay, Julia, we're going to help you."

I couldn't believe this was the same Leanne. "I'll deal with the passengers and get supplies," I said, as I started to clear the area of onlookers.

The passengers in the first few rows near the toilets were delighted with their move to the Upper Class bar. We then draped blankets around the overhead lockers and spare seats to create a private cubicle space for the woman.

I gathered plastic aprons, surgical gloves, face masks and cloths from our first-aid supplies in the galley and returned to the scene with more crew to help. Once dressed in our protective gear we were safe to enter the toilet cubicle.

Julia was sobbing, doubled over with her head in her hands. "Okay, Julia," said Leanne, crouching by the toilet and lightly touching Julia's upper arm. "We're going to help you out of here."

Julia, clearly in pain, lifted her head. "Thank you."

Very gently, Leanne led Julia out of the toilet into the cubicle space where, for the next half an hour, we cleaned her up, gave her feminine products and a fresh pair of Virgin pyjamas to wear, then settled her beneath blankets onto a seat.

"My husband, can I see my husband?" asked Julia, her pretty heart-shaped face a luminous white.

"I'll get him for you," offered Leanne.

As Leanne left the makeshift cubicle I took a seat next to Julia, raising the armrest that separated us. "Is there anything you need?" I asked.

She slipped a weak arm from beneath the blanket. "Will you hold my hand?"

I folded her hand in mine. "Of course I will," I said.

On touchdown at Heathrow, Julia and her husband were whisked away in an awaiting ambulance. I felt so sorry for her. A miscarriage is traumatic enough, let alone enduring one in an aircraft toilet at 35,000 feet. The toilet was in such a mess we had to seal it off.

One thing that had amazed me, however, was just how well Leanne had coped with the trauma. She was brilliant, switching from jaded flight attendant to Florence Nightingale in the space of seconds.

I reminded her of this as we travelled back to Gatwick on the crew bus. "That was really tough, Leanne. I don't think I could have coped with that on my own, but you were amazing."

Leanne pinched the bridge of her nose. "I've got a bitching headache now, though."

And just like that, Florence Nightingale turned back into Leanne.

It was mid morning when I finally arrived back at my little pebble-dashed house, barely able to place one foot in front of the other. I dumped my luggage in the hallway, walked into the lounge and fell onto the sofa. I was exhausted, emotionally drained – and what was that awful smell? I lifted my forearm to my nose, sniffed the sleeve of my jacket and nearly heaved. It was a strong aroma, like stale pasties mixed with … farts. Eau de Boeing, just as Leanne had predicted.

Memories of the last forty-eight hours reeled through my mind: the flight out, the W Bar, phone sex, sightseeing and shopping, pizza in my face and poor Julia. I had a whole day of rest ahead of me, then I'd be doing it all over again. I lay back on the sofa and sobbed.

CHAPTER FIVE

REST DAYS

The first few months were tough. After that first traumatic flight back from New York, I questioned whether I was actually cut out to be a stewardess. I cried myself to sleep on the sofa and woke up with a crippled back, banging head and eyes the size of Ping-Pong balls. My first thought when I looked in the mirror and saw my puffed up mascara-stained face was: I might have to quit this job.

But I'm a Northern lass and made of sturdy stuff, and as the tiredness subsided, the fond memories of New York, meeting Laura and the fun we'd had, spurred me on. After all, there'd be plenty more fun times ahead, right? They'd warned us in training to allow ourselves six months to settle in. I also had another good reason for not quitting. I'd finally heard back from Brighton Police regarding the charges I'd pressed against Neil for beating me up that night after the Jamiroquai gig. The sergeant said the charges had been dropped because the police officer dealing with the case had taken too long to prepare it. "She ran out of time," he explained. He then asked me whether I wanted to lodge an official complaint against her, or seek compensation. I declined. Neil was out of my life for good now and pursuing a lengthy battle against the cops would only serve as a brutal reminder of that awful night. What I hadn't forgotten, though, was how proud and liberated I'd felt when I'd landed this job – I'd set myself free from Neil and that was my revenge. If I gave up now, he'd win.

So I wiggled my size-ten bum back into my red skirt and got back on that big white bird.

It was gruelling. I was doing two long-haul flights in eight days with one or two night stopovers and one day's rest in between in the UK. Including the security briefings and occasional delays, my working day could sometimes be up to twenty-six hours long – and most of this time I'd spend on my feet without any breaks. The in-flight supervisors in those days were incredibly strict. We weren't allowed to be seen eating in uniform, so if we did want a snack, it had to be eaten in the privacy of the galley with the curtains firmly drawn. There were no seats in the galley, so as soon as the metal bar boxes were empty we'd use them as stools – sometimes padded with a cushion nicked from an empty passenger seat if you wanted to be posh. Then the in-flight supervisor would come along and tell us to put all the boxes back.

My body clock was completely screwed up from the time zone changes … not to mention all the partying down-route. It's no wonder many new recruits threw in the towel within the first few weeks of flying, or ended up getting sacked for screwing up. Like Sarah, from my Ab Initio course, who got the boot for falling asleep on the job. She was travelling home from Orlando – her second trip – when, so overwhelmed by tiredness, she decided to steal forty winks. Thinking no one would notice her absence, she found an empty passenger seat, curled up and nodded off beneath a blanket. When the purser found her and shook her awake, bleary-eyed Sarah barked, "Don't touch me, I'm trying to sleep." Instant dismissal.

There was nearly always a drama on board, usually involving demanding or insolent passengers, who thought it was perfectly acceptable to belittle and abuse crew. This happened again during my second flight to New York, while I was serving coffee to a woman in Economy. She was one of those types who obviously couldn't afford to travel Upper Class or Premium, but really thought she belonged there – mid thirties, wearing a beige dress from a high-end high street store, knock-off designer shades perched on her head, loads of costume bling and looking down her nose at everyone around her. "Would you care for tea or coffee, madam?" I'd said politely, stopping the cart by her seat. Without looking up she pointed at her cup on her tray, blurted "coffee" and continued reading *Marie Claire*. She even didn't say thank you when I filled her cup.

"Is there anything else I can get for you, madam?" I said.

Then she glanced up at me, took one look at my name badge and sneered: "Mandy Smith? You've come down in the world, haven't you. Didn't you marry some millionaire rock star?"

The ignorant bitch thought I was the model-cum-pop star Mandy Smith, who married, then divorced, Rolling Stones bassist Bill Wyman.

"Yep, that's me," I said with a smile. "Still keeping it real by working – the bills don't pay themselves. Now, is there anything I can get for your children?"

The woman sneered and turned to speak to her kids, two girls aged around nine and eleven sporting matching purple velvet dresses. "See that, girls," she said, nodding in my direction. "That's where you'll end up if you don't do your homework and do well at school – serving tea and coffee on a plane."

Unfortunately, this kind of attitude towards crew is prevalent among some passengers. Many believe our sole duty is to dish out meals and pour coffee. Some of them never see what goes on behind the scenes – when we're cleaning up after miscarriages, restraining violent passengers and, in some cases, saving lives. If that woman had been on my flight back from Delhi the following week, for instance, she might have witnessed me cleaning up and restitching a gentleman's five-inch stomach wound, which had burst open mid flight following a recent operation. On the plus side, however, I was discovering that many perks came with this air hostessing lark. Just eight weeks into my career I'd flown to New York, Orlando, Johannesburg and Delhi – and I was discovering a beauty treatment gem at every destination. In Joburg, at the luxury Sandton Sun Intercontinental Towers Hotel, I could get my hair cut and styled at a snip of the price I would back home – plus an amazingly soft paraffin wax treatment. Delhi's Hyatt Hotel was for threading – an eyebrow shaping there set me back no more than eighty-five rupees, which is about eighty pence in Sterling. I'd also heard you could get your bits waxed to perfection at a bargain price in San Fran, but I was yet to travel there being so new (flight routes are all about seniority).

I was also making lots of new friends, and with every flight came a whole new set of faces. My social life had gone from a few drinks down the local pub on a Friday night to riotous parties all over the world in the matter of weeks.

My social life at home in the UK was becoming more hectic too. In addition to the crazy room parties down-route, there were also crew house parties happening all over Sussex, which were equally as outrageous, involving lots of nudity, drinking and sex – as I discovered when I attended my first one at Laura's house.

I was just home from Joburg, enjoying my rest day, curled up on the sofa watching *Some Like It Hot* while my washing churned in the machine, when Laura called.

"Hey Mandy, please tell me you're not jetting off anywhere today," she said, her voice loaded with excitement.

"Not today – just back from Joburg yesterday – Vegas tomorrow. Why?"

"House party at mine tonight – you've got to come – all the girls will be here and I want you to meet them."

I was tempted. For once I wasn't feeling too tired – and Jonathan was in the Caribbean so I had no date fixed with him, and no other plans except to get organised for the following morning. And Laura had told me so much about the girls – the BA hostesses she lived with, Sally and Joanne, and her best Virgin dolly pals Felicity and Suzy, whom I was itching to meet. But partying the night before a ten-hour flight was probably not a wise idea.

"I don't know Laura. I've got to check in at ten in the morning."

"Ah bollocks, that's plenty of time. Bring all your stuff for tomorrow and you can leave from my place in the morning. Stop drinking by midnight and you'll be fine."

"But what if ..."

"I'm not taking no for an answer. It's not going to be a wild one – just us girls, pizzas, face masks, manicures, few glasses of vino. A few others might be popping in later but I've not told that many people about it. Come on, Mands ... I'll do your nails for you for tomorrow."

How could I resist?

"Okay, but I'll need to be semi sensible."

"Great, see you about five."

"I'll be there."

I arrived at Laura's bang on five. Best to start early and crash early, I reasoned. I wasn't entirely sure what the appropriate dress code was for a house party so I opted for a smart yet casual knitted brown dress with knee-length boots and tights.

"Maaandy," shrieked Laura, flinging open the front door, glass of white wine in hand, looking stunning as ever in a gun-metal halter-neck satin dress.

I trotted in with my wheely case, squealing. Laura haphazardly rested her glass on the hall radiator shelf and threw her arms around me. I hugged her back and we rocked from side to side, giggling and screeching.

"Come into the lounge," she said, when we eventually let go of each other. "Jo and Sally are here – the others are on their way. Can I get you a drink? I'm so excited to see you."

"Me too."

"Come," she added. "We can take your stuff upstairs after you've met everyone."

I followed Laura into the lounge where Joanne and Sally were sitting on the sofa by a fireplace decked with twinkling white fairy lights, their feet up on a pouf, with pedicure separators between their toes. Both girls were blonde – one had a bob and the other had long hair pulled into a low side ponytail that was draped over her shoulder in a glistening sheet.

"We've just been having a little pedi session, like," gushed Laura.

I walked further into the room, hand outstretched. "Hiya, I'm Mandy, I've been so looking forward to ..."

I was interrupted by something moving out the corner of my eye that almost made me jump out of my skin. I turned my head sharply and gasped at the view. For there on the floor, staring back at me from a huge cage, were two giant rat-like creatures with bushy tails and enormous ears.

"Bloody hell, Laura," I said clutching my chest, "are they Gremlins?"

Everyone laughed.

"They're chinchillas," explained Laura, crouching by the cage and making funny faces at the animals. "Mandy, meet Sonny and Cher."

"Hi Sonny, hi Cher," I cooed.

"Want to hold one?" asked Laura, reaching for the cage door.

"Oh no, no, it's okay … I mean, later, maybe? Sorry, they made me jump, that's all."

"No need to apologise. That's the first time I've seen Sally smile today," said Laura, crawling across the floor and tickling one of the feet on the pouf.

The girl with the bobbed hair retracted her foot sharply. "Stop it," she giggled.

"Twice," declared Laura triumphantly.

"You must be Joanne then," I said, extending my hand towards the other girl.

"Just call me Jo. Lovely to meet you."

"Yes," added Sally, reaching forwards to shake my hand, "Laura's told us so much about you. Come and sit down," she added, patting the cushion to her right.

"Drinks, everyone?" said Laura, as I took my place on the sofa.

Sally knocked back her half glass of wine in two generous gulps then lifted her glass in the air. "Fill her up."

"We've been having a bit of a conference, Mandy," said Laura, taking Sally's glass.

"Wine, beer, spirits – what d'ya fancy?"

"Here, I've got a couple of bottles of red in my bag," I said, rising to my feet.

"Don't be daft, sit down. Chat to the girls – I'll get you a drink and take your bags upstairs for you."

"Thanks, Laura – wine's in my crew bag. What's the conference about?"

"Fucking men," said Sally, biting her bottom lip. "Bastards."

I glanced at Jo, not really needing an explanation.

"Sally split up with her fella yesterday," she said. "They were together almost a year."

"Fucking bastard, wanker, cunt," added Sally, shaking her head. I noticed her eyelids were swollen beneath layers of pearly pink shadow. "Sorry, Mandy, I don't normally use that word – but for him I make an exception."

"Cunt," repeated Jo.

"Utter 'see you next Tuesday'," said Laura, appearing in the door frame carrying a tray loaded with drinks.

"What did he do?" I said.

Three glasses of wine later I'd heard the whole sorry tale. Sally had been seeing her ex, a BA steward called Alex, for "eleven months and twelve days". They met on a flight from Heathrow to Chicago and spent the entire trip holed up in a room overlooking Lake Michigan at the Hilton Hotel, ordering room service and shagging. On the flight back they joined the Mile High Club in the crew rest area – he was the best lover Sally had ever had, sensitive, passionate and very complimentary. "He said I had legs like a dancer's," sighed Sally, "and breasts like perfectly moulded jellies." It had been the perfect relationship and Sally had even suspected Alex was on the verge of proposing. Then she discovered, via a reliable source, that Alex had cheated on her with, not just one, but two other air hostesses, Lisa and Annette, in a threesome in Barbados. "He didn't even deny it," Sally said incredulously between slurps of wine. "He didn't apologise. All he said was, 'It's been over between us for a while now. It's time to move on.' He'd obviously been thinking about ending it – and I'd been looking at bloody bridal magazines."

"Well, it sounds to me like you're well shot of him," I said. "What a dick."

Poor Sally. She seemed like such a genuine, gentle person. And she was so pretty: diamond-shaped face and soft violet eyes, little ski-jump nose spattered with honey freckles. I imagined how I would feel if Jonathan cheated on me and shuddered. I'd be devastated – and the humiliation, being the last person to find out ... at work. It didn't bear thinking about.

My thoughts were interrupted by the doorbell ringing repeatedly, prompting some peculiar high-pitched barking noises – girly barks, almost – from Sonny and Cher.

"That'll be the girls," said Laura, leaping from her armchair.

There was another flurry of excitement as Felicity and Suzy teetered into the room, carrying plastic bags full of chinking bottles.

"Sally."

"Flis."

"Jo."

"Suze."

"Sally."

"Jo."

"And you must be Mandy," said one of the new arrivals – a tall blonde resembling Christie Brinkley in her "Uptown Girl" days – as she leaned forward to peck my cheek. "I'm Felicity, Flis."

"Suzy," said her friend, kissing my other cheek. Busty with masses of long blonde hair, she looked a little like Abi Titmuss ... only far prettier.

I liked all four girls instantly – Laura was right, they totally were PLU. It was like gaining a new family – a chosen family. The drink flowed and the conversation returned to Sally's broken relationship. "I hope he's caught a nasty disease," she slurred.

"He deserves to have his bloody dick cut off – do a Bobbit on him, hon," Felicity suggested. "Arsehole."

"Arsehole," echoed Suzy. "I think you've been far too lenient on him, Sal. If Jimmy did the same to me I'd kill him."

Jimmy, I discovered, was Suzy's boyfriend – another Virgin steward. "This is him," she said, fishing her purse out of her bag and flipping it open to reveal a cheesy photo booth picture of her with her man, a man I recognised from my previous Delhi trip – the same man I'd mentally nicknamed Jimmy Forsyth, because he had a huge jutting-out chin like Bruce Forsyth's. I hadn't warmed to Jimmy. I thought he was a bit of a knob, and he hadn't mentioned anything to me about having a long-term girlfriend.

"Oh my God," I said, peering at the photo, "I flew with him the other week."

Suzy looked up at me all dreamy-eyed. She was sitting on the floor in front of me, legs curled beneath her, nestling in an overly shaggy shocking pink rug. "He's lovely, isn't he?" she cooed, dropping her purse back into her handbag.

"Yeah, he's great," I lied.

I was having such a nice time getting to know the girls that I didn't really notice the room filling up. People had been arriving in dribs and drabs. But somewhere between my third and fourth glass of wine I became aware of the fact that our little posse had morphed into a crowd of at least thirty, spilling into the hallway. Hed Kandi tunes were pumping from the stereo and I could barely hear what Suzy was saying to me. Sally and Jo were getting their feet rubbed by a first officer called Simon, and Felicity was wedged into an armchair with a black-haired guy, snogging for Britain. Another couple were practically having sex up against the wall by the chinchillas' cage when, out of nowhere, two girls wearing nothing but G-strings and heels came bouncing into the room, arms linked, boobs jiggling. They bounced around for a few seconds, laughing hysterically, then turned and ran out again. I'd seen shows of this nature several times down-route – normally occurring during games of truth or dare. Nearly all of the dares involved getting naked and running around hotel corridors. A cabin crew party isn't a party without at least one fleeting nude episode.

"'Nother drink?" shouted Sally, slapping her hand on my thigh as she attempted to peel herself off the sofa, her upper body swaying. I took hold of her hand. "Fancy some fresh air?"

Sally looked at me, her eyes struggling to focus. "What's your name?" she said.

I helped her up and guided her through the crowd of revellers into the hallway, where more people were gathered. Sally could barely walk. "Shoes. I need my shoes," she insisted, then pointed at a door beneath the stairs. "There." At least she knew where her shoes were.

"I'll get them for you, babe," I said. "What do they look like?"

I opened the door on a surprising scene: a Henry vacuum cleaner, a pile of shoes and a girl giving a guy a blow job. He was completely starkers and she knelt tightly to the right of him, head bopping up and down and making little humming noises. He was stroking her hair as if to say, "good girl, stay there, keep going". What was I supposed to do? Ask them to stop for a moment while I rummaged around for Sally's shoes? I shut the door. I didn't even think they'd seen me.

Sally slumped her head on my shoulder. "I feel sick," she groaned, followed by a hiccup.

I hooked my arm under her armpit. "Where's the bathroom?"

"Upstairs."

"Excuse me, coming through," I yelled, jostling Sally past the bodies in the hall. It took a huge amount of effort to get Sally up the stairs – she practically fell up them, falling asleep halfway, her limbs limp and heavy. We only just made it into the bathroom in time – and had to kick another frisky couple out in the process. Sally let out a faint moan and slumped to the floor next to the toilet bowl, her arms floppy and rubbery. I crouched by her side, pulled her hair back from her face and gently rubbed her back. "You'll feel better after you've been sick, babe," I said, my voice all mumsy. Sally grasped the toilet seat, retched, spewed – pure white wine pumping from her stomach, slapping the toilet water, spraying the sugar-pink porcelain rim. When she'd finished she started sobbing, fat, inky mascara tears streaming down her face, snot dribbling over her lips. "He thinks I'm ugly. Do you think I'm ugly?" she asked, wiping her nose on the sleeve of her dress.

I flushed the chain and wrapped my arms around her. I could smell vomit on her breath. "You're not ugly, babes. You're beautiful."

"I want to go to bed," she sniffed, her hair glued to her face with fresh vomit.

"Me too," I said. "I've got a Vegas tomorrow."

I would've loved to have carried on partying, but I knew if I went back downstairs it would be too tempting to stay. So I washed Sally's face, found the room with my luggage in it, and slipped into bed beside Sally, as the party throbbed beneath us … right round to the following morning.

I woke early – just before seven – showered, changed into my uniform, did my hair and make-up and headed downstairs, into the post-party carnage. It didn't look as though anyone had made it home, the hall and lounge strewn with sleeping bodies. There were empty bottles lying everywhere and party food mashed into the carpets. I found a space in the hall to leave my case and crew bag and made my way through the human obstacle course, stepping over the crashed-out revellers, following the scent of burning toast.

I walked into the kitchen to find Laura, in her dressing gown and slippers, with a towel turban wrapped around her head, eating toast and reading a magazine.

"Morning," she breezed, leaping from her seat. "Did you sleep okay? Would you like a cuppa, some toast?"

"I'll do it," I offered. I was ravenous.

"No you won't. Sit," ordered Laura.

Over breakfast Laura filled me in on the events of the previous night.

"It was pretty tame, actually – neighbours banging on the door at 3am, threatening to call the police, few broken ornaments, live sex shows in the lounge. Flis left about 1am with that fella she was playing tonsil tennis with all night ... and, erm ..." Laura's voice trailed off, her eyes drifting skywards, acrylic nails drumming the table. "Dan came over. We had sex then he dashed off – said he had a flight today. He was acting a bit strange, to be honest. Bloody men."

"How?"

"I don't know, he didn't seem that, well ... into it, if you know what I mean."

"Maybe he was just tired," I said.

Our conversation was interrupted by my Virgin mobile ringing in my handbag. I delved into my bag and grabbed the phone.

"Hi, is Mandy there, please?"

"Yes, speaking," I sang.

"Hi Mandy, it's Jim from Crewing ... where are you?"

"Oh hi, Jim," I said brightly. "I'm just having breakfast."

"Breakfast? Mandy, you were supposed to check in five minutes ago."

I glanced up at the clock on the wall. It was only 8.35am. What was he talking about? "Check in isn't until ten," I said. "I've got plenty of time."

"We're on the winter schedule now, Mandy – it switched last week."

Oh bugger. I took a slurp of tea. "Sorry – I swapped onto this flight. I'll be right there."

"Fuck," I cursed, throwing the phone back into my bag. "I need to go."

"I'll see you out," said Laura, springing from her chair.

Fortunately, Laura lived close to the Flight Centre. If I hurried I'd make it. But after stumbling back through the human debris in the hall, another obstacle thwarted my exit: the front door was locked and Laura had no idea where the key was.

"Shit," said Laura. "It was my key – it was in the lock last time I checked. Shit."

"What about the back door?" I suggested.

"You can try, but it's like Steptoe's yard out there – there's a heap of junk blocking the side gate."

"Let's give it a go," I said, scooping my case up in my arms.

One of the girls who'd been sleeping on the hall floor stirred, sat up and peered down her top.

"I've got a squashed sausage roll in me cleavage," she giggled.

Laura grabbed my crew bag from the floor. "Let's get you out of this bloody madhouse."

Laura hadn't been exaggerating. Their back garden really was like Steptoe's yard. Stacked against the wooden gate leading to the driveway – the only way out – was a complete bathroom suite, broken table and chairs piled in the bath, an industrial-size tumble dryer, a knackered lawnmower and piles of broken tiles, among other dilapidated odds and sods.

I stared at the wreck before me. "Right," I said, "I'll climb up and you pass me my bags."

I wedged my feet into a pile of tiles then climbed onto the rim of the bath, holding on to the top of the gate with one hand. "Ready," I called.

Laura lifted my case. "Be careful, Mandy," she warned.

I grabbed the case, heaved it over the gate, followed by my hefty crew bag and handbag, trying desperately not to lose my balance. Then I climbed onto the tumble dryer, hoisted my skirt and vaulted over the gate, landing neatly in the driveway.

I could hear peals of laughter from the other side. "Are you okay, Mands?"

"I'm fine, Laura. Better dash – I'll call you in the week, hon."

Then I ran through the streets of Horley, my ground shoes skating over the frosty pavement. I arrived at the Flight Centre just as the bus engine chuckled to life. "Vegas, here I come," I said under my breath as I clattered towards the bus door. I'd made it – and I hadn't even snagged my tights.

CHAPTER SIX

GALLEY FM

There's nothing cabin crew love to do more than have a good old gossip. When the passengers are fed and settling down for a kip or watching the in-flight entertainment, we huddle in the galley, perched on our bar boxes, and giggle over the outrageous stories doing the rounds. Cabin crew are renowned for their zany and promiscuous proclivities, both down-route and on board, and their japes kick the galley gossip mill into overdrive. There are no secrets at Virgin – every antic is noted and talked about. Some stories are true, others turn out to be hyped-up rumours. Some of us even started rumours about ourselves, to see if they ever got back to us – and they did. There's a phrase we use for the discussions that go on behind those soundproof galley curtains: Galley FM – and trust me, you don't want to make the bulletins.

Some crew members made quite a name for themselves as a result of their debauched shenanigans. One of them was Paula, a raging nymphomaniac with frazzled blonde hair who went through men like tights. She was a popular Galley FM topic because she was always getting drunk and making a show of herself down-route or on nights out. I flew with Paula a few times in my early days, although I felt I knew her better through Galley FM. Every time I saw Paula she looked different. She had a weird routine: get married, get fat, get divorced, get her stomach stapled and then get hitched again. She'd done this at least four times that I knew of.

Once, on a night out in Hong Kong, she got so drunk that she wet herself. She didn't even try to conceal it. Standing legs astride, she simply let it all out and then laughed, pointed at the puddle on the floor and exclaimed: "I've just pissed me self." When she'd finished, she whipped off her soggy knickers in the middle of the packed bar, spun them above her head by her finger and hurled them across the room, where they landed on a startled Chinese businessman's head.

In another equally shocking incident, Paula found herself passed out in a bush in Brighton, knickers round her ankles and smeared in dog muck. A couple of stewards found her, fished her mobile from her bag and called her then husband, whose response was: "You can fucking well keep her – I've had enough." So the guys had to carry her home with them, reeking of dog poo.

But Paula's finest moment happened when she was caught performing a blow job on a popular boy-band singer at 35,000 feet. She'd forgotten to lock the toilet door and a passenger walked in on her mid job. She was handed her notice after that one.

I also encountered a few alcoholics, one being Sharon. On trips she would just stay in her hotel room alone, drinking. She also had a tendency to steal items from hotels – usually random things. I remember being on a trip with her in Shanghai where she was caught trying to nick a bolster cushion. Hotel staff saw the cushion hanging out the side of her case as she walked through the foyer. Some were amazed that she kept her job.

Crew were forever injuring themselves. Drunken accidents led to broken limbs, backs and necks – people diving into swimming pools from balconies, cliff diving or injuring themselves on quad bikes and banana boats down-route. A steward called Jack was actually sober at a room party in Cuba, but he was hoisted on someone's drunken shoulders and he fell head-first into a large television cabinet, embedding his teeth in the wood and fracturing his neck. In the same week a pilot and his purser wife were so tired after a night flight that they crashed her car and landed upside down in a ditch, resulting in the pilot's neck being broken.

One accident that really got tongues wagging was when Tina broke her neck during a shower romp with a fellow dolly, Millie. It all began in the Jacuzzi at our crew hotel in LA. After several shots of tequila, Tina and Millie – both proud owners of giant plastic boobies – peeled off their bikini tops and put on a lesbian show for the lads by fondling and kissing each other's boobs. When two of the guys joined in, they decided to continue their sex show in the privacy of Tina's room. But when they got there, the girls only seemed to have eyes – and hands – for each other, to the point that they thought it'd be rather fun to try out the strap-on Tina had brought with her. Moments later, after Tina had strapped on her ten-inch black dildo, she and Millie were frolicking in the shower over the bath while the lads perched on the side of the bath and watched. Apparently Tina then tried to angle the dildo into Millie and, as she did so, slipped and fell flat on her back, dildo still vibrating, her neck twisting and cracking as her head smashed against the corner of the bath on her way down.

Millie called 911 and Tina was stretchered out of the hotel with her ten-inch plastic erection still in place. She never lived that one down.

Sex stories were common, especially those involving mile-high escapades. Many crew often popped into the Premium Economy toilets for a quickie. It's the most spacious toilet on board an Airbus A340, with a handy fold-down baby-changing table to rest your bum on. Some colleagues also used the crew rest area bunk beds for their steamy liaisons. My friend Suzy had an unfortunate experience in the crew rest area on the Boeing. She was giving a steward a blow job when violent turbulence caused the plane to drop about twenty feet from the sky ... just as he came. She said she was almost sick.

A few crew members soon spotted an entrepreneurial opportunity in the rest area. For £250 an hour, they hired out the space to amorous passengers wishing to join the mile-high club. This went on for some time before their scam was rumbled by management. Understandably, they were all sacked on the spot. The crew rest area is strictly off-limits to all passengers.

It's a known fact that the airline industry is an incestuous environment. Casual bed-hopping is rife and crew sexploits are rarely kept secret. A group of lads – straight, party-hard stewards nicknamed the Vengaboys, most of whom had joined up to be the only straight man on a trip with twenty girls – had a "rugby boy" style competition going to see who could shag the most crew. There were about seven of them in total and they shared a huge house in Smallfield, Surrey, along with a hostie called Gill, who slept in a tent in their living room. The Vengaboys charted their sexual conquests on a whiteboard, which they kept on the kitchen wall and showed off at every party. Red wings were awarded for shagging a junior, brown wings if she let you shag her up the bum, white for an in-flight beauty therapist, black for a flight service manager and pink for gay sex. And to prove that they'd actually done the deed, they had to bring home a souvenir from each woman – usually a pair of knickers or a bra.

It was always fun going on trips with the Vengaboys, although they never got any work done and were constantly playing pranks; one of their favourite pranks was to hide in the overhead lockers. The first time I flew with Greg, the head of the Vengaboys, he filled up my flight bag with sugar and replaced my life jacket with a regular one for my safety demo. Every crew member had a tale to tell about the Vengaboys – they were hot gossip on Galley FM.

Some of my colleagues' idiotic antics ended up being broadcast beyond the galley curtains ... in the national news. In January 2002 – just four months after 9/11 – a French steward was charged with writing phoney bomb threats in the aircraft toilet on a flight from London to Orlando, which forced the 747-400 to make an unscheduled landing and take-off at Keflavik Airport in Iceland. The plane was searched but no bombs were found, and the plane safely proceeded to Orlando.

He was arrested at Newark International Airport two months later, as he was about to board a flight to London. His arrest came after an FBI investigation that included analysis of fingerprints left on a toilet mirror and air sickness bag on which the threats "Bin Laden is the best, all Americans must die" and "There is a bomb on board – Al-Qaida" were scrawled.

He was sentenced to five years' probation and a $176,000 fine, to be paid to cover our costs at Virgin Atlantic. As a result of the case, security rules became even stricter on crew for all US flights, and the guards in Orlando hated us more than they had done before. We were all so shocked – we couldn't believe one of our own crew could do such a thing.

Two other attendants, Nick and Allyson, made national headlines in 2007 when they became stranded at sea during a visit to Richard Branson's paradise home Necker Island. They survived for eighteen hours after going overboard in the shark-infested Caribbean Sea, being hurled into the water after their canoe capsized during a storm. They clung to lob-ster pots for seven hours then swam three-and-a-half miles in the dark, through ferocious waves, to an uninhabited island. After a further seven-hour wait on the isle they were saved in a rescue operation spearheaded by Richard himself.

Nick was one of the many flamboyant characters at Virgin Atlantic. He often appeared on flights in fancy dress. One morning he turned up to an Orlando flight with only a Winnie the Pooh costume in his bag but got swapped onto the Vegas route. He wore the costume all around Vegas and ended up getting invited on stage during a show. I also heard that he once wore a ladies sari for a Delhi flight instead of his uniform – Nick was such a character he was the only person who could ever get away with this; anyone else would have been disciplined for turning up to work out of uniform.

Of course, another name that frequently cropped up during Galley FM chats was Richard Branson. Many dollies threw themselves at Richard; he was often seen at functions with attractive hosties draped on his arm.

Richard was also renowned among his staff for his generosity; he was always inviting crew to Necker Island and enjoyed partying with us when-ever he was down-route. He once offered two of our crew the chance to get hitched on Necker Island, after they'd announced their engagement to him in a conversation at the bar on a New York–bound flight but told him they had no money to get married just yet.

Richard is such a good sport; he doesn't mind making fun of himself. On our inaugural trip to Toronto – where a star-studded party was thrown in a huge lavish marquee on the tip of the harbour bay – the Weather Girls were performing "It's Raining Men" and he was dancing on stage with the other hunky choreographed dancers – pulling his clothes off in unison with them to reveal Union Jack shorts as the finale. He attracted more attention than Ronan Keating, who also performed at the party – the Canadians had never heard of Ronan, so it was just all of the crew who sat at his feet on the stage, swooning and singing along with him. We were all over the moon when he joined us for a drink later after his performance, because he was such a gentleman.

Many celebrities were cherished by the crew, because you knew you would have a laugh when they were on board: Scottish actor and comedian

Billy Connolly was well known for giving impromptu comedy shows in the Upper Class bar. And of course there's "the Hoff" – David Hasselhoff – who is such a good sport and always up for a laugh; I once walked into the galley to find him and the other stewardesses swapping shirts for a bet.

Some passengers have even been known to write letters of complaint to the ground managers about the explicit conversations overheard through the galley curtains. One letter in particular raised a few eyebrows. It was from a passenger who'd typed up the whole conversation and had been horrified to hear a hostie discussing her detailed sex life, including failed attempts at anal sex.

Galley FM still continues to this day, and I'm sure my name has popped up from time to time. Just remember though: like most headlines, not everything you hear behind those "soundproof" curtains is true.

CHAPTER SEVEN

JOBURG HIGH JINKS

You don't go to Johannesburg for an early night and a mug of Horlicks. You go there to party ... hard. And boy, did we kick the arse out of it. As soon as you saw Joburg appear on your roster you knew exactly what fun lay ahead: drinking, eating superb food, sunbathing, shopping ... and the wildest room parties ever.

You could have either a two- or five-night trip to Joburg in those days, depending on which aircraft you flew out on. There's no drastic time zone change to deal with, so there's absolutely no excuse not to get rat-arsed. And because Joburg has a dizzying altitude of almost 6,000 feet above sea level, the booze shot straight to your head in minutes.

Staff at the Sandton Sun Intercontinental Towers Hotel must have dreaded our visits. We caused mass disruption and chaos there. It wasn't really safe to go out in Joburg, so our shocking misdemeanours often happened within the hotel. It had everything we needed: spa, pool, bars, restaurants, Nelson Mandela Square – which was just through the sprawling shopping mall and full of more restaurants and bars – and a walkway linking us to the BA crew hotel and our gym. Room parties at the Sandton were wild affairs and there was always one person who'd take things too far. Once, a steward threw a sofa out of a window from the thirtieth floor. It crashed onto the street below and, miraculously, no one was injured, but I heard on Galley FM that the steward was sacked.

With so much hedonistic fun to be had down-route in Joburg, it was always a bonus if you could share the experience with your friends. So in February 2000, Suzy, Jonathan and I requested a trip there together. It couldn't have come at a better time. I'd barely seen Jonathan recently and our break would take in Valentine's Day. I'd even bought some props to spice things up a bit: the *Kama Sutra*; a 3D Mould-a-Willy kit; edible knickers; raspberry sorbet edible body paint and a couple of racy negligees from Ann Summers. My case was like a travelling sex shop – the security guards at Heathrow had a field day scanning my case, giggling and nudging each other like children.

I wasn't the only one anticipating some action. Suzy was in the late recovery stages of a bitter relationship break-up – the phase where she was re-immersing herself, with newfound verve and confidence, in the dating game after weeks of crying and not eating. Jimmy "big chin" Forsyth had dumped Suzy after falling for another crew member. For a while we were extremely concerned for Suzy. It hit her hard. But after lots of TLC from us girls, her depression gradually lifted. Now she was spreading her wings – and her legs – by embarking on no-strings-attached flings with a number of stewards. In our previous week's crew briefing on our way to St Lucia, she realised she'd slept with every steward in the room. It was payback time for Suzy. "I'm chewing them up and spitting them out," she said.

This particular trip to Joburg was a five nighter – and we planned to make the most of every minute. There were some gregarious characters among our crew: our captain Nathan, a towering six-foot-four figure, well spoken but bumbling, with a penchant for fancy dress; Sindy and Katie – both big-time exhibitionists who appeared to be joined at the hip, and Adam, who had Mediterranean looks, fancied himself as a bit of a stud and was itching to bed Suzy. About fifteen other equally flamboyant and colourful personalities completed our merry throng.

Our first night began in a civilised manner with a slap-up dinner and wine at the Butcher's Shop steak house in Nelson Mandela Square. From there the group fragmented. Some headed up to Nathan's suite for a room party, while the rest of us shimmied along to the hotel bar for cocktails, where we managed to piss off a group of over-the-hill BA hosties sporting floral Laura Ashley-esque dresses and reading glasses. They took one look at us glamorous young Virgin girls strutting in and immediately looked the other way. They were even more infuriated when the two pilots they'd been sitting with decided we were far more interesting than them. The two men – both in their mid fifties – couldn't leave their seats quickly enough and were soon mingling with our mob, gathering at the bar. One of them, who introduced himself as David, "pilot for British Airways", sidled up beside Suzy and me. There's a standing joke among hosties: "How can you tell who's a pilot at a party?" The punchline being: "Because he will tell you."

"Can I get you lovely ladies a drink?" David said, his crinkly eyes fixed on Suzy's huge cleavage.

Suzy instinctively rippled her body like a pole dancer into an S-shape, flashing David a treacly smile. "We'll both have Screaming Orgasms, please."

David self-consciously rubbed the back of his neck with his left hand. I noticed he was wearing a wedding ring. "Two Screaming Orgasms coming up," he said with a nervous laugh, then shuffled to the bar, crossing paths with Jonathan, who was headed in our direction holding two goldfish-bowl-size glasses of Pinotage.

"Who's that?" he said, cocking his head over his shoulder.

"Ah, that's David," I said. "He's a BA pilot ... he's off to get me and Suzy a Screaming Orgasm."

"I'll give you a screaming orgasm you'll never forget later," said Jonathan, handing me one of the glasses.

"I'll hold you to that."

I sipped my wine, enjoying the sensation of the velvety liquid trickling down my throat. A fog of laughter and high-pitched conversations filled the room, drowning the languid background jazz music. I spotted David's friend, smoothing down his wispy comb-over and chatting up a vampish hostie, whose fake boobs were popping out of her little black top. I glanced over at the BA hostesses, who were still shooting us hostile looks that screamed: "We were once like you." It made me smile.

"Here, Suzy," I said, motioning towards them with my glass. "Do you think that'll be us one day?"

"Hell no," she laughed. "We'll still be partying when we're ancient."

Just then David returned with our drinks on a tray. "Two Screaming Orgasms," he said.

"So, David," I said, reaching for my glass. "I see that you're married."

"Was married," he said hesitantly.

Me and Suzy exchanged knowing looks. Of course he was still married – we'd heard this old chestnut many times before.

"Does you wife not understand you?" I said with a sarcastic tone.

I took a sip of my Screaming Orgasm, then another sip of wine. "David, meet my boyfriend, Jonathan. He's training to be a pilot too. We'll leave you two alone to talk planes – thanks for the drink."

Then I edged into the crowd with Suzy, leaving Jonathan and David to their geeky aircraft chat.

A few drinks later and we were becoming far too rowdy. The drinking games had started and we were getting foul looks from some of the other guests who were trying to enjoy a civilised tipple in a relaxed environment. The BA hosties had long gone and, when Sindy and Katie started kissing and fondling each other in an overly dramatic manner "just for a laugh", we decided that was probably a good moment to make our exit, too.

"Let's take this upstairs," shouted one of the stewards as the two girls broke away from each other in fits of giggles, lip gloss smudged clown-fashion around their mouths. Drinks were downed in record time and off we clattered like a drunken, cacophonic marching band, through the lobby, into the lift and up to Nathan's suite to wreak more havoc. Realising he wasn't going to pull, David had made his excuses and left. His mate, however, must have got lucky; he was nowhere to be seen when we left – and the vampish girl he'd been fawning over had vanished, too.

Nathan answered the door to his suite wearing a ten-sizes-too-small salmon T-shirt dress, which left nothing to the imagination. He was also wearing a rabbit shower cap with inflatable ears and holding a glass containing a scarlet drink resembling mouthwash that was garnished with a cocktail parasol.

"About bloody time," he beamed, flinging open the door. "Come on in."

"Fucking hell," said Adam, staring at Nathan's bulging crotch as we spilled into the room, "What yer come as this time?"

Nathan glanced down at his groin, bunny ears drooping forwards. "I must say, it does feel rather snug down there."

Adam shook his head. "See all yer meat and two veg in that, mate."

"I've exchanged clothing with Natasha," Nathan explained in a serious tone. "She's wearing my chinos and polo shirt."

But Adam had now lost interest in Nathan's dress and was raiding a table loaded with booze bottles along with Suzy.

"You look a million dollars in that, Nath," I said, standing on tiptoe to kiss his cheek. "Fantastic figure."

"Knockout," added Jonathan, patting his shoulder as we walked by.

Nathan laughed loudly – he had one of those booming upper-class laughs that reminded me of a character out of *Blackadder*. "I do like to keep in shape. You know what they say: a moment on the lips equals a lifetime on the hips."

Nathan's suite was huge. Pilots always get the best rooms, and that's why they're used for so many crew parties. The main room – a sprawling lounge with its own office space – was a hive of activity. There were bottles and items of clothing strewn across the floor, and Puff Daddy's "Come with Me" was uh-huh-ing and yeah-ing from the stereo. People were laughing and counting out loud, as a girl with bubbly blonde curls, wearing nothing but a pair of bikini bottoms and a diving mask, was performing a headstand against the wall. Others sat on the huge window ledge, smoking cigarettes. On a giant television screen, encased in the ornate solid teak cabinet, a peroxide-blonde woman was giving a streaky-haired guy a blow job, as a long-haired man pounded into her from behind. The whole porn-in-the-background thing actually started as a prank played on many nasty pilots whom no one liked – we would drink their room bar dry and order porn so they had a huge room bill – but it had actually caught on and became a common background scene at a lot of our room parties. On one of the sofas in the room, a girl was simulating a deep-throat blow job on a banana as her friend fell about laughing.

"Forty nine, fifty," chanted the headstand spectators. The girl's legs fell to the floor over her head so that all we could see was her arse swallowing the tiny triangle of orange bikini. She stood up, picking the fabric from her bum. "I feel all dizzy," she said, reaching for a miniature of rum resting on top of the teak cabinet. "Someone else's turn now."

Suzy returned from the table with three glasses containing a viscous beige liquid. "I've made Mudslides," she declared, her eyes radiating mischief.

"She's taking it up the backside now," said Jonathan, nodding at the television.

The semi-naked headstand girl came skipping towards us, her boobs now covered by a white T-shirt that was so thin you could see the brown tinge of her nipples through it. "We're all playing truth or dare," she said excitedly. "Come and join in."

I don't think I've been to one room party that hasn't involved a game of truth or dare. They're inevitable. I tended to opt for truth rather than dare. It was a no brainer: firstly, you could lie through your teeth, and secondly, everyone was so off their tits they wouldn't remember anything you'd said anyway – although this did backfire on occasion. I wasn't a prude; I did my fair share of dares. I just didn't see much point in flashing my wares to all and sundry every time.

This time though, emboldened by Mudslides, vodka, Screaming Orgasms and wine, I accepted a dare from Nathan, which, astonishingly, didn't involve flashing or streaking, or performing naked headstands.

"I dare you to fill up the lift," said Nathan, motioning towards the door with his bunny ears.

This was a common pursuit on trips – to pack the elevator so full of furniture that no one could get in. Sometimes we'd even stack furniture outside hotel room doors so the boring crew who hadn't come to the room parties couldn't get out. It was all taken in the lighthearted way it was meant.

"Easy peasy," I said, handing my glass of mud to Jonathan.

One by one I carried and dragged pieces of furniture from the hallway and Nathan's suite along the corridor – a chest of drawers, coffee table, two swivel chairs, an armchair and a standard lamp. I was spotted by a few guests leaving their rooms as I assembled the furniture by the lift. "We're just moving things around – having a change around," I said with a terrible South African accent. When the corridor fell silent again, I made my move. I called for the elevator, praying no one was inside it. I watched the floor numbers flash by on the digital display, giggling to myself, until the doors pinged open. The lift was empty. I blocked the door with the armchair and set about filling it up. I couldn't stop giggling. As I heaved the last piece of furniture – a chest from the corridor – into the lift, I heard a door close followed by hurried footsteps. *Fuck,* I thought, *I'm going to get caught here.* I tried to crouch behind the armchair still blocking the door but there was hardly any space to stand, let alone crouch. I'll just walk out, I reasoned, and act shocked. As far as anyone else was concerned, I could have found the lift in this state. So I casually stepped out of the lift ... and bumped into Suzy, naked aside from a skimpy pair of black knickers tied at the sides.

"Ah, Suze," I said, "Thank God it's just you."

"I got the topless knock-down ginger dare," she said, peering into the lift and laughing. "Looks like you've passed your dare – no forfeit for you."

Then she turned, hammered three knocks on the door opposite the lift and sprinted down the corridor giggling. I heard voices calling after me as I darted back into Nathan's suite.

The party continued, getting louder and wilder as the hours slipped by. Every drink I guzzled was a different colour: red, green, blue, pink, yellow. More and more people were stripping off. A hostie called Francesca was flashing her recently purchased double-D implants, saying, "Go on, touch them," to anyone who was interested, like they were just hats she had bought. We were all pulling moonies at the window and one guy did a full strip and ran down the corridor and back with his cock slapping his thighs.

It was almost 4am when a security guard arrived to "investigate a number of complaints". He'd been knocking on the door for some time but no one had heard him. It was only because Nathan had noticed the phone ringing that he knew he was there. Nathan turned the stereo off and answered the door. The security guard – a stocky South African man – did a double take when he saw Nathan, who was still sporting his salmon dress and bunny cap.

"Can I help you?" said Nathan, covering his groin with his huge shovel hand.

The security guard walked into the room, almost tripping on an empty Bacardi bottle at his feet.

"You're the Virgin Atlantic party?" he said, stating the obvious.

"Yes, that is correct," replied Nathan.

Drunken sniggers filled the room.

"We've received some complaints. May I speak to your captain?"

"Well of course," said Nathan, removing his bunny cap, "I am the commander."

The security guard shook his head. "You're disturbing our other guests. And the furniture in the elevator ... is that from here?" He glanced around the room, searching for missing pieces, his eyes momentarily fixing on the lesbian spanking scene now playing on the television.

"I'm terribly sorry," said Nathan. "We'll clear everything up – and you won't hear another peep from us."

The security guard raised his hands. "Please keep the noise down."

"Of course, of course," vowed Nathan, ushering him out the door. "Like I said, not a peep."

It was midday when Jonathan woke me, planting feathery kisses over my face. "Happy Valentine's Day, gorgeous," he whispered. I blinked a few times until his face came into focus. He was lying beside me on top of the covers, his head propped in his hand, a towel wrapped around his waist.

"Happy Valentine's, babe," I croaked.

"Look what I've got," he said, pulling a tube and a paintbrush out from under his pillow. "Strawberry flavoured body paint."

"I don't believe it," I said, "I've brought some too ... raspberry sorbet."

Jonathan threw back the duvet and rolled on top of me. "How do you fancy breakfast in bed? Chase away the hangover."

Hangover? I was still drunk. "Oh yeah," I moaned, sliding my hands beneath his towel, "colour me in."

He unscrewed the tube and squeezed the red paint onto the brush. He then painted "I" on my left breast, "love" on my right and "Mandy" across my midriff, adding a kiss below my belly button. He took a moment to admire his work, smiling proudly, as if he'd just created a masterpiece. I looked down at my graffitied skin and laughed. "Now you're going to have to eat those words."

"I intend to," Jonathan said, already lowering his head to my breasts. He rolled back on top of me and, very slowly, kissed a path from my boobs to my navel, devouring the paint. I looked like a murder victim by the time he'd finished, my torso smeared red. And Jonathan looked like Hannibal Lecter after a three-course meal with his strawberry-stained lips and face.

We stayed in our room all afternoon playing with our Valentine's toys. Jonathan was thrilled I'd bought him a copy of the *Kama Sutra*. We mastered the Erotic V position – which involved me sitting on the edge of the dressing table with my feet hooked around Jonathan's neck – the Catherine Wheel and the Splitting Bamboo, which gave me the most intense orgasm. But I nearly broke my neck attempting the Suspended Scissors position. This was the trickiest and involved me suspending my body with one hand on the floor, lying sideways with my feet resting on the edge of the bed. Jonathan's job was to step over my left leg, hold up my right leg, then, with his other hand supporting my waist, enter me from behind. It was impossible – each time Jonathan tried to step over my leg my arm gave way and my head crashed to the floor. "I don't think this is happening, babe," I said, collapsing again after our fourth attempt. "Maybe we should move on to the Ship ... or the Landslide?"

We worked up huge appetites – I was so hungry I ate my edible knickers. They weren't exactly sexy: white, plastic and surgical-looking. After our Suspended Scissor disaster we were both too exhausted to try any more positions, so we ticked off the ones we had conquered and made a note of the ones we'd try next time. As we lay in our paint-stained sheets, flicking through the book, the phone rang. I answered it. It was Suzy.

"Happy Valentine's Day, hon – I hope you've been naughty like me."

"Why, what have you done?" I asked in a voice that really said, "I know what you've been up to."

"Adam has only just left my room," she said in a loud whisper, as if he was still in earshot.

"Why are you whispering?"

"He came back after the room party – I haven't been to sleep yet. Fuck me he's a goer: huge cock, very ... girthy."

"Worth going back for more?"

"Maybe. Unless someone better comes along to test drive. Anyway, enough about him, what are you up to?"

"Oh, you know, nothing much. Sitting in bed, covered in strawberry and raspberry body paint, reading the *Kama Sutra*."

Suzy giggled. "Well, get yourselves ready – we're all meeting in the bar in an hour."

She hung up before I could reply.

Another night in Joburg turned into another debauched night in Joburg, ending with another room party interrupted by security. This time Nathan was wearing a Fred Flintstone costume when the guard arrived. "I'm terribly sorry," he explained again. "Would you care for tequila?" It's a good job the security guards had a sense of humour.

The days all seemed to blend into one in Joburg. We hardly slept and the amount of drink we got through was criminal. On our final day – our only sober day – a few of us went on a safari tour at Pilanesberg National Park, near Sun City. Set in the crater of an extinct alkaline volcano, and fringed by concentric ridges, the park is home to every South African mammal, including the "big five": lion, leopard, black-and-white rhino, elephant and buffalo. We were told this by our tour guide, Ryan, who looked as though he too should've been roaming among the wildlife. He was so hairy: a mop of curly black hair, furry arms, woolly neck and hands. There were even hairs sprouting from the bridge of his nose, but strangely he suited it and was actually quite handsome – in a Neanderthal kind of way.

The Jeep crawled along rugged paths, past forested ravines and rolling tawny grasslands where rhinos lay on their sides, lazy and heavy against the trees, and zebras pranced along the plain. Every time we thought we'd spotted a lion it turned out to be nothing more than a mound of moving dry grass. Ryan got us into a little spot of difficulty en route to the Main Lodge house for lunch. We were driving along a tree-lined road – he was singing along to that annoying song "The Bad Touch" by the Bloodhound Gang, which was blaring from the radio, and trying to get us all to join in – when a baby elephant emerged from the trees and trotted alongside the Jeep, swinging its little trunk with a cute smile on its face. Ryan continued along the path, singing, oblivious to the calf, driving us almost head-on into the calf's mother, who charged out from the trees, flaring her ears, screaming and trumpeting. We all screamed. Ryan shouted, "Holy fuck," slammed on the brakes and reversed the Jeep at top speed. Fortunately the three-tonne elephant didn't give serious chase – she just wanted to put herself between us and her baby – but it was still terrifying how close she had come to ramming us.

We couldn't even go on safari without a drama occurring. And there was a further drama on the flight home. No one had seen Sindy or Katie since our first room party. We hadn't thought much of it at the time; it was perfectly normal for some crew to do their own thing on trips and Sindy and Katie went everywhere together, anyway. But they reappeared in the hotel lobby when the crew bus arrived, looking a little drained and stiff. I noticed Sindy struggling to lift her flight bag, flinching and clutching her chest every time she tried to hook it onto her arm. "Shall I take that for you?" I offered.

"I'll be okay," she said with a grimace. "I want to look normal."

"Have you injured yourself? You don't look very well, babe."

"No, I'm fine," she said. "I think I overdid it in the gym yesterday, that's all. I'm perfectly fine."

But halfway through the flight Sindy was forced to admit to our flight service manager, "I've had my boobs done," after her new implants had exploded mid flight. During our trip to Joburg, Sindy and Katie had been under the knife, which explained why they'd gone AWOL. After Sindy's trauma mid flight, Katie also confessed she'd had a boob job and they were both taken off duty. They thought they'd saved themselves a fortune getting top surgery at a snip of a price in Joburg, but their new inflatables ended up costing them dearly. When they got home they were sacked. Honestly, the lengths some girls will go to ... all for a pair of fake boobs.

CHAPTER EIGHT

THE FLOWER GIRLS

I blame my naked antics in Barbados entirely on Felicity. She's always had a bizarre fascination with skinny dipping, taking her clothes off and running around in the buff. But who can blame her for showing off her size-eight figure and gigantic GGs? Now it seemed Felicity's love for streaking had rubbed off on Laura and me. It was late evening – approaching midnight – and the three of us were completely starkers, standing by a pool at the lavish Tamarind Cove resort, giggling hysterically with the local tall Heliconia Wagneriana flowers sandwiched between our butt cheeks.

We'd just been skinny dipping in the waters of the Platinum Coast – where a cast of mischievous crabs had moved our clothes along the beach – and we were running back to our hotel, ducking behind plant pots and palm trees, when Felicity suggested a further prank.

"Let's do a dare," Felicity said, reaching into the plant pot and yanking three of the long-stemmed flowers from the beautiful tropical display. "I say we stick these flowers in our bum cheeks and swim across every pool in the resort. Anyone who drops the flower has to perform a forfeit."

"You're fucking mad, you," Laura said, snatching one of the flowers. "How am I supposed to fit this in me crack? My bum's virtually non-existent."

"Easy, I'll show you." Felicity turned around, poked her slender bum in our faces and slid the flower between her cheeks, snorting with laughter as she did so. Laura and I were clutching on to each other, giggling.

"You have to clench," Felicity added, squeezing her bum and waddling forwards. "Just like this – squeeze and clench, squeeze and clench."

"Oh fuck it, I'm game if you are, Mands," Laura said.

"Honestly, the stuff that girl gets us doing," I said, having no trouble positioning my flower between my ample butt cheeks. "Let's just pray no one sees us."

Leaving our clothes in a pile behind the floral display, we climbed into the amber-lit pool and tried to swim to the other end. It was an impossible task – the only way to keep the flowers in place was to keep our legs together and use only our arms to swim – and we couldn't do that for laughing. We made it across the pool, despite losing our flowers several times, and then repeated the process in the second and third pools before dashing back for our clothes, our flowers now soggy and droopy in our backsides.

"I think we've all earned forfeits," Felicity said, scooping up her clothes.

"Bugger that," I said. "That was a forfeit in itself."

We then ran, dripping wet, clothes clutched to our chests, past the bar terrace and guests' rooms, through the hotel lobby, where we were greeted by a red-faced receptionist.

"Morning," chirped Felicity as we jiggled and slipped through the lobby, our feet making wet slapping noises on the marble flooring.

"Don't mind us," I sang.

The receptionist didn't know where to look. She just nodded and turned her eyes to some paperwork. We pattered up the stairs, still giggling and pulling on items of clothing, and returned to the room party we'd nipped away from ... all dressed in each other's clothes.

It was late July in 2001, and Felicity, Laura, Jonathan and I had used one of our two monthly requests to jet off to Barbados together, along with Laura's then BA pilot boyfriend, Dan.

Barbados is a beautiful teardrop of an island with dramatic cliffs, ocean views and exotic wildlife: turtles bobbing in crystal waters and monkeys lolloping by the roadside. The Tamarind Cove resort was a blissful oasis of calm, with red tiled buildings, fountains and tropical gardens opening out to a glorious Bounty advert crescent beach where the waves ruffled at the shore like can-can girls' knickers. It was such a quiet, tranquil resort ... until us lot tarnished it with our Club 18–30 style behaviour. The local nightlife left a lot to be desired in those days (although it's a lot livelier now), there wasn't much else to do in hurricane season, when there was more hotel staff than guests. So we amused ourselves.

It was good to let our hair down and enjoy some light relief. The flight out to Barbados had been rather solemn. The day prior to our departure, a Concorde had crashed just minutes after taking off from Roissy Charles de Gaulle airport, killing all 109 people on board and four people on the ground. One of our crew, a steward called Spencer, lost one of his best friends in the disaster. She was an air hostess on board the Air France aircraft, who had just found out she was expecting a baby and hadn't told her manager yet, as she was due to be grounded for the rest of her pregnancy following that fateful flight. Spencer cried all the way to Barbados. He was heartbroken. "I only spoke to her two days ago," he explained to me in the galley, tears trickling down his cheeks. "Why did it have to happen, Mandy ... why?"

I couldn't answer his question, but I could offer a shoulder to cry on. "You know, you didn't have to come to work today; you shouldn't be working – you're grieving, it's natural," I told him.

He looked at me with his red-rimmed eyes and, with a sad half-laugh, said, "I need the money, Mandy."

We were all worried about Spencer. He didn't leave his room on our first day in Barbados. He said he wanted to be alone so we respected his wish ... but called his room from time to time to check in with him.

Meanwhile, back in the Mandy and Jonathan love bubble, there was cause for celebration in Barbados. On our second morning, after my naked flower-in-the-bum escapade, Jonathan asked me to marry him. It took me completely by surprise. We'd now been together for two years and although our relationship was strong, he'd never brought up the subject of marriage prior to this. It was bizarre how it happened. We'd just had sex – the *Kama Sutra* position of the day for us being the Lotus Flower – and I'd asked Jonathan to hold my feet while I did some sit-ups on the floor. It was a routine I performed prior to hitting the beach: 250 sit-ups to flatten the tummy.

"You really don't need to do all these sit-ups," Jonathan said, kneeling between my knees as he held my ankles. "You've got a beautiful body."

"I don't think the receptionist would agree with you after last night's episode," I joked.

"I'm still gutted I missed that."

"Serves you right for not coming skinny dipping with us. Prude."

I raised my upper body, kissing Jonathan's lips as I came up. We did this 250 times – sit-up, kiss, sit-up, kiss, and after my final sit-up, as I lay back on the floor, Jonathan popped the question. He rested his dimpled cheek on my knee and smiled. "I love you, Mandy."

"I love you too."

"Marry me."

This made me sit up again. "Are you serious?" For some reason I thought Jonathan was joking.

"Of course I'm serious. I want to marry you. I want you to be my wife, Mandy."

Images of wedding gowns, a vintage Bentley and dress shopping with the girls whizzed through my mind. I threw my arms around him, shrieking: "Oh my God, oh my God," over and over.

"I take it that's a yes, then?"

"Yes. Yes, yes, yes, yes, yes," I shrilled. I was ecstatic. "I can't wait to tell the girls – they can all be bridesmaids. Would you prefer a church wedding, or registry office ... or we could get married abroad, here maybe? On the beach: won't that be romantic? Although personally I like a good old-fashioned church wedding. And we should tell our parents – they're going to be thrilled – let's call them now. What time is it back home? I wonder whether I'll go for ivory or white. Vintage or modern? What about a ring ... I don't have a ring."

Jonathan's smile faded. "I'll get you a ring. I'll save up for one, but I don't think we should broadcast our news. Let's keep it quiet for now, eh? Keep it between us two."

His words punctured the tyres of my vintage Bentley. "Can we not just tell our parents? My mum and dad will keep it under their hats," I fibbed, knowing full well the moment I broke the news to Mum she'd be on the phone to Jeanie Mac and the rest of the family, saying, "My baby's getting married."

"It's just for now, Mands. Let's not rush things. We've got plenty of time."

"Okay, but don't be angry if it accidentally slips out. I'm just excited, that's all."

"Me too," Jonathan said. "Now, let's get to the beach – the others will be wondering where we are."

As soon as I saw Laura, her tiny, toned figure lost in a vast, comfy sun-lounger, I ran towards her in the hot sand, arms flailing, shrieking: "I'm getting married, we're engaged."

Laura sat up, looked around through her oversized Prada sunnies, searching for my voice, then spotted me. "I'm engaged," I cried again. Laura was with Dan, and about a dozen other crew members, all in a line on the beach facing the sun – and all were looking in my direction. They looked like the cast of *Baywatch,* a landscape of mountainous boobs, tanned six packs and hummock bums.

Hearing me the second time Laura sprang from her sun-bed and ran over to greet me, screaming and clapping. "Oh my God, I can't believe it. Congratulations," she said, slinging her arms around me, and then shouted over my shoulder, "Congrats, Jon."

In my moment of excitement I'd forgotten about Jonathan. I'd ignored his mutters of "Mandy, please don't," when I'd dropped his hand and bounced down the beach towards Laura. He strolled up beside me. "I thought we'd agreed to keep it quiet, Mandy," he muttered into my ear.

"I've only told Laura," I said with a light laugh, as the rest of the crew whistled and clapped.

I joined Laura on her sun-bed and Jonathan sat with Dan. Everyone was firing questions at us.

"So, when's the big day then?" Dan said.

"Let's see your ring?" asked one of the implanted girls whose name I couldn't remember.

"Did you get down on one knee, Jonathan?" Laura said. "Knowing you it was romantic."

"I was doing me sit-ups," I replied. "And he popped the question."

"Can I be a bridesmaid?" requested Alex, who was fastening a Slendertone belt around his waist with one hand and swigging a vodka Diet Coke from the other.

"Course you can, sweetie," I said with a wink. "You can join my girls." I turned back to Laura, "Obviously you, Felicity and Suzy are going to be my chief bridesmaids."

"Eee, that's great, I'm made up for you both."

"Talking of Flis," I added, "Where is she? I thought she was meeting us here."

Laura grinned. "She's gone off with that water sports instructor ... local guy ... what's his face? The one she met yesterday."

"Denton?"

"Yeah, that's the one."

The previous afternoon, as we'd sunbathed, Felicity had seen Denton – a tall, dark, muscular figure – emerging from the sea. She rose to her feet from her sun-lounger, and declared: "I'm having him." She sashayed over to him – stomach sucked in, boobs pushed forwards, untying her long blonde hair and shaking it free – and shook his hand, then disappeared along the beach with him. That had been around two o'clock. We didn't see her again until eight o'clock when she turned up at the room party, still wearing her bikini and a miniscule denim skirt, her face flushed chilli red and sporting a pair of flip-flops, which she'd borrowed from Denton for her walk of shame back from his equipment hut, where she'd spent the afternoon "shagging his brains out".

Although it was hurricane season, we'd been lucky with the weather so far: blue skies, temperature averaging around twenty-three degrees, with a gentle breeze. The atmosphere today was chilled. Dan and Jonathan went to the bar and returned with a tray of cocktails, while Laura and I stretched out on the double sun-bed, chatting about weddings.

"You're not going to make us wear hideous dresses, are you?" Laura asked.

"I'm thinking tangerine orange taffeta with puffball sleeves."

"Or you could go for the slutty ballerina look," added Alex, perching on the edge of our bed. I glanced over at him. He was fiddling with the control pad on his slimming belt.

"Why are you wearing that thing?" I said. "You are not fat."

Alex wouldn't have looked out of place as an extra in Wham!'s "Club Tropicano" video: waxed, tanned body; skin the colour of Red Leicester cheese from frequent visits to spray-tan booths; his teeth Hollywood white; and his brown, quiffy hair streaked with hay highlights.

"Are you kidding me, girlfriend? I need to lose at least a stone. My Jamie will look elsewhere if I'm not careful. I've not eaten any carbs in a week and still I can't shift this gut," Alex sighed, glancing morosely at his flat stomach.

"Let's have a look at that thing," I said, shuffling down the bed on my bum. "What setting have you got it on?"

"Number two, I think. The instructions said to start on a low setting and gradually build up the intensity."

"Maybe we should crank it up a bit?" I offered. I leaned forward and pressed the up-arrow button a few times. The vibrations intensified. "How does that feel?"

"Good, really good. Let's go higher."

I jabbed the button several times. The vibrations were now travelling through the bed.

"I can feel it working now."

"Crank that up some more," added Laura, rotating onto her belly.

"It feels proper good, that."

So I continued jabbing the button until the belt reached full speed. "How does that feel, babe?" I said.

Alex grabbed the edge of the bed with both hands, his whole upper body convulsing. "I ... think ... I'm ..."

He couldn't get his words out and I noticed his Red Leicester face was turning a sickly shade of green.

"Are you okay, Alex?" I said. "You look a bit off-colour."

"I think ... I'm ... going ..."

He then heaved violently, leaned forwards and spewed into the white sand. I ripped the belt off him, trying not to laugh. Laura snorted loudly as Alex vomited again. I rubbed his back. "I'm sorry babe, maybe I took that a bit too far."

Alex wiped his mouth with his hand. "Well, that's one quick way to shed the pounds," he said.

As he recovered, Alex seemed quite chuffed that he'd emptied the entire contents of his stomach and celebrated by ordering a club sandwich. "I can afford the calories now," he beamed.

We stayed on the beach until sunset. A few cocktails were downed, although we couldn't drink too much ahead of our flight home the next day. This didn't deter some, though; a few went on to party in Bridgetown.

Laura was pissed off when Dan decided to join them. "I thought we were going to have a quiet night," she said, as we trundled across the sand towards the beach restaurant. "I've got to work tomorrow – I can't get hammered."

"I haven't got to work, though," was Dan's response.

I wasn't too keen on Dan. Laura had invited him to Barbados on one of her free-of-charge staff travel tickets, and now he was abandoning her on her last night by buggering off with a bunch of people he'd only just met. I wondered what Laura saw in Dan at times. He wasn't exactly Mr Personality; compared with Laura's effervescent nature, he was relatively dull and hardly made any effort to get to know her closest friends. He was quite good looking, I suppose: mid thirties, about six foot with a gym-buff body and a moody, handsome face. But his lack of charisma somehow cancelled out his good looks.

So Dan vanished with the Bridgetown-bound posse and Laura came to the restaurant, where we celebrated my engagement to Jonathan over a couple more cocktails, just "for the road", spending the last of our trip allowances.

I couldn't sleep that night – I was still buzzing after Jonathan's proposal, and when I did eventually drop off, I drifted into a wedding anxiety dream. It was the day of my wedding, which, bizarrely, was due to take place at Whiteleys shopping centre in Bayswater, London. But, for some reason, I was at JFK Airport, where our flight had been delayed, then cancelled, and I still hadn't bought a dress. Felicity was there ... and Laura, I think. I was running around the airport, trying to find a shop to buy a calling card, but everywhere was shut. An announcement was put out over the tannoy – it was Jonathan's voice: "Urgent call for Miss Mandy Smith – your wedding has been cancelled ... I repeat, your wedding has been cancelled."

I woke up mumbling: "But it's my special day." It took me a moment to realise where I was. We stayed in so many hotels that they all tended to blend into one after a while. This room had apple-green walls decorated with a few contemporary-style Caribbean paintings – an up-close image of a fuchsia, another depicting a sunset over the ocean – and archway doors leading to a balcony overlooking the Platinum Coast. It was 9am.

Jonathan was still sleeping, his arm curled around his head on the pillow, mouth agape. I kissed his forehead and left him to sleep.

On my way down to breakfast I bumped into Laura in the corridor. She emerged from her room, slammed the door behind her and then turned and stuck her two middle fingers up at the door.

"Hey Laura, are you okay?" I said, even though it was blatantly obvious something was bugging her. She turned round, her face set in a tight scowl. "He's a fucking idiot."

I gave her a hug. "What's he done now?"

Laura pulled away and linked my arm in hers. "I'll tell you over brekkie."

We loaded our plates at the breakfast buffet and settled at a table on the outdoor terrace. "So he didn't come home last night," said Laura piling a forkful of eggs Benedict into her mouth. "He rolled in at eight o'clock this morning – said he'd only just got back from Bridgetown. I didn't have an issue with this – we all party round the clock. But when he was in the shower the phone rang. It was some tart, asking to speak to 'Dan, my boyfriend'. She said he'd left his watch in her room."

"Shit, did you confront him? What did he say?"

"I didn't bother confronting him ... there's no point."

"Surely you're not going to let him get away with it, though?"

Laura shrugged. "It's okay. While he was still in the shower I cancelled his ticket home. He knows nothing about it – he won't find out until he checks in."

I laughed. "Good for you, babe. I can't wait to see his face."

"Mmm, look behind you," Laura said, her chirpy grin returning.

I looked over my shoulder. It was Felicity, sporting a naughty grin and a sexy black fitted playsuit. She fell into the seat next to Laura and, before she said anything, pulled an ivory pair of knickers out of her bag and threw them on the table, narrowly missing Laura's eggs Benedict.

"Mind me food," Laura said, shifting her plate away from Felicity's underwear.

"Do we have to look at your smalls over breakfast?" I added.

Felicity then explained how she'd spent a night of passion with Denton in his equipment hut. "We got up to all sorts in a three-man inflatable kayak," she said. But when she'd woken up that morning, she couldn't find her knickers. "I couldn't find them anywhere," Felicity added, reaching for Laura's coffee. "I woke Denton up, and said, 'Hey, what have you done with my pants?' And he denied knowing anything about it until I had searched high and low for them, then he produced a jar, rammed full with women's knickers – mine included."

"Weirdo," I said.

"He then said he wanted to keep my knickers as a souvenir. 'I will smell them and always think of you,' he said."

Orange juice spurted from Laura's nostrils. "What did you say to that?"

Felicity sat back in her chair, folded her arms across her breasts and said, "I told him, 'You can't keep them – they're part of a matching Bravissimo bra and pants set.'"

Everyone on the terrace turned to look at us – we were all laughing so hard.

"So," Felicity added, wiping a tear from her eye, "what's been happening with you girls?"

Laura composed herself. "I've binned Dan, and Mandy's engaged," she blurted, and then burst out laughing again.

"Bloody hell," Felicity said. "I can't leave you lot alone for five minutes."

This was what it was like on trips. No matter what dramas occurred, we always laughed. It was our coping mechanism. We laughed again later that day when Dan tried to check in at Barbados International Airport. Our crew watched as he argued with the woman behind the desk, thumping his fist on the counter and saying, "I'm a pilot for British Airways."

"Come on, let's go," Laura said. "What a knob-head."

On cue we all extended the handles of our Delseys, turned and walked in a sassy red line towards security.

"Laura, wait," yelled Dan, running behind us. "There's a problem with my ticket – they're saying I'm not on the flight."

We all stopped, and as though rehearsed, looked over our shoulders, and with big, cheesy smiles, sang, "See ya," then carried on walking through security.

CHAPTER NINE

THE MILE HIGH CLUB

"**M**arathon ground control, this is November niner niner, eight zero Delta, requesting clearance for take-off." Jonathan's voice flooded my ears through the headphones like a powerful aphrodisiac.

"This is Marathon ground control. November niner niner, eight zero Delta, you are clear for take-off."

I reached over and gave Jonathan's bare thigh a gentle squeeze. "Chocks away," I said with a cheeky giggle.

Jonathan pushed in the throttle and the little Cessna chuckled along the tarmac.

"Airspeed alive," he called out as the plane gathered pace, his brow knitted in concentration. God, he looked sexy – so authoritative, masterful. The Cessna thrashed down the runway, engines growling, vibrations tickling my bum through the seat until the plane leapt into the clear Florida sky like a giant tin locust. I peered out of the window and watched the Keys shrink beneath us, surrounded by waters of varying shades of turquoise, cyan and teal.

"It's a lovely clear sky out there," said Jonathan, "Perfect for VFR [Visual Flight Rules] flying."

"Sure is," I said, stroking the soft blond hairs on his leg. He looked so handsome – unshaven and rugged, which was unusual for him. He was showing me how to check the horizon to make sure we flew straight. I gazed at him not hearing a word ... I had only one thing on my mind that day: sex.

It was mid July 2001. Jonathan was still a trainee pilot and was building up his flying hours in Florida in order to gain his commercial pilot licence, so I'd taken a week off work to join him there. It was a rare treat for us to spend some quality time together away from the pressures of work and home. After Jonathan's marriage proposal – which turned out not to be as half-hearted as it seemed – in Barbados, we'd had a good long chat about our relationship and agreed that, if we were to get married at some point in the future, we really should try living together first. Within three weeks we'd moved in to a little two-up, two-down house on a new estate in Westergate, Chichester.

Living together had many perks: being able to walk around the house naked without the fear of bumping into flatmates – or disturbing them with our noisy sex sessions – snuggling up in front of the TV, and showering together. There was no more PMT-features Becky crashing the Hoover around at all hours or screaming about unpaid bills. But, like most couples who cohabit for the first time, we were also discovering some habits about each other which were less appealing. Jonathan found it irritating – and hurtful – that I never wanted to speak to him when I returned home from trips. But the last thing I needed after a ten-hour flight of small talk was to discuss avionics for the Cessna 172, or hear him prattle on about how many job rejections he'd received. I just wanted to relax in the bath with a glass of wine.

What niggled me about Jonathan – not that it was a major issue – was that he was rather tight with money. It always seemed to be me who was paying out for things around the home. When he called me from trips abroad, it was always a half-minute call to say: "Can you ring me back?" Whenever he bought me flowers they were always anaemic, limp carnations from the local garage. But despite his frugal proclivities, I loved him dearly and I was thrilled to come to the Sunshine State with him ... even if it did mean kipping in a basic dorm at the Huffman Aviation flight school, which was another money-saving brainwave of Jonathan's. "Saves splashing out on an extortionate hotel," he said.

Our first few days in Florida had been magical: flying over the Keys, exploring Venice and the vast, pristine beaches of Sarasota where the sand is as white as icing sugar. We visited fantastic restaurants and feasted on lobster claws and steak and giant prawns. We made love in the sand dunes, collected sharks' teeth and swam in the Gulf of Mexico. It was like a mini honeymoon ... if you took the flight school accommodation out of the equation.

Our excursion to Marathon had been equally as romantic and decadent: picnicking on the palm-lined shore of Sombrero Beach, feeding each other succulent slices of cantaloupe, sunbathing and burying each other in the sand. We'd shared salty kisses in the Atlantic, Jonathan wading in languid figures of eight as I clung onto him, legs clamped around his waist, his hands creeping into my bikini bottoms under the water.

By the time we left Marathon I was highly aroused. My body felt like an erotic solar panel, drenched in sexual energy from the sun. I was in the mood for something risqué.

As the Cessna climbed further into the sky, and my hormones continued to scream "take me now", I remembered a conversation I'd had with Jonathan a few weeks back about joining the Mile High Club.

"I can't believe we've not done it yet," I'd said, as we lay in bed that Sunday morning after attempting the suspended scissors position from the *Kama Sutra* (we were still trying to master that one).

"Done what?"

"Joined the Mile High Club ... I mean, it's embarrassing really – we both fly for a living ... and we've had plenty of opportunities when we've been on trips together. We've no excuse."

"I don't think it's something you can just do on a whim, Mands. It requires a certain amount of planning."

"Planning? Don't be ridiculous. That's the whole point of it – you just sneak into the toilet and go for it – that's what makes it so exciting."

"It's a technical point, Mands."

"Go on," I'd said, suppressing a little laugh. I couldn't imagine what was so technical about bonking in a plane – unless it involved performing the Suspended Scissors position, of course. That was difficult enough on the ground.

"Well, technically you shouldn't really do it at 35,000 feet. It's called the Mile High Club so it should happen at 5,280 feet –exactly a mile high. It's logical when you think about it."

This had all sounded rather geeky to me at the time. Now, however, I was beginning to warm to his theory. We'd been in the air for almost ten minutes, which, according to my estimation, would mean we must be a mile high by now. I glanced over at Jonathan, surveying the space between his groin and the yoke. It was tight, but doable. His voice flooded my ears again.

"You okay, Mands?"

Very doable.

I nodded. "How high are we flying?"

Jonathan narrowed his eyes, studied the altimeter. "About 5,000 feet – still climbing."

The timing was perfect.

"November niner niner, eight zero Delta," I purred, unsnapping my seatbelt. "You are clear to fly me."

In a series of sleek, rapid movements I removed my headphones (they wouldn't be needed), kicked off my flip-flops, pulled my T-shirt over my head and untied my silver bikini top. Jonathan shot me a sideways grin. He was saying something but it was impossible to make out his words over the engine noise without my headphones on. I wriggled out of my shorts and bikini bottoms, unleashing a deposit of sand, and reached across to unfasten Jonathan's Bermuda shorts. He was flying commando – and more than ready for action.

My next manoeuvre was tricky. I had to weave my whole upper body under Jonathan's right arm and over his left shoulder, and angle my head to avoid obstructing his view. Then I threaded my legs through, knelt on his lap and, using my hand, gently guided him into me. The sensation was exhilarating, almost tantric. Jonathan was in no position to thrust because he couldn't let go of the yoke, and I didn't want to cause a crash by going for it cowgirl style. So I took it slow, rocking my hips backwards and for-wards, side to side. I could touch him but he couldn't touch me. It was like a lap dance in the air ... with extras.

Jonathan's body was rigid against mine, his legs tense, pelvis tilted, hands still firmly gripped to the yoke. I could feel his heart accelerating against my breast. I turned my head sideways to catch a glimpse of his face. His eyes were glazing over, mouth open and jaw jutting forwards. It was an expression I knew well – that I'm-going-to-come face. The plane hopped and bumped through the air, adding to the thrill; even in the best flying conditions, it's very rare to experience a smooth ride in a two-seater Cessna. I continued to grind and rock as the Cessna climbed and swayed, burying my face into the crevice of Jonathan's neck. He smelt of the sea ... and Nivea Factor 15. Sunlight flooded the cockpit, warming my back. Jonathan's chest heaved and blood rushed to my head – I had to grab the back of the seat to steady myself. Seconds later I came, followed closely by Jonathan. It was the most ethereal orgasm I'd ever encountered, shivering throughout my entire body for what seemed like an eternity.

When I'd recovered I weaved my quivering limbs back to my seat. Naked, weightless and giggling uncontrollably, I slipped my headphones back on to check in with the pilot.

"November niner niner, eight zero Delta: did you reach the required height?"

Jonathan grinned, glanced briefly at his lap. "This is November niner niner, eight zero Delta: roger that, correct height confirmed."

"I must say," I said, "I'm most impressed at your ability to maintain full control of your joystick."

"It's all part of the service, madam," he said. "Now, if you wouldn't mind dressing and preparing the cabin for landing."

"I was thinking I'd just stay as I am," I teased. "Land of the free, and all that?"

"That'll give the guys at Venice Air Traffic Control something to smile about."

As Jonathan began our descent I slipped back into my beach gear. As much as I found the idea of me climbing out of the Cessna in the buff highly amusing, I didn't fancy getting arrested for indecent exposure – that would've ruined our perfect day out.

We touched down at Venice Municipal Airport with a succession of bumps. I couldn't wipe the smile from my face. Finally, after two years flying round the world, I'd joined the Mile High Club in a fashion I'd never imagined. I couldn't wait to tell the girls.

"Did we really do it at 5,280 feet?" I said, as we parked up.

Jonathan flicked a switch, twiddled a couple of knobs and buttoned up his shorts. "We sure did – I was watching the altimeter. It was bang-on."

He switched off the engine. "That was fucking amazing, Mands. Do I get a kiss now?"

So there we remained, for the next ten minutes, kissing passionately in our little love plane. Outside the early evening sky was beginning to flush pink, and I thought to myself, *This is the life.*

CHAPTER TEN

9/11

I managed to call home just in time: moments after American Airlines Flight 11 slammed into the North Tower of the World Trade Center, just before the phone lines crashed and cyberspace froze. Moments after people inside that doomed skyscraper made unimaginable heart-wrenching final calls to loved ones. In that brief shell-shocked pocket of time before the world descended into chaos.

When the horrific news broke, I was in Florida, hung-over and tucking into the all-you-can-eat breakfast buffet with my crew mates in the lobby restaurant at the Marriott Orlando Airport Hotel. Prior to this we'd been having a giggle – recounting embarrassing stories from the previous night when we'd pushed the mild-mannered bar staff to near-breaking point with our brash drunken antics. Jokes were also flying around about Hurricane Gabrielle which, according to the local radio station, was currently brewing in the Gulf of Mexico and was about to batter Florida with a vengeance. "All airports could be closed," warned the newsreader.

"Looks like we might get to Disney World at this rate," joked our captain, Steve, in between mouthfuls of sloppy maple syrup–saturated pancakes. "If this storm gets going we could be looking at spending a good few days here. Get ready to party, kids."

And it was literally at that point, as the word "party" spilled out of his greasy crumb-stippled mouth, that the haunting image flashed up on the giant TV screen behind his head: A slick silver skyscraper – such an iconic feature of the New York skyline – engulfed in flames with plumes of smoke billowing from a gaping black hole in its side.

The breakfast din of subdued chatter and cutlery scraping china came to an abrupt stop as everybody stared at the screen in stunned silence. And suddenly, memories of busty Julie whipping her top off and dancing on the table in the Kicks Bar didn't seem remotely funny anymore. And the hurricane and Disney World and the all-you-can-eat breakfast buffet all paled into insignificance.

A cataclysm of Armageddon proportions was going down in Manhattan ... and my parents thought I was there in the thick of it all; I'd been due to fly to JFK on September 10, but I'd swapped flights with a colleague, Debbie, at the last minute because she was desperate to see her boyfriend, Tom, who lived in New York. Only I hadn't told Mum and Dad that I'd switched. There had been no need to tell them, as they hardly ever knew where I was, and I routinely swapped flights. But I had been to see them the previous weekend and told them I was off to New York, so I knew that wherever they were and whatever they were doing at that precise moment in time, Mum and Dad would have heard the news and they'd be going out of their minds with worry. So, as the frantic eye-witness accounts flowed, and the grainy footage of what looked like a plane hitting the tower filled the monitor, I fled to my room to make that call.

"Please be home, Mum," I said over and over, as I furiously punched the ten-digit code from my international calling card into the bedside phone.

The line crackled then connected. The ring tone purred into my ear. "Please pick up, please pick up," I said out loud. But the phone rang out and connected to the answer phone. I heard Mum's cheery voice: "You've reached Sue and James. We're out just now, but do leave a message. Thank you."

I waited for the loud bleep to end and left a message. "Hi Mam, hi Dad," I said, trying to sound calm. "I don't know whether you know what's happened over here yet, but there's some horrible stuff going on involving planes in New York. I just wanted you to know that I'm safe and well. I swapped my New York flight and I'm currently in Orlando. I'll try and call later. I love you."

I hung up and tried calling Jonathan, but by the time I'd dialled the code again, the lines had crashed. I stayed in my room for a while, thinking about the tragic scene that had just played out on CNN downstairs in the lobby restaurant. It was totally incomprehensible, like we'd been watching a scary movie, or somebody had hijacked CNN's airwaves and broadcast fake footage. I couldn't erase the harrowing image from my mind. Outside I could hear the early rumblings of Hurricane Gabrielle. I looked out of the window. I'd stayed here dozens of times on trips but I never tired of the view. You could see for miles – across the vast car park and man-made lake all the way to Cape Canaveral, where monstrous charcoal storm clouds were now looming, making ever-changing scary faces in the sky. The palm trees were being whacked out of shape in the wind, and the fountain on the man-made lake became distorted. Cars jiggled in the car park, threatening to take off. The room darkened. The air con pumped frosty breaths on the back of my neck and the flagpoles squeaked and chimed eerily in the storm.

Walking back to the bar, I felt as though I was trapped in a dream world. The hotel had hosted one of those hideous child beauty pageants at the weekend and the contestants were out in force – in the corridors, the foyer, turning cartwheels on the garish swirly-patterned carpets and belting out Broadway hits. They looked like mini Dolly Partons minus the boobs – dolled-up to the nines in layers of make-up and fake tan, masses of big hairdos, dressed in revealing spandex costumes or frothy dresses akin to those worn by the dollies that sit on toilet rolls. They were like the product of a genetic experiment gone wrong. And as they twirled and strutted and posed and sang, a second plane hit the South Tower.

In the lobby restaurant more misery emanated from the television: people leaping from the towers, others running for their lives, coated in grey dust. It didn't make for good viewing but none of us could tear ourselves away from the screen. We had around two hundred crew members in New York and no way of contacting them. What if any of them had decided to visit the Twin Towers that morning? It didn't bear thinking about. All of us had stayed in New York at some point in our flying career, but I had done so many flights there every month, I now classed it as my second home – bumping into more friends walking down Fifth Avenue than I ever would at home. Most of us were too shocked to speak … apart from Steve, who started chanting lyrics from "Bob the Builder" when the South Tower collapsed. We all looked at him in disbelief. Obscenities such as "knob-head" and "wanker" were muttered. For once, a wave of realisation spread across Steve's face – he knew he'd been bang out of order this time.

"Sorry guys," he said, sheepishly.

Steve was one of the fat, bald pilots who fancied himself as a Casanova and had a bit of a God complex – one of the ones quick to brag about the fact he has "at least 400 people's lives in my hands". He was always trying to get the young stewardesses into bed, labouring under the misapprehension that they'd be happy to oblige just because he could fly a plane.

The ghastly footage continued to roll: the smoking Pentagon, crumpling like a house of cards; the White House evacuated; reports of United Airlines Flight 93, headed for San Francisco, crashing into a field in Pennsylvania; the work of terrorist hijackers; that fuzzy shot of a plane striking the North Tower relayed over and over again to the soundtrack of yet more eyewitness accounts. We were hearing reports of airline crew fighting off the hijackers – and that one passenger had had their throat slashed. A nightmare was unfolding in front of us.

None of us moved from the restaurant until the early hours of the following morning. We were glued to the screen, cut off from the world with only each other for company. The mood was solemn. We felt for the crew who had lost their lives – how they'd gone to work that day and just never returned. This played on my mind as I drifted in and out of sleep later that morning, Gabrielle performing a raucous dawn symphony outside my window. I wondered whether I'd ever really contemplated the risks involved in this job. During training we'd been taught how to deal with potential hijack situations, but none of the scenarios put to us had involved planes crashing into major landmarks. "Hijackers normally have only one goal in mind: to seek asylum," we were told. "Listen to them, don't antagonise them and, in most cases, nobody gets hurt."

The previous day's events affected some crew members more badly than others, one being Nicole, a new recruit who was only nineteen, and who woke me from my restless sleep when she called my room at 8am, sobbing down the phone.

"I can't cope," she said, her voice trembling. "I've not slept all night ... I want to go home." She sounded so fragile.

"Come up to my room," I offered. "I'll stick the kettle on."

Five minutes later Nicole arrived, looking as white as a sheet, with red-rimmed eyes.

"I'm so sorry," she whimpered, dabbing at fresh tears with a soggy, disintegrating tissue, cardigan slipping from her delicate shoulders as she stretched the sleeves over her hands.

"Don't be silly, hon," I said. "Come, sit down and I'll make you a cuppa."

As I made the tea, Nicole's emotions gushed out.

"It's so awful, Mandy ... what's happened. And I can't speak to my mum ... or my boyfriend. I don't have one of those phone cards – and the woman at reception said the lines are still down, anyway ... and I can't go out because of the hurricane ... and ..."

She shivered, caught her breath, "I just don't know what to do ..."

I left the tea to brew, sat next to her on the bed and gave her a cuddle.

"... and that tea's shit, we can't even have a proper cuppa," I said, and Nicole laughed, just a little.

"Anyway," I added, "I've got a phone card with loads of minutes still left on it. As soon as the lines are back up, you can use it – to call whoever you want."

She rested her head on my shoulder. "Thanks Mandy, that means the world to me."

And then, through more sniffles, she announced: "I can't do this job anymore."

"Yes, you can," I insisted. "You're just in shock. We'll get through this, you'll see."

Another long day lay ahead of us at the Marriott Orlando Airport Hotel. At lunchtime we were called to a meeting in the conference room. The outlook was grim. "American airspace remains closed to all flights," said one of the flight service managers. "And even if it reopens, the hurricane could also ground us. You're all on standby every morning until 10am, when you'll receive a wake-up call to your rooms. You'll either be stood down or invited to a meeting for an update."

The good news, however, was that the national phone lines were now up and running and contact had been made with our colleagues in New York. They were all safe and well. Although we were told some of them had witnessed some horrific sights after going to the scene of the atrocity to offer first-aid support.

We were stuck in Orlando for nine days in total, trapped in the hotel with those freaky kids, who seemed to pop up everywhere we went – the bar, pool, lobby, in the toilets "fixing" their hair and make-up – there was no escape from them. We couldn't leave the hotel (because of the hurricane), although a few of our posse attempted to venture out to Denny's for breakfast one morning, only to return five minutes later complaining of being hit by "flying shrubs". We had no clean clothes because we'd anticipated staying for only one night, so the hotel staff let us use their laundry room, where us girls killed time painting our nails while watching our smalls spin round and round. The only other place to go was the restaurant, where the news had now turned to the clean-up operation in Manhattan: the brave firefighters, scenes of rubble and deformed steel girders and repeated messages of "God bless America" flashing up on the screen. And despite the pre-9/11 "batten down the hatches" warnings, the tornado had completely vanished from the news schedule.

Each day turned into a morbid drinking session after the ten o'clock stand-down call. There was nothing else to do. People began to niggle at one another – a combination of cabin fever and spending too much time together in such a fraught environment. The lack of communication with the outside world didn't help either; back then there was no Facebook or Twitter and we rarely used our mobile phones abroad because it was too expensive or could get no signal. Only when the international phone lines resumed did the mood lighten. Nicole was delighted, but even after speaking to her parents she was still intent on giving up her job.

I also called home. Mum picked up on the second ring. I could tell she'd been crying.

"Mam?"

"Oh my God, baby. Have you seen what's happened? You need to get home."

"It's okay, Mum," I said, "I'm safe. I'm not in New York, I'm in Orlando – I swapped flights with someone – I left a message on the answerphone."

I could hear Dad in the background, bombarding Mum with questions.

"She's okay, James," she told him. "She's still in Florida but she's safe – sounds like she's just round the corner."

"Florida? What's she still doing in Florida?" I heard Dad ask. "When is she coming home? Ask her when she's coming back."

"I don't know James, but she's okay."

This happens every time I call home – I get cut out of the conversation and end up just listening to Mum and Dad.

"Mum," I said, "Are you still there?"

"I'm just letting your dad know you're okay. He wants to know when you're coming home."

"Not sure, Mum," I said. "There's talk of all flights being grounded from here anyway because of the hurricane, and now this has happened I'm ..."

"Hurricane?" She shrieked, "What hurricane?"

Dad grabbed the phone.

"Mandy," he said, "For the love of God. Pack that bloody job up. Can't you see what it's doing to your mother? She's worried sick about you."

"Dad, it's okay," I assured him. "I just wanted to let you know that I'm safe."

"Safe? Have you seen what's just happened in New York, Mandy? How do you think we felt? We thought you were there – we watched those planes crashing into the towers and there was no mention of which airlines were involved and we hadn't heard your voice message at that point and ..." Dad paused.

"Dad, are you there?"

He continued: "I was watching the footage over and over on my laptop Mand ... just zooming in to see if I could make out the name of the airline. Then Mum heard your message – we were going out of our minds with worry, pet. We thought you were ..."

"I'm sorry, Dad, I tried to call you. I'm so sorry ..." I said. "I'm in Florida and I'm fine. I just wanted to make sure you got my message, you don't need to worry anymore."

Dad sighed and cleared his throat. He could never stay upset with his little princess for long.

"Well you just look after yourself, Mandy. And no going outside in that hurricane. I've got enough grey hairs – I don't need any more." I could tell he was trying to make light of the situation so I didn't feel as guilty for putting them through what must have been a horrible afternoon. So I played along.

"I will, I won't," I said. "Love you, Dad."

"Love you too, pet. Just ... be careful, that's all."

I hung up and dialled my home number. No one picked up. I left a message for Jonathan, saying that I was safe and well and hoped to be home soon. He had been due to fly to Japan on September 11.

My next call was to Debbie's hotel in New York. I was sure she'd mentioned that her boyfriend worked in the North Tower of the Trade Center.

Debbie answered the phone, her voice hoarse and small.

"Oh Mandy, it's awful," she said. "We didn't even know what had happened. There was a blackout at the hotel so we had no access to the news. All we heard was that there had been some kind of accident at the Trade Center – so a few of us headed up there on spec."

"Are you okay?" I asked, "Is Tom okay?"

"I'm fine, pretty shaken, but fine. Tom's fine too – can you believe he'd booked the day off work? What if hadn't? What if he'd been one of those ..." Debbie started crying.

"I'm here for you, babe," I said.

"I've never seen anything like it, Mandy. We went to the towers to help with first aid. There were people leaping from the buildings and dangling from windows, trucks rolling past loaded with dead bodies. Then the first tower collapsed and I couldn't see a thing for the dust – people were running in all directions, screaming and crying. Those images will haunt me forever."

We talked until my minutes ran out. I was paralysed with shock when I put the phone down. I couldn't move; I just sat there staring at the phone, unable to comprehend anything Debbie had just told me.

The following day we got the all-clear to leave Orlando. Normally we'd be laughing and joking on the crew bus, recounting all the fun tales from our trip. This time we travelled in silence.

The night flight home was also a solemn affair. We were one of the first flights to leave and were only given basic supplies, just bottles of water and enough food for one meal service. The passengers appeared petrified, nervously scanning the cabin for would-be terrorists. I noticed that nobody was reading a newspaper, which was understandable given the circumstances. I recognised a few of the kids who had travelled on our flight out – children with life-threatening illnesses who had been sent out by the Make-a-Wish Foundation, a charity that grants the wishes of dying children – their wish was to visit Disney World and it broke my heart to see their sad little faces, knowing they'd probably not made it there. We'd had so much fun with them on the way out, running draw-your-favourite-crew competitions, handing out Disney toys and performing Mickey Mouse impersonations over the PA system. We had no idea of the terror that loomed ahead of us then.

There wasn't much to do during the flight home. Most people slept or watched the in-flight entertainment. I was working in Economy with Nicole. I'd got to know her well over the last week, so it was nice to spend some extra time with her. We made ourselves comfy in the galley – well, as comfy as we could be sitting on empty bar boxes – we closed the curtains, huddled together and nattered all the way across the Atlantic.

"Are you sure you want to give all this up yet?" I asked her.

She nodded, tucking a stray wisp of blonde hair behind her ear. "It's just not for me. I thought it was, but ..." Her voice trailed off. "Wow," she added, pointing at the window in the emergency exit door. "Look at the sky."

We shifted our boxes closer to the door to admire the view: miles and miles of ruby sky, tinged with streaks of deep turquoise and violet.

"It's gorgeous, isn't it?" I said. "We must be crossing the time zone – flying into dawn. We've got our own time machine."

We sat for a while, transfixed by the ever-changing hues: ruby smudging into pink, orange, yellow. It truly was the most beautiful thing I'd seen all week.

I hugged Nicole goodbye at Gatwick. "Keep in touch," I told her.

"I will," she said. "And thanks for everything, Mandy."

I never saw her again after that day.

Back home the headlines were still dominated by what was now being called 9/11. And when I saw the first mug shots of Osama bin Laden, I recognised him from some photographs we'd been shown during our Virgin security training at least a year prior to the terror attacks. "If you ever see this man boarding a flight, contact ground security immediately," we'd been warned. How on earth had he slipped through the net for so long?

It also emerged that the Twin Towers hijacker pilots, Mohamed Atta and Marwan al-Shehhi, had attended the Huffman Aviation centre in 2000 to learn how to fly small aircraft. It was the same flying school that I'd stayed at with Jonathan just one month before the terror attacks.

About six weeks after 9/11, I took Mum and Dad to New York for some Christmas shopping, using my complimentary flights. We visited Ground Zero to pay our respects. The vastness of destruction was unbelievable – far worse than it had looked on television. The mountain of rubble that occupied the spot where the towers had stood had now been fenced off. There were photographs taped to the fences of missing people, along with notes saying, "Have you seen this person?" There were wreaths of flowers and American flags, photographs of dead fireman. And, disturbingly, there were people nearby who had set up stalls, flogging glossy Twin Tower souvenir brochures – among other tacky pieces of memorabilia. It felt more like a tourist attraction than a site of mass murder. That was the one and only time I went to Ground Zero.

Air travel changed dramatically following 9/11 and our cabin crew training manual was practically rewritten. We had to undergo an updated rigorous course of SAS-style security training and Virgin's entire fleet was modified in line with heightened security rules. The flight decks were fitted with bulletproof doors, walls and security cameras. Security keypads were also added to the flight deck, the rotating entry code being revealed only to a select few staff per flight. There were armed marshals on board and the days of kids being able to visit the flight deck were well and truly over. We were taught code words and phrases that would be used in cases of emergency – secret messages that could be relayed to crew via the PA system if, for example, there was a terrorist on board.

The extra training paid off. In March 2002 – just three months after Richard Colvin Reid attempted to blow up American Airlines Flight 63 from Paris to Miami with a shoe bomb – an incident happened at Heathrow on board a San Francisco-bound flight.

We were preparing for take-off. The cabin doors were closed and the safety demo was about to begin. But something was unnerving us. Two crew members and I had been watching two guys towards the rear of the cabin. One was sitting in the middle row of seats, the other in a window seat a few rows behind. A few things had triggered our curiosity, they looked rather shifty, very conspicuous – all jumpy and irritable and staring at other passengers. I alerted my flight service manager and checks were swiftly made with ground staff. Alarm bells started ringing when we discovered they'd booked their tickets on the same credit card but had chosen to sit separately. The jetway was reattached, police stormed the cabin and the two men were handcuffed and escorted off the plane. When we informed the passengers that they too would have to leave the aircraft, some of them went berserk, demanding compensation and threatening to complain to Richard Branson.

The sniffer dogs entered the cabin and headed directly for the suspects' seats. It later transpired the two men in question were on the FBI's most wanted list and were suspected sleeper terrorists, who apparently travelled on every airline, to suss out airline security measures. The plane was grounded. No compensation was paid.

The effects of 9/11 almost crippled Virgin Atlantic. There were loads of redundancies and cutbacks. Quite a few of the girls, including Nicole, quit altogether, many forced to leave because their partners or husbands thought their lives were at risk – and marriages fell apart for some who defied their husband's wishes. Times were bleak, but I knew one thing for certain: this dolly wasn't ready to hang up her red skirt.

CHAPTER ELEVEN

DUSK 'TIL DAWN

Hong Kong trips in those days were like mini holidays: five days and nights of sightseeing, sunbathing, eating, drinking and, most importantly, shopping. The dichotomies of Hong Kong Island have always fascinated me: gleaming steel skyscrapers leaning against lush green mountains; humble vendors serving up bowls of bird's nest soup from rickety stalls next to a McDonald's or Starbucks; and the sweet, musky fragrance of incense mingling with the sickly stench of durian fruit. It truly is a spectacular city.

Shopping in Hong Kong is a must; I never returned from a trip empty-handed, as there were too many bargains to be had. As well as the obvious shiny mile-high shopping malls lined with Clarins and Tiffany's, there are whole shopping malls with only electrical shops over the causeway bay in Kowloon. Then there's Ladies Market along Nathan Road, also in Kowloon, which is a girly shopper's paradise, rammed with stalls selling anything from trinkets and CDs to replica designer handbags, sunglasses and jewellery. We girls went there so often we became known to most of the vendors. One of them, Jimmy – whom we nicknamed "Jimmy the Handbag Man" – made so much money from Virgin crew alone, he eventually quit his stall and set up a secret shop in his flat with daily pick-ups just for us.

Jimmy operated an efficient service: he had taped a Virgin duty-free carrier bag – with his phone number written on it – to the interior wall of a payphone near the market, and whenever we were in town, we'd call him. Within minutes he'd turn up and take us back to his huge, grey fortress of a flat for a shopping spree. The building was very basic, with concrete walls and metal grids shielding doors, while the lift that took us up to Jimmy's thirtieth-floor "shop" was so small that only two people could fit inside at a time. The flat itself was an Aladdin's cave of goodies and consisted of four rooms – all lined with shelves neatly loaded with fake designer handbags, purses and jewellery. There was no bathroom or kitchen, just a single mattress hidden behind a desk. Jimmy was great; he didn't mind us browsing and his prices were good: a copied Rolex for £30, Chanel handbag for £20 – depending on its grading. Sometimes we'd spend a whole afternoon in his flat, trying on jewellery and prancing around, swinging handbags. Visiting Jimmy's shop was the highlight of some of the Christmas trips, so we were gutted when Jimmy and his carrier bag vanished one day. We tried calling the various numbers he'd previously displayed but none of them worked. We could only presume he'd been busted.

Unfortunately, I also associate Hong Kong with a not so pleasant, humiliating experience, involving a first officer whom, until this trip, I'd considered to be a good friend of mine. His name was Tom, a giant two-metre man in his late thirties, with Tom Selleck looks: jet-black hair threaded with tinsel strands, coarse moustache and eyebrows, and dimpled cheeks.

I'd been on a few trips with Tom and had always enjoyed his company. Unlike some other first officers and captains, he wasn't sleazy or arrogant. He was good fun, kind-natured and appeared to be happily married to his wife, Sophie, an attractive Virgin Atlantic flight service manager. In LA I'd once helped Tom shop for nappies for their newborn baby boy at an outlet store. He'd proudly shown me photographs of baby Jake: Jake sporting an all-in-one bear suit; Jake in the bath, his little pink head topped with foam; Jake sleeping in his pram; and Jake enjoying "snuggles" with Mummy, nanny Violet and a whole cast of other smiling relatives. "I tell you, Mandy," Tom had said on that flight to LA, "Becoming a parent is the most wonderful experience. I only have to look at Jake and my eyes well up."

"He's adorable," I'd said, thinking, *Tom's definitely one of the good guys*. Although as it transpired, he wasn't one of the good guys – not in the slightest. For on this Hong Kong trip, he turned into a lecherous, violent lunatic during a night out in the red-light district of Wan Chai.

It was the summer of 2003. By now I was a senior junior and climbing up the career ladder. I had been selected for promotion and was due to sit my senior exams, which, if I passed, would mean a fatter pay packet and the opportunity to work solely in Upper Class.

The hours prior to that particular night in Wan Chai had been filled with fun. We were on our penultimate day in Hong Kong and had decided to make the most of the scorching weather by taking a junk boat cruise around some of the outlying islands. The scenery was spectacular: chiselled granite shards covered in green moss formed a beautiful maze for us to sail through, and we passed majestic mountains swathed in forests rising from crystal aqua waters – it was like sailing through a fairy-tale landscape.

There were about fifteen of us on the cruise, including Tom and his mate Jacques, a French first officer who owned the boat – he worked for Air New Zealand and lived on Hong Kong Island. We took bottles of vodka and plastic cups onto the boat and by mid morning we were all very merry. Laura was there, and she and I kept the rest of the crew entertained by singing Northern folk songs, assailing the serene vista with strangled-cat renditions of "Blaydon Races" and "Fog on the Tyne".

At lunchtime, cross-eyed and staggering, we stopped off at Lamma Island for a bite to eat at the pigeon restaurant Han Lok Yuen, which probably wasn't the best choice of eatery considering there were five vegetarians among us, who were horrified when our food – all chosen by Tom and Jacques – arrived. There were pigeons, roasted whole with their beaks agape, deep-fried wrinkly chicken feet and chicken testicles. One of the girls had to dash to the toilets to throw up.

Bizarre delicacies aside, we were having a wonderful time – albeit very drunken. Everyone was in high spirits, faces bright red from too much sun ... and alcohol. As we clambered back onto the junk boat, vodka-pigeon (with a hint of chicken feet) soup swirling in my stomach, I realised how lucky I was to have a job that enabled me to explore so many exotic countries and experience new and diverse cultures; I couldn't think of many professions that would enable you to eat chicken testicles at two in the afternoon on Lamma Island.

"We're so lucky, aren't we," I said to Laura as we leaned over the side of the junk boat on our journey back to Hong Kong Island. "I mean, look at this place," I added, motioning towards the sea, my plastic cup cutting a clumsy arc through the air, vodka leaping into the waters below. "It's bloody stunning."

The sun was setting over Hong Kong Island, cradled by the silhouetted mountains, the last of its rays scoring the violet clouds.

"It's fucking beautiful, babe," said Laura, hiccuping.

"Magical," I said.

"We're very lucky, Mands."

"Very, very lucky," I slurred.

"Sooo lucky."

Once ashore, we continued our party at the Dusk 'til Dawn nightclub, where we literally did party from dusk 'til dawn. It was one of our regular haunts in Wan Chai: open until the early hours, the booze dirt cheap, and always heaving with expats, locals and crew. As our group fractured into smaller groups, Laura and I found ourselves stuck by the bar with Tom and Jacques, who was a complete sleazebag. Stocky, with a grubby tan and hirsute arms, he was full of cheesy chat-up lines, playing up his French accent in an attempt to sound all seductive and sexy but failing miserably.

"French lovers are ze best in ze world," he said, touching my arm with his clammy hand. "Do you have a lover? *Voulez-vous coucher avec moi?*"

"No, thanks," I said turning my back in disgust.

Tom burst out laughing and, randomly, groped my arse. "He's just teasing you, Mandy."

I was confused; the caring, mature family man I knew and liked had suddenly turned into a boorish lad. And since when did he think it was acceptable to grab my arse? He'd never done that before.

I turned to Laura. "Just tell 'em to '*va te faire foutre*'," she advised.

"What the hell does that mean?" I said.

"It means 'fuck off' in French."

So I looked Jacques in the eye and in a thick Hartlepudlian accent shouted, "*Va te faire foutre.*" I grabbed Laura's arm and we moved onto the dance floor, where we boogied for hours to Beatles and Monkees hits played by a local live band, knocking back bottles of Smirnoff Ice and Hooper's Hooch, sweating pure alcohol. All was well until Tom and Jacques reappeared. I was singing and dancing to "Love Me Do" with some of the other crew when they came thrashing onto the dance floor, swaying and bumping into everyone, which wasn't a huge problem – we were all pretty wobbly by this stage. But there was no excuse for what they did next. It happened just after Laura disappeared to the loo.

As "Love Me Do" blended into "Daydream Believer" and we all started swaying our arms over our heads, Jacques slithered his arms around me from behind, grabbed my hips and started grinding his groin against my bum. I wrenched his hands off me and tried to break free from the crowd, but Tom blocked my way, gripped my wrists and yanked my arms above my head, just as Jacques' hands came creeping around me once more – this time at my chest. I twisted my body, bent my knees and tugged hard with my wrists, but the harder I fought, the tighter Tom gripped. A warped merry-go-round spun past me, a swirl of jeering faces and oscillating bodies, the chirpy strains of "Daydream Believer" becoming increasingly dissonant and mocking. I felt my feet leave the floor as Tom lifted me up by my wrists. Then Jacques pulled my top down to my waist, slithered between Tom and me, and started motor-boating my boobs, his greasy face slapping against my cleavage and rubbing against my white bra, as Tom looked down, laughing. He had an evil glint in his eye that I'd never encountered before, a look that compelled me to fight back with renewed vigour. I lashed out with my dangling feet, kicking Jacques' knees until he buckled and fell back against Tom, and only then did he let go of my wrists. I pulled up my top, turned and forced my way out of the club, elbowing my way through the sea of revellers, tears streaming down my face. I should maybe have gone to find Laura, but I felt so humiliated and violated – I just wanted to leave. Sure, hosties were always flashing their boobs in public, but the big difference here was that I hadn't chosen for this to happen. And what Tom and Jacques had just put me through was a sexual assault.

Outside the club I jumped in the first taxi I saw. Dawn was breaking but the neon-lit streets were still buzzing with energy: partygoers spilling out of bars and clubs nestled beneath rundown office blocks, people thronging fast-food shops and local vendors setting up ramshackle market stalls with corrugated roofs. The incident in the club had sobered me up. I was numb with shock. Why had Tom's behaviour changed so suddenly?

Back at the hotel, I furiously scrubbed myself clean in the shower before calling Jonathan. We hadn't been getting along as well recently; before I'd left for Hong Kong we'd quarrelled. I never really had blazing rows with Jonathan – mainly because he didn't stick up for himself, which, ironically, was the reason for most of our arguments. The problem was his mother, Margaret, who detested me with a passion. She was forever interfering in our relationship and criticising me. She controlled Jonathan, and he caved in to her every demand. Her latest trick was to let herself into our house uninvited (Jonathan had given her a set of keys against my wishes), snoop around and rearrange things to how they *should* be. All I wanted was for Jonathan to man up about it and stop giving in to her.

He sounded grumpy when he answered the phone. "What time is it? I was sleeping," he said.

"Six in the morning – ten o'clock your time."

"Is everything okay? Has something happened?"

Through floods of tears I relayed my traumatic experience. "I don't understand why Tom would do this to me," I concluded.

"I'll kill him – and that French bastard," said Jonathan, his breath jagged. "What were they thinking? You have to report this, Mands ... promise me you'll do that?"

"Okay," I sniffed, thinking, *Why can't he be this assertive with his mother?*

I spent the following day and night in my hotel room with Laura, watching movies and ordering room service. I wasn't in the mood for mixing with the rest of the crew and the thought of bumping into Tom and his slimy French mate made my blood boil. I didn't even feel up to shopping, which was rare for me. Laura was shocked when I told her what had happened.

"I was looking for you when I came back from the toilets," she said. "Tom said you'd left because you were tired. I knew that French bloke was an arrogant arsehole but, bloody hell, Tom? You should tell his wife, Mandy. She deserves to know."

"Maybe," I sighed. "I'm going to report it, anyway – Jonathan said I should definitely do that."

I never did spill the beans to Tom's wife ... although I was very tempted. But I did perform one act of revenge that made me feel slightly better about the whole sordid episode. On the flight home I was supposed to be working on the upper deck, in Premium Economy, but that would have meant looking after Tom in the flight deck. So I requested a move to the "R4" position with a duty-free bar at the back of Economy. It's the least desirable job on the aircraft – as you're rushed off your feet dealing with the constant demands of duty-free orders – but if it meant I wouldn't have to speak to Tom, I was more than happy to do it.

As the meal service got underway, Laura came to visit me in the back galley. "Look what I've got," she said, an impish smile on her face. She placed a tray on the counter. "Smoked salmon with crème fraiche and rocket leaves, wild mushroom stroganoff with a creamy risotto, orange juice and chewy Belgium chocolate cake – all for our darling Tom."

I flashed her a look that said, *Are you thinking what I'm thinking?* "I think Tom's meal is lacking something," I said.

"Me too," said Laura, cocking her head to one side and pressing her index finger to her lips. "I'm thinking a phlegm garnish would add a superb kick to that risotto."

"Definitely – it'll complement the earthy mushroom flavours."

I cleared my throat and turned my back to Laura. Clearing my chest, I vacuumed as much mucus as I could muster into the back of my throat, swung back round, gobbed a huge, green globule of catarrh smack into Tom's risotto, and burst out laughing. Laura clutched her stomach, giggling wildly. I grabbed a fork, my body shaking with laughter, and stirred my spit into the risotto.

"Dinner is served," I declared, prompting another round of giggles.

Laura wiped the smile from her face and picked up the tray. "Bon appétit, Tom," she said, and swished out of the galley.

Although spitting in Tom's food had given us a laugh, I still couldn't erase the seedy memory of that night in Dusk 'til Dawn. My armpits and wrists were still hurting days after I returned to the UK. Taking Jonathan's advice, I reported the incident to my ground manager, who didn't seem overly concerned. She told me I could take the matter further if I wished, but it'd probably result in a futile battle of his word against mine. What she could offer, however, was assurance that I would never have to fly with Tom again. So, in order to avoid any confrontation, I accepted this offer ... at least I would never have to clap eyes on Tom again.

A week later my manager contacted me again. "Occupational Health would like you to see a psychiatrist," she said. "It'll help you recover from your ordeal."

"Psychiatrist?" I said, laughing. "I'm not mad. He's the one who needs to see a shrink, not me."

"It's company policy. No one's suggesting you're mad," she replied.

I went to see the shrink. I travelled all the way to his office in Bournemouth where he conducted his business in a little office adjacent to his shabby cottage. His name was Philip, a scrawny bloke in his late sixties, with wispy white hair and broomstick-thin shoulders nudging upwards through his cable-knit cardigan. He made me feel like such an idiot. After explaining in detail the events that occurred in Hong Kong, he proceeded to ask me a string of totally unrelated psychoanalytic questions. I think he thought he was Sigmund bloody Freud.

"Tell me about your childhood, Mandy," he said, steepling his hands beneath his chin.

"What has that got to do with anything?" I said.

"What's your relationship like with your father?"

This was getting ridiculous. "Look, Philip, I appreciate you're just doing your job, but I really don't think I need to be here – I don't need therapy."

"Why do you think you don't need therapy, Mandy? Do you think you're above needing help – do you feel there's something wrong, perhaps ... the fact you feel no one can help you?"

At that point I stood up, thanked Philip for his time, and left. And that marked the end of my "counselling" sessions.

I was still appalled about being treated in such a degrading manner by Tom and Jacques, but there was a light on the horizon. After I complained again to management about the shambolic counselling session, I was put on a three-month buddy roster with Laura, meaning that we would do all of our trips together. I also passed my senior exams with flying colours. Things were looking up.

CHAPTER TWELVE

CARIBBEAN QUEENS

We had so much fun during our three-month buddy roster. Laura and I went everywhere together: LA, Vegas, Joburg, New York, Japan, Hong Kong, laughing our way from country to country.

In our first month, we were deemed Caribbean Queens – because our roster consisted predominately of Caribbean trips: Barbados, St Lucia, Grenada, Tobago and Antigua. We thought the Caribbean trips were great, because you got extra cash and stayed at beautiful, luxurious resorts. Not many other seniors liked these trips, because a lot of them preferred to visit their rich boyfriends in New York or Los Angeles – and the smaller Upper Class cabin made it much harder work. Which meant Caribbean trips were easy for us to get, even with my low seniority. At the Colony Club, Barbados, you could swim straight from your hotel room to the swimming pool, via a small stream off your balcony, lined with stunning waterfalls and plant life. Most of our days were spent sunbathing, partying on catamarans and scuba diving.

On one trip to Barbados, Laura and I were invited to represent Virgin Atlantic at a promotional event held at the exclusive Sandy Lane resort. We met a few celebrities – Cilla Black, the late Bob Monkhouse and the perma-tanned TV presenter Dale Winton. Sir Cliff Richard, who also owns a house in Barbados, was there, playing a charity tennis game. It was the perfect opportunity to rub shoulders with the rich and famous, whom we were supposed to be promoting our new Upper Class service to, but all Laura and I were interested in that night was the free champagne.

We always had good parties in the Caribbean, especially during hurricane season when high winds and sheet rain battered the islands. That's when we had some of our wildest room parties; we couldn't go out or sunbathe so we just drank ... and drank.

After a month of living it up in the Caribbean, Laura and I were put on a few New York trips. New York trips are all about shopping, which we did a lot of. All the money I'd saved in the Caribbean was soon frittered away on Sephora products and more handbags from Guess – I had enough shoes and bags to open my own shop.

On our first New York trip, Laura, who'd stayed single since dumping Dan, found herself a fuck buddy, aptly named Randy, a graphic designer who owned a swanky loft apartment in the up-and-coming Meatpacking district. "I think it's the best sex I've ever had," Laura had said. "It's proper throw-down stuff – and he's got the biggest dick."

Richard Branson came on our New York trip, and, as usual, requested that the whole crew from all six flights that day attend a glitzy function down-route. He popped into our briefing before the flight. "Right, guys," he said, "Donald Trump's invited us all to a party tonight ... I'd like you all to be there if possible. Girls ... and boys, wear something sexy, flirt and just have fun." Lots of smiling faces nodded at Richard and even the boys seemed to be excited at the thought of a high society party in Manhattan.

"I'm not going to that bloody party," said Laura as we bounced along the jetway. "I'm seeing Randy. No more phone sex for me; in approximately ten hours' time I'll be going for it like the clappers. God, it feels like forever since my lady chamber has been serviced."

"You only saw him last week," I said.

"A week is a long time, Mands. I need my Randy fix."

Just hearing Laura say his name made me laugh. "Trust you to have a boyfriend called bloody Randy."

Laura grinned and jiggled her eyebrows. "Randy by name, randy by nature. Bring it on."

"I'll be thinking of you when I'm guzzling champagne at Trump Tower tonight. Can't you come for a little while? It won't be the same without you there."

We stepped onto the plane and turned left – we were both working in Upper Class that day.

"Sorry Mands, no can do. Let's go for breakfast tomorrow morning though – I'll fill you in on all the juicy details – then we'll hit the shops."

"If you can still walk," I said.

Richard greeted the passengers as they piled onto the plane, laughing and joking with them and signing autographs. But once we were airborne he did his usual disappearing act to the crew rest area, where he slept until touchdown. Richard had even gone to the lengths of taking the legally required SEP exams to enable him to use the crew rest areas on board every aircraft, so he could get a good night's sleep without being disturbed.

After checking in at the Helmsley Hotel, I showered and headed along to my colleague Ruth's room, where a party was already underway. I took all my gear – make-up, clothes to wear for the Trump party and, most importantly, my two complimentary miniatures of vodka. I walked in on the usual chaotic scene: girls screaming and giggling, swapping clothes, doing each other's hair and make-up and MTV blaring from the television. Laura came in for a drink, looking stunning in a jewel-encrusted black satin dress and heels, and then disappeared to meet Randy. "Wish me luck," she said, hugging me goodbye.

"I don't think you need any," I said. "You look incredible. Randy won't be able to keep his hands off you."

From there the night was a blur. I was half-cut when we arrived at Trump Tower. I can remember seeing a throng of paparazzi outside as we rushed into the building, and Richard arriving alongside us with two more pretty stewardesses from his PR team, his arms snaked around their nipped-in waists. I also remember seeing him leave the party early with his leggy companions. And I have foggy memories of a room party back at the Helmsley afterwards, where I woke up around 8am stretched out on the floor with a huge pizza next to my head and a girl lying across my legs. I'd mixed vodka, champagne, rum ... and probably much more.

I felt rough as hell, but I'd arranged to meet Laura at 9am for our breakfast, so a lie-in was out of the question. I shook the girl off my legs, peeled myself off the floor – my legs now dead – limped back to my room, showered, painted over my dehydrated face and headed down to the lobby. *A plate of stodge and some sex chat from Laura should pick me up*, I thought.

After waiting half an hour for Laura to show up, I figured she'd opted for morning sex with Randy over breakfast with me. I couldn't wait any longer – my stomach was growling.

I sauntered along Forty-Second Street, the sound of the traffic assailing my delicate head, and the aromas of freshly brewed coffee, cinnamon and bacon sending my taste buds into overdrive. I was starving: I hadn't eaten dinner the previous night or even touched any of the canapés at Donald Trump's party. I walked to the nearest deli and was about to go in when I heard a screeching siren behind me, followed by a voice screaming, "Mandy, Mandy." I turned around to see Laura hanging out the rear window of a New York Police Department car, arms flailing, her long dark hair whipping her face. In the front seats were two remarkably gorgeous officers of the NYPD.

"Quick, get in," cried Laura, flinging the door open. These lovely fellas are going to take us for a ride."

The officers had been on a routine patrol when they'd spotted Laura on her walk of shame from Randy's apartment, wandering aimlessly in a dodgy area near the Coyote Ugly bar they had been to the night before. After explaining she was "a tad lost", they'd offered to drive her back to our hotel.

"You're mental," I said, climbing into the car. Laura laughed. She was still wearing the same dress she'd gone out in the previous night. "Mandy, meet Brett and Jeff, two of New York's toughest crime busters." Laura reached up and twiddled a dial on the ceiling, setting off the siren. "How cool is this?"

"Nice to meet you, Mandy," Brett and Jeff drawled.

"Hiya," I said. "Can I have a go at the siren?"

Brett and Jeff took us for a spin round the block, giving a comedy-style guided tour, while Laura and I played with the siren and rolled around on the back seat, giggling. "To your left you'll see Harry's Deli," Jeff said, "He's been on Forty-Second Street since 1954 – serves the finest waffles in town."

"And ahead on the right, you can see the Chrysler Building," added Brett, "and a lamp post."

It was a great laugh – we didn't want to get out of the car when the cops pulled up outside our hotel. "Can't we stay for a little while longer?" asked Laura.

"Sorry, girls," said Jeff, "We'd love for you to stay but we've got some serious crimes to fight today."

Laura set the siren off one last time and we clambered out of the car. "Thanks for the ride," I said.

"Phwoar, I wouldn't mind playing with their truncheons," Laura said, as we stood on the sidewalk, waving goodbye to the handsome cops.

"What about Randy?"

Laura looped her arm through mine, a secret smile tickling her lips. "I'll tell you all about that over breakfast."

Although I was having a ball down-route, my home life wasn't so peachy. My relationship with Jonathan had deteriorated rapidly in recent weeks. Our sex life had dwindled and no more was said about our engagement – Jonathan still hadn't bought a ring. "I'm saving up for one," he'd say whenever I brought up the subject. There really wasn't much point in us being engaged if I couldn't even discuss it with my mam.

His mother, Margaret, was still being a pain, letting herself into our house when we weren't there and constantly telling me I wasn't good enough for her precious son. I remember one conversation we had after I'd booked a romantic getaway to Paris for Jonathan's birthday. We were eating Sunday lunch at the time at his parents' house. "I'm taking Jonathan to Paris for his birthday," I'd enthused. "I've booked a lovely hotel on the Champs Elysees and dinner at the Eiffel Tower."

Margaret shot me a derisive glare over her bifocal lenses. She waited until Jonathan was out of earshot then blurted out: "Who is paying for this Paris trip? Jonathan has better things to spend his money on than you."

In the end – after trying to make the relationship work for a considerable length of time – I knew it had run its course. I'd thought about ending it for a while, but there always seemed to be some obstacle or other in the way: Jonathan's birthday, or Christmas or Valentine's, or he was sitting his pilot licence exams or applying for jobs, and I didn't want him to mess all that up. Becoming a pilot was his dream. So I waited until he'd passed his exams – and landed a job as a first officer at Flybe – before I finally broke up with him.

I'd just returned from a five-night Hong Kong trip to a cold and empty house. I could tell Jonathan hadn't been living there in my absence. All the food in the fridge was exactly where I'd left it and had gone off. The contents of the fruit bowl were shrivelled and mouldy, and the furniture and surfaces speckled with dust. I called Jonathan. "Where have you been for the last five days?" I said.

"At home, why?"

"You couldn't have been. Everything is exactly how I left it – plus, all the food is rotten, there's dust everywhere."

Jonathan paused, let out a deep sigh. "I just stayed at my mum's for a few days, that's all. I'm on my way home as we speak."

I told Jonathan we needed to "talk" and hung up.

I was waiting for him in the lounge when he came home, tissues at the ready. I heard the key tinkle in the lock, the door clicking shut, followed by Jonathan's cheery voice singing, "Mandy, I'm home."

"In the lounge," I called, trying to disguise the nervousness in my voice.

He walked into the room, dressed in his Flybe uniform, arms outstretched. "Give me a hug then," he said.

I looked down, wringing my hands in my lap. "Sit down, Jonathan," I said slowly. "There's something I need to tell you."

His face dropped. He sat down next to me on the sofa and reached for my hands. "What is it, Mandy?" he asked. "Please don't tell me anything bad."

I looked at him. His face was a mixture of fear and hope. "I'm sorry, Jonathan, I don't think this is working. I – I ..." It was hard to find the words. "I think we should split up."

Jonathan let go of my hands, covered his face and wept, his voice breaking as he said, "No, please no."

I hugged him. There were no words left to say. I held him in my arms, his strong shoulders collapsing inwards as he sobbed. After a while he looked up at me, his eyes bloodshot and pained, bottom lip quivering. "Please, Mandy, can we at least give it one last try? We've been through so much together. Please don't throw it all away."

It killed me to see him so upset, but I'd made up my mind. After contemplating this for more than two Valentine's Days, I couldn't stay with him out of pity; that wouldn't be fair on either of us. "I'm sorry, Jonathan," I said, tears now streaming down my cheeks. "I can't."

Ending our relationship was the hardest thing I had ever done. We'd been together for years and, as Jonathan had pointed out, we had been through a lot together. I moved out of our house and stayed with my Mum and Dad for a while to sort myself out. Jonathan was in bits. He called me every day for weeks, crying and begging for me to take him back. He told me the break up was affecting his work. "I sat in the first officer's seat and just cried for an entire flight, Mandy," he said. "The captain wasn't very happy – he said I could get a disciplinary or the sack if I do it again."

But there was nothing I could do to help him. "I'm so sorry, please just try to move on," I said. "I'm sure it will get easier."

Although I had to show a strong front to Jonathan, being the one who had made this decision, inside I was hurting. But I also felt like a huge weight had been lifted from my shoulders, and I was enjoying being single again. After our break-up I went on a trip to Vegas with the girls and some other crew to celebrate my thirtieth birthday. I partied hard. We hired a canary-yellow 22-seater Hummer limo and cruised along the strip, drinking the bars dry. We hired speedboats on the Hoover Dam and hit every nightclub in town. It was great to let my hair down and flirt a little – and not have to worry about pleasing someone else. I felt independent, happy and strong again. I also booked a few weeks off work and travelled to Thailand on my own, where I'd arranged to meet some of my RAF friends in Pattaya, who took me to watch a local kick-boxing tournament. I swam through death-defying cave tunnels and trekked through a rainforest on Ko Phi Phi Leh to the beach where the movie *The Beach* was filmed. I also gained my advanced diving certificate on Ko Tao.

When I returned from Thailand I felt like a new woman. I bought a new convertible VW Beetle and my own house in West Sussex, and returned to work feeling invigorated, confident ... and ready for a fresh start.

CHAPTER THIRTEEN

SMOKE AND MIRRORS

It's a good job we're expected to look cheerful in this line of work. I was staring ahead while doing the in-flight safety demonstration, and one of my colleagues, Stacey – whom I'd only just met – was flashing her boobs at the back of the cabin. The passengers couldn't see her, as they were all facing me, but I was getting a right eyeful. I could barely keep a straight face. She'd unbuttoned her jacket and blouse, pulled down her bra and was now holding a boob in each hand, bouncing them in time with the beat of the voice over the PA system, her neat, threaded eyebrows darting up and down in mock surprise at the words "oxygen masks will drop from above." Ever the professional, I continued the demonstration, suppressing my laughter as I placed my life jacket over my head and tied the straps around my waist. But when I glanced towards the back of the aircraft again, Stacey was now flashing her bare arse. She was bent over, skirt hitched at her waist, support tights and knickers at her knees, wiggling her suntanned bum. I couldn't help but laugh now.

It was nothing I hadn't seen before. Crew were always putting on strip shows to distract their colleagues during demos. Next time you see an air hostess or steward laughing uncontrollably as they go through the demo, look behind you, and you just might catch a glimpse.

As Stacey's bum disappeared behind the galley curtain, I began my slow walk down the aisle, glancing from side to side, checking all seatbelts were fastened, trays stowed and seats upright. There were too many seniors on the flight and I had volunteered to help out in Economy, so took a little longer to secure my zone in the unfamiliar cabin. As always, I had to ask a few passengers to turn their iPods off or fold their trays away. I reached the end of the cabin and entered the galley, where Stacey was re-buttoning her jacket and giggling to herself.

"Hey, what was all that about, Dita Von Teese?" I said, giving her a playful jab in the ribs.

Come to think of it, Stacey did resemble Dita Von Teese, with her glossy black hair, hourglass figure and pouty red-painted lips.

"Thought you'd like that. I was going to go for full frontal but I'm due a wax," she said.

Today's destination was Miami – another party city. All we ever did in Miami was sunbathe and hang out at cheesy nightclubs on South Beach.

"We should go to Mangos tonight," Stacey said during takeoff. "I always pull there."

Mangos, on Ocean Drive, was a regular haunt for cabin crew. It was right up our street: flamboyant, with tropical rainforest decor and staff clad in leopard-print cat suits who danced on the bar.

"Yeah, I'm up for that," I said. "Do you know anyone else on this trip?"

"Only one of the girls in Upper Class who I've flown with a few times, but she's a bit of a princess, to be honest ... not a huge fan."

I bonded instantly with Stacey. She was one of your all-round, fun-loving, up-for-anything hosties who didn't take herself too seriously. I didn't know any of the other crew on board so I was glad to have made another friend. We chatted excitedly about the trip ahead until we left our jump seats to prepare the first meal service. This is the moment passengers do look over their shoulders, and it usually fills them with a sense of relief to see that we're up and about.

Back in the galley, Stacey and I got down to business, heating up the Economy meals – the usual beef bourguignon and chicken with rice – and caught up on a bit of Galley FM while we stacked our carts.

She told me about a recent trip to St Lucia where one of the dollies had invited a group of rugby lads back to her hotel room for a party in her hot tub. "The Jacuzzi couldn't take the weight," she said. "And the tub crashed through the balcony and landed on the balcony below. Can you believe she actually got a disciplinary for that, I mean wasn't her fault, was it ...?"

I told Stacey about the escapade Laura and I'd had with the NYPD cops and, of course, she'd already heard it on Galley FM ... only her version involved us actually copping off with the coppers.

"I was told it ended in a foursome back at the station," Stacey said. "I was proper jealous."

I laughed. "No, it wasn't that exciting, it was just a bit of a giggle and totally random."

"So, are you seeing anyone at the moment?"

"No," I sighed, "I mean I was ... we were engaged, but we split up not so long ago. We were never really properly engaged though; I didn't even have a ring and he wouldn't let me tell anyone."

"Shit, I'm sorry to hear that," she said, bending down to load the cart.

"It's okay. It was never going to work, his mum was a total nightmare. I'm moving on: young, free and single again."

Stacey looked up and winked a heavily made-up eyelid. "Stick with me, Mandy. We're going to have so much fun in Miami."

Surprisingly, there were no demanding or unruly passengers on board, which made a nice change. Normally we'd be bombarded with complaints about the food, or the in-flight entertainment, and at least one drunken air-rage incident was guaranteed. But today's flight was going smoothly, apart from a little turbulence, which often occurred over this part of the Atlantic. Then, about four hours into the flight, something happened.

Stacey and I were back in the galley, making a start on the duty-free service and moaning about the crap commission we received, when our flight service manager, Sam, poked his head around the curtain.

"Sorry to interrupt you, girls ... have you got a minute? There's something I need to tell you." He was calm and collected, as flight service managers always are – one of the old-school types, in his early fifties with a balding head.

"Sure," I said.

"I need everyone to assemble in galley two for a briefing. I'll brief the right-hand side of the plane first, then the left. See you in five."

Stacey and I exchanged worried glances. We knew what "assemble in galley two" was code for: it meant there was an emergency of some description.

"Now I don't want to worry any of you," Sam said, once we were all assembled in galley two, "but we've had an engine fire in engine three."

There was a brief silence, interrupted by a hostie, who asked, "Does that mean we can't go to Miami?"

"Never mind Miami," added a gangly steward. "What about the fire, is it spreading?"

Sam hushed everybody down and continued. "It's okay, it's electrical. The captain has turned off the electricity on that engine, which has got rid of the blaze. However, as per regulations he's going to try and turn it back on again in the hope it doesn't reignite. But under the circumstances he's decided to redirect back to Gatwick – it's too costly to get the engine fixed in Miami. We're still in the green zone, so we're safe to head back. We'll have to dump fuel though."

Sam paused.

"We still have three good engines, though?" I asked.

"Indeed. As I said, it's nothing to worry about. The captain will be making an announcement shortly, and the passengers will be told about the fire. Some of them may freak out so we'll need to reassure them everything is fine. In the meantime, we carry on as normal."

We headed back to our respective doors, faces beaming. "Keep calm and carry on" was the message. Strolling down the aisle, I was stopped by a few passengers, wondering what had happened to the duty-free cart. "I ordered 200 Rothmans ages ago," said one guy.

"I'll be right back with them, sir," I sang, as I swished past.

None of them could have noticed the engine fire – otherwise they wouldn't have been moaning about packets of fags. Then we had a fifteen-minute breather – just enough time for the other crew to be briefed and to deal with a few of the duty-free orders – before the captain made his announcement. I was in the aisle handing a passenger her change when his voice came over the PA: "Ladies and gentlemen, this is your captain speaking. I'm afraid we've had a bit of an engine fire. The situation is in hand, but as a precautionary measure, we'll be diverting back to Gatwick to deal with the problem there. We apologise for any inconvenience this may cause. Arrangements will be made for you to travel on the next available flight to Miami."

Pandemonium struck. People started screaming and crying, gawping out the windows looking for flames and shouting one question after another: "Are we going to crash?" "Which engine is it?" "If it's normal then why are we diverting?" Crew paced up and down the cabin, repeating reassuring messages as advised. Stacey and I dealt with the passengers in our aisle. "It's okay," I said calmly. "The fire is contained. Everything is perfectly safe. Just try to stay calm."

Just after I'd said that, a massive plume of smoke billowed from one of the wing engines on the right side. More screams filled the cabin. "You call that 'normal'?" yelled a bespectacled man, getting out of his seat. At the front of the cabin a woman sitting in an aisle seat started sobbing uncontrollably. I went over to her and crouched by her side. Her head was in her hands and her thin legs were pulled tautly together and trembling.

"It's okay, madam," I said. "There's nothing to worry about. In a few hours we'll be back on the ground."

She let her hands fall into her lap. Her face was rigid and pale, like a bleached wood carving. "I'm sorry," she sobbed. "I'm not normally like this. But when the captain mentioned an engine fire it panicked me. I've got two young children at home."

"And you'll be back with them in no time."

She blew her nose and nodded. "I hope so."

"Listen," I added. "I'm the best person to speak to about engine fires. I used to work in the engineering department so I know a lot about engines and how they work. We don't actually need four engines; three is more than enough. The fire has gone out now – the captain has turned that engine off, so it's no longer a problem."

"But what about the smoke?"

"That was probably just the captain testing the engine again, It's all switched off now by the looks of it, and we're quite safe to land with three engines. Most cross-Atlantic flights only have two engines on the aircraft anyway – but all of our Virgin planes have four, so we actually still have one spare."

She began to relax and even managed a little laugh. "I feel rather silly. I watched that film *Alive* the other night, the one where the survivors of a plane crash eat each other's flesh. I had visions of that happening to us.

I'm so stupid – I know I shouldn't have watched that film. I'm sorry for being such a wreck."

"You're not a wreck. It's natural to feel scared," I said, then, with another reassuring smile, added: "You should see the passengers down the back of the plane ... it's like a scene from the *Airplane* movie down there – there are nuns playing guitars and a queue of people slapping them 'n' everything."

She laughed again. "Ask them to play a number for me."

Most passengers gradually began to accept the situation and calmed down ... except for a handful, who started going on about compensation and complaining that their holidays had been ruined. The captain made another announcement reiterating that everything was under control, we had turned around and our landing at Gatwick was rescheduled for four hours' time, and, for a while, things did return to normal, especially when we wheeled the drinks cart out.

It was approximately two hours prior to landing when we were hit with a second drama: turbulence ... *severe* turbulence. It started while we were serving drinks – a few bumps and skips, nothing out of the ordinary for this part of the Atlantic. But the bumps rapidly became thumps and the aircraft started shuddering, dropping altitude, rising then dropping again. Drinks were being spilled, cups flying off trays. A few passengers started reaching for their sick bags. The seatbelt lights were illuminated and Stacey and I made our way back to the galley with the cart, crashing into seats as the plane jolted and trying to control the movements of the floating cart. By the time we reached the galley, the back of the plane was swinging erratically from side to side in a looping motion. We secured the cart in its stowage, grabbed some biohazard sacks and went back out to the cabin to clear up the debris. But now most of the passengers were vomiting – filling up bags, vomiting into the aisles and over each other like some sort of chain reaction – as the plane dropped at least a hundred feet, steadied itself then shook violently. People were handing us sick bags full of warm vomit, faces sage green and stark white, and we were slipping on the puke-splattered carpet. The smell was overwhelming: acrid and choking. Stacey stumbled to the galley and returned with all the spare sick bags we had, passing them round the cabin. Then the captain announced that this was only clear air turbulence – nothing to do with the technical difficulties we had experienced earlier, but that all crew were now to return to their jump seats.

I'd never experienced turbulence that brutal before – and it lasted for over an hour. We used every sick bag and every biohazard sack on board, and people were still throwing up even after the turbulence subsided. We made an emergency landing at Gatwick and were greeted by a fleet of screaming fire engines and ambulances. The passengers – exhausted, traumatised, their holiday outfits soiled and reeking of sick – were let off the plane with the assurance they'd be placed on the next available flight to Miami. We put the biohazard sacks, filled with regurgitated food, in the toilets, ready for the poor cleaners to deal with.

Stacey's strip show at the start of the flight now seemed like a distant dream after eight hours of trauma. However, we soon bounced back to our flirty, fun-loving selves when the hunky firemen came on board – we were falling over ourselves to help them, and Stacey even managed to line up a date. "I'm impressed," she said as we walked through the terminal building. "I can still pull even when I smell of sick."

All crew on board that disastrous Miami-bound flight were expected to be ready for the same flight, on the same aircraft with the same passengers the very next day. I requested a few days off work after speaking to my manager, however. Not once during the engine fire flight had I panicked – I had automatically slipped into "Smiley Stewardess" mode. But the following day the impact had really hit me, and I was plagued by negative thoughts of what could have happened if the fire had not been contained. The blaze would then have spread to the wing and fuselage, which probably would have led to the plane ditching in the Atlantic. We had been extremely lucky.

An internal investigation was later launched after it emerged a hostess who had been working in another cabin had gone through the emergency door procedure with her passengers, demonstrating the brace position and telling them what to do if anything should happen to her. Nothing came of it, though, as she had basically thought she was just being thorough and hadn't realised how much she had scared the living daylights out of her poor exit row passengers.

I seemed to be going through a phase of attracting dramas on board. When I returned to work, I found myself dealing with two incidents in as many weeks.

I had recently been promoted to purser and was flying from Shanghai, China, to the UK when the first episode occurred. It was night time, and I'd just returned to the galley from a break in the crew rest area. Most of the passengers were asleep but I noticed four call lights were illuminated in the galley, where a few of the national crew girls were sat on bar boxes nattering in Mandarin. When I asked them why they hadn't answered the call bells, they just shrugged their shoulders. "I didn't notice any calls," said one of the girls, then turned back to her heated conversation.

"I guess I'll answer them then," I sighed.

It turned out one of the calls had been made by a Dutch gentleman in his late fifties who was suffering from chronic arrhythmia (an irregular heartbeat). When I got to his seat he was in severe pain, one hand clutching the chair, another pressed to his chest. He could barely breathe and couldn't speak, but fortunately his wife was with him.

"Does he have any medical history?" I asked her as I felt for her husband's pulse.

She handed me a huge folder full of graphs and medical notes dating back several years.

I could only just feel his pulse. It was faint and irregular.

I hurried them back to the galley and instructed the national crew to lay blankets on the galley floor. "One of those calls you ignored came from an extremely ill passenger," I said. "We need to get the defib. Clear the galley. You two stay to help."

I was fuming that they hadn't answered the call bells. I put a message over the PA system requesting the mobile defibrillator be delivered to the L4 door and, with the help of the man's wife, we slowly led him into the galley. We lay him down on the galley floor and I unbuttoned his shirt. His face was as grey as his beard and his eyes were beginning to glaze over. I gave him oxygen straight away and kept him in the galley to monitor him for the remainder of the flight. He was strapped to the defibrillator, and it kept saying, "no shock advised". He never lost consciousness, but his heartbeat was so faint I could no longer feel it. His wife knelt by his side, stroking his soft grey hair. The flight service manager came back occasionally to check up on him, and we eventually moved him into Upper Class for a more comfortable lie-down. An ambulance greeted us at Heathrow on arrival, and the couple were extremely grateful for my help. They gave me their phone number in Shanghai, where they lived. "Any time you want to visit, just call," they said.

The second incident I encountered was far less serious, yet far more dramatic. Mid flight – en route to Johannesburg – a rotund Indian woman, robed in a violet sari, came bursting into the galley, doubled over and groaning loudly. She pushed past me and grabbed hold of the counter, panting and sweating and clutching her stomach. She looked like a woman in labour.

"What's the matter, madam?" I asked. "Is it your stomach? Can you show me where the pains are?"

She rubbed her hand over her lower stomach. "All over here," she gasped.

It was obvious to me this woman was suffering from a severe case of trapped wind – a common ailment associated with flying. "Madam," I said. "I know it doesn't sound very ladylike, but I think you have trapped wind. The best thing you can do is kneel on all fours and try to break wind."

I handed her a few Rennies from the first-aid kit and pulled the curtain across.

"Now," I said calmly, "I'm going to leave you alone. This is your space – no one's going to come in. You can do whatever you want in here, or if you would feel more comfortable, you could go to the toilet?" But as soon as I left the galley she come flying out again in a flash of violet and sequins, arms flailing, screaming at the top of her voice. By the time I reached her she was thumping the emergency exit door and pulling at the handle. "Madam, do not touch the door," I warned, pulling her away from the exit and back into the galley.

"Hands off, hands off," she yelled, lashing out with her elbows. It was like trying to restrain a pit-bull. At that point my flight service manager, Angela, came into the galley and together we managed to calm the woman down. But she was still complaining of pain in her midriff.

"I think it's trapped wind," I told Angela.

"Mmm, I'm not so sure – let's do a PA call for a doctor."

There were two doctors on board – male and female. The male doctor took one look at the woman, mouthed "trapped wind", rolled his eyes and walked out of the galley. The female doctor, however, decided the woman must be suffering from something far worse and proceeded to stick a morphine drip into her arm. But in the doctor's haste, she forgot to close the valve and a fountain of blood came spurting from the woman's arm, prompting another screaming fit. We had to put on our biohazard aprons and protective masks and gloves in order to help the woman further as her blood sprayed everywhere.

Once the doctor had closed the valve and the morphine kicked in the woman began to mellow – in fact she looked blissfully happy. She returned to her seat but continually rang her call bell for the rest of the flight, asking for drinks and more Rennies, and making sure we'd arranged for an ambulance to meet her in Johannesburg.

There's no doubt about it, trapped wind can be agonising – at worst it can feel as though your insides are about to explode – but this woman was a drama queen. She loved all the attention. There had been no need to give her morphine. The only thing this woman had needed to do to alleviate her pain was some good old crop dusting.

CHAPTER FOURTEEN

DOWN UNDER

Brad: a stunning Australian Qantas pilot. Mid twenties, chiselled features, super-sexy body, a real little muscle muppet. He had the most amazing cock. It reminded me of a banana: long, but not agonisingly so, generous girth and a slight inwards curvature, which made it the perfect G-spot teaser. Orgasms with Brad were euphoric, explosive and earth-shattering. I couldn't get enough of them.

I met Brad during my first trip to Narita, Japan, about two months after I separated from Jonathan. But our love affair didn't start there. Although I found Brad incredibly attractive, I played hard to get, making him sweat. And believe me, it was worth it; when we finally did get together, the sex was dynamite and an eighteen-month global sexfest ensued.

I was singing our Virgin crew anthem "Like a Virgin" to a boisterous crowd of fellow crew members, at Narita's karaoke bar, The Truck – a drinking hole contained in an old truck in the car park of the ANA Crowne Plaza Hotel – when I first spotted Brad. He was standing with some of our crew, laughing as I hopped around the stage in my little denim shorts screaming suggestive lyrics with the microphone lead tangling round my legs. I was high as a kite after downing numerous shots of lemon hais – hence the reason for my karaoke performance – but sufficiently compos mentis to notice that this guy, with his oatmeal Bart Simpson-style hairdo, couldn't take his eyes off me.

As I handed the mic over to the next singer, a Qantas stewardess who'd requested "I Will Survive", one of our girls, Hayley, darted from the bar to greet me, flapping her hands in front of her chest. "Mandy, don't look now but I've just met the sexiest guy," she squealed. "He's a Qantas pilot, Paul. He's with his friend – also a pilot and equally as hot – who's dying to meet you."

"That's just what I need ... another pilot," I said, looking directly at the guy with the Bart Simpson flat-top, whom I could only presume was the "hot" guy Hayley was referring to.

"But he's gorgeous, Mandy. C'mon, I'll introduce you."

Before I could argue, Hayley had linked her arm through mine and was hustling me across the gluey floor to where the two men were standing.

"This is Mandy," said Hayley, her eyes lingering on the taller, surfer dude–looking guy.

"Hi, I'm Brad," said the man with the flat-top, extending his hand. I shook it. "You were amazing up there, Mandy?" he added. He had that Aussie upward inflection going on, where every sentence sounds like a question.

"That's me," I said. "Karaoke queen. People pay good money to stop me ... er I mean hear me sing back home."

"Paul," said the surfer dude, offering his hand. "Top effort, Mandy."

Our conversation was then momentarily aborted by the demonic noise the Qantas girl was making. It sounded like she was being tortured, half-shouting, half-wailing her way through the song. Tall, with muscular Tina Turner-esque legs and pixie-cropped black hair, she cut an imposing figure as she hollered her way through the song, pacing back and forth and stabbing a dagger-like finger in the direction of an embarrassed guy perched on a bar stool. It got worse. As she reached her finale she started screaming, "I will fucking survive," over and over again, tears cascading down her cheeks. Then she threw the microphone on the floor and crumpled to her knees, sobbing. Friends swarmed, helping the devastated Qantas girl to her feet and leading her out of the bar as she yelled, "You bastard, you bastard."

I looked at Brad. "Well I think she outshone my performance," I said.

He smiled. "That's Miranda."

"And that's her ex, Kenny," he nodded in the direction of the guy sitting on the bar stool. "Usual story: he cheated on her. She's taken it badly."

"No shit. That was some show."

On the surface Brad seemed like a nice guy. He was happy to buy all the drinks, which is unusual behaviour for a pilot. Our pilots hardly ever bought the crew drinks. They also had a nasty habit of ordering four-hundred-pound bottles of wine at dinner, which they'd keep up their end of the table, guzzle, and then expect us all to chip in when the bill arrived. So Brad scored highly in the generosity department. He also told me that he was thirty-one and loved all sports, especially surfing. He said he lived in an "ace" apartment on the North Shore in Sydney.

"It's totally awesome," he said. "You should come and stay sometime."

He was strikingly handsome: forget-me-not blue eyes – blue with a dash of chrome yellow around his pupils – and tanned skin. I could tell he was the type who enjoyed showing off his physique. He was wearing a tight white T-shirt that accentuated every ripped muscle in his upper body – a body that looked as though it was made solely for sex.

Brad was highly flirtatious, and so persistent. Within ten minutes he was asking for my phone number. "I've only just met you," I said, "I'm not just handing over my phone number."

Several lemon hais later, I found myself boarding the shuttle bus back to his hotel for a room party. I didn't really want to go. I was feeling quite hammered and was dubious about getting involved with another pilot so soon after Jonathan. But Hayley was desperate to get her claws into Paul and had practically begged me to tag along for moral support. "We can just stay for a little while," she said.

A "little while" turned into at least four more hours' drinking with Qantas crew at Brad and Paul's suite at the Radisson Hotel. It wasn't the usual riotous room party – just a handful of people lounging around chatting. Paul – in a blatant attempt to woo Hayley – sat on the bed playing his guitar, singing along to songs such as "Stairway to Heaven", a few Oasis numbers and an excruciatingly cringeworthy version of Eric Clapton's "Wonderful Tonight". During one awkward moment, after his rendition of Damien Rice's "The Blower's Daughter", Paul bowed his head and in a pained, breaking voice sang the final line before letting out a huge sigh that indicated his performance had left him emotionally drained. I had to stop myself from laughing out loud. It was so obvious he was putting on an act to impress Hayley, which had worked. Paul's serenading appeared to send her into a dreamy trance, her eyes transfixed on his long, strumming fingers.

Meanwhile, Brad's mission to get my phone number continued. "If you won't give me your phone number, then I'll make do with an email address?" he persisted. "We can message each other?"

Eventually I caved in. "Okay, you can have my number," I sighed. "But I don't have a pen."

"I'll get a pen, I'll get a pen," he said, springing to his feet. I'll admit, when he ran into the next room I couldn't help but check out his bum. It was so high and firm I imagined it to resemble sculpted marble in the flesh. He returned a few minutes later, pen in hand and an eager smile on his face. "I've got a pen, Mandy."

I snatched the pen out of his hand. "Oh dear, I don't have any paper."

Brad slapped his forehead. "Bloody hell. I forgot about the paper ... I'll find some."

"Don't worry," I said, pen poised, I'll write it on your T-shirt."

Brad recoiled. "No way, man, this is my favourite T-shirt."

"Forget it then," I laughed, throwing the pen on the floor. "You can't like me that much after all."

This is the last flashback I have of that party: throwing the pen on the floor and watching Brad's muscular face drop. I must've passed out soon afterwards. I woke up mid morning curled up on a sofa ... with Brad spooned behind me. *The cheeky so-and-so,* I thought. I left him there sleeping and caught a taxi back to our hotel, my head spinning, stomach churning.

It was my last day in Narita ... and I spent it with my head down the illuminated toilet bowl, lemon hais, noodles and bean sprouts exploding from my gut, water spraying my face every time I flushed the loo. It was one of those state of the art Japanese sensor toilets that squirted water up your bum when you flush. I couldn't keep anything down – not even water. I had to cancel my planned trip to Shinshoji Temple; I was in no fit state to go anywhere. Thank God I'd packed so much in the previous day. In the morning Hayley and I had hit the charming wooden shops of Narita town, where I'd treated myself to a kimono, several Japan Airlines fridge magnets and a few Hello Kitty knick-knacks. The afternoon had been spent trying on puffy dresses at a wedding fair at our hotel. No one had even questioned the fact neither Hayley nor I were wearing engagement rings. She was to be a "winter" bride and I was due to marry my heart surgeon fiancé at a lavish summer ceremony in the Cotswolds.

Later the next day, when all I could bring up was stodgy, acrid bile, I heard a knock at the door. It was Brad.

"What are you doing here?" I said, ushering him into my room before anyone spotted him. "How did you get my room number?"

I had no make-up on and bean sprouts in my hair ... I looked terrible.

"Hayley gave it to me," said Brad. "She's still with Paul ... I thought I'd give them some space. They've been at it all morning – you should've heard them. It sounded like someone was being murdered in Paul's room."

Brad strode over to the window. He seemed far too energetic and fresh for someone who'd been on the lash all night. "Lovely view," he said, then, flashing me a cocksure smile over his shoulder, "Not as lovely as you though."

I shook my head. "You don't give up, do you."

He stayed for a while and we got along fine, discussing trips and surfing and exchanging snippets of crew gossip. When he left he asked, very politely, "Can I kiss you, Mandy?"

"You don't want to kiss me," I said. "I've been throwing up all day."

"I don't mind," he said. "Please let me kiss you."

I couldn't kiss him. I hadn't even brushed my teeth. However, I did scribble my email address on a napkin. "You can email me if you want," I said, passing him the napkin.

"Unreal," he said, and pecked me on the cheek.

I had an inkling I wouldn't hear from Brad ever again. I assumed a man as good looking as him would have women throwing themselves at his feet and, after my refusal to put out, would simply move on to the next, more willing, candidate. But the day after I returned to the UK, I was surprised to find my inbox flooded with messages from Brad. "Hey Mandy," he wrote in one email. "I can't stop thinking about you. I really feel as though we connected and I would love to see you again."

In another message he urged me to think about visiting him in Sydney. "I'll cook for you," he wrote. "I'm an awesome chef."

Inwardly, I was thrilled Brad was still pursuing me. His messages were funny and sweet, and I realised I'd maybe been a bit harsh towards him in Japan. So I wrote back, and over the next few weeks, our messages went from being mildly flirtatious to highly erotic. We began instant messaging on MSN, describing what we'd like to do to each other. He told me about a spot on the beach where we could have sex. We discussed orgasms and sexual positions. "I can't wait to make you come," he said. "I have to see you again." And on that note, I requested a trip to Sydney.

From the moment I left Heathrow I was beside myself with excitement; all I could think about was getting to my destination and having hot, passionate sex with Brad. I was to meet him at the Shangri-La Hotel, where he'd booked us a plush suite overlooking the Opera House.

During the two night stopover in Hong Kong en route to Sydney I pampered myself at the local spa: facial, full body massage, leg wax, bikini wax – if there's one thing a pilot deserves it's a clean, tidy landing strip – manicure and pedicure. Some of the girls were going for colonic irrigations and tried to persuade me to join them. I declined – the idea of having a tube shoved up my bum and watching my poo being sucked out of me ahead of meeting my new boyfriend didn't really appeal. What would I say to Brad? "Go easy on me love, I'm feeling a little delicate – just had a colonic." I don't think so.

The flight from Hong Kong to Sydney was torturous, my excitement building to an almost agonising level as ten hours passed slowly. Just before we began our descent into Sydney Airport I nipped into the loo to slip into the sexy new underwear I'd bought: black silk-and-lace sussies, matching knickers and sheer black, lace-top stockings. Well, I was hardly going to rock up for my steamy liaison wearing my support tights and Bridget Jones pants. I touched up my make-up, restyled my hair, sprayed perfume on my wrists, neck, inner thighs, navel and boobs – all the spots I anticipated Brad's lips to explore – and floated out of the toilet.

We touched down in Sydney just after 7am local time and, surprisingly, I didn't feel tired. During the taxi ride to the hotel, stuck in rush-hour traffic, Brad texted: "Hey sexy, can't wait to see you. Head straight to the presidential suite when you arrive. Hurry up, I'm waiting ..."

I wasn't sure what impressed me most: the sight of Brad's bare legs, or the view of Sydney Harbour through the floor-to-ceiling windows behind him. "Welcome to Sydney, babe," he said, opening the door to the presidential suite. He was wearing one of his tight muscle T-shirts and surf shorts, skimming thighs that could have been crafted by Michelangelo. I'd never seen such a magnificent set of pins: smooth, defined, golden. The next moment we were in each other's arms, slow dancing around the room, kissing. His mouth was minty and gentle, and he smelt so manly and fresh – a spicy, woody aroma. My hands ventured down his back, pressed into the dip at the base of his spine and fanned his taut bum as his hands crept beneath my jacket, under my shirt, up over my breasts. I pulled him closer, stepping backwards until my back was against the door. Brad reached behind him, peeled my hands off his bum and tacked them to the door above my head, his lips travelling down the side of my neck. My heart walloped. I was so turned on – and slightly hypoxic after the flight – I thought I was going to faint. Every arousal point in my body hummed. I was light-headed and breathless, and only when I started seeing black dots dancing before my eyes and my knees began to give way did I have to ask Brad to stop.

"I think I may have to sit down for five minutes," I said, letting out a deep breath ending in a weak laugh.

Gently, Brad lowered my hands, kissed my forehead. "It's so great to see you, Mandy," he said with a hedonistic smile. "I'll warn you though, that was just a warm-up."

I laughed. "Glad to hear it."

"Come here, let's get you a glass of champagne. I've got some gifts for you, too."

Brad had transformed the presidential suite into a lovers paradise. There were bottles of vintage champagne on ice, a table topped with crystal bowls filled with chocolate-coated strawberries, and square plates loaded with seared beef carpaccio and figs. Beside a sumptuous white sofa bopped three heart-shaped red helium balloons.

"Wow, you've gone to so much effort," I said, wandering over to one of the giant windows. The view was phenomenal: the harbour waters glistening like a trembling sheet of silver and ice-blue sequins in the morning sunlight; I could see the Harbour Bridge, the Opera House and little yellow water taxis whizzing across the harbour.

I heard a cork pop behind me. "You're worth it," said Brad. "Champagne?"

"Please."

While Brad poured the champagne I slipped off my shoes, jacket and made myself comfortable on the sofa.

"God my feet are killing me," I said.

"I'll massage them later," he said, passing me a flute of bubbly.

He knelt at my feet and we chinked glasses. "Cheers," we harmonised.

The fizz warmed my stomach, an instant hit, dissipating through my body, melting every muscle.

"Ready for your first present?" said Brad.

"You didn't have to buy me anything."

"This is just a little something I put together for you – I've got more gifts for you in the bedroom."

"Is that a promise?"

Brad reached beneath the sofa and produced a thin square parcel, beautifully wrapped in fuchsia satin paper tied with purple ribbon.

"A CD?" I guessed.

"Open it and see."

"It's so pretty," I said, tearing off the paper. It was indeed a CD – a blank CD in a clear case.

Brad folded his arms on my knees, grinning expectantly. "Like it?"

"It's fabulous – just what I've always wanted," I said, staring at the blank CD.

"It's some tunes I threw together – songs that make me think of you. Want to hear it?"

I laughed. "Sure."

Brad strode over to the stereo and popped the CD into the tray. *How sweet,* I thought. No man had ever made me a compilation CD before. I was then overcome by fits of giggles as the over-indulgent strains of Luther Vandross boomed from the stereo. Even the helium balloons appeared to dip their foil atriums in embarrassment. Brad turned round gradually, hands outstretched, and, with closed eyes, crooned along to "All the Woman I Need", which made me laugh harder. Then he danced out of the room, motioning with his head for me to follow.

Brad's dance led me to the bedroom, and onto the four-poster bed where a cluster of glossy gift bags had been assembled among a scattering of red rose petals.

"What's all this?" I said, climbing onto the mattress. There were bags from Agent Provocateur, Bulgari, Billabong, Godiva – it was like the product of a shopoholic's final spending spree sprawled before me.

"I wanted to spoil you," said Brad, kneeling on the bed opposite me. "Go on, open them."

I picked up the black Agent Provocateur bag. "This looks sexy. I didn't know they had an Agent Provocateur in Sydney."

"I ordered it online."

Inside the bag, wrapped in tissue, was a skimpy gossamer black negligee.

"Wow, this doesn't leave much to the imagination," I said, pinning the spaghetti straps to my shoulders.

"That's the idea," said Brad, reaching for my face. He leaned across and kissed me, gently pushing me backwards onto the bed until we were horizontal. Brad lay on top of me, his mouth delicately slugging mine, and soon we were moving in fervent rotations over the bed – him on top, me on top, him on top again, steam rolling gift bags, the Opera House coming in and out of focus with every turn. In the next room Brad's CD played on – Terence Trent D'Arby was singing "Sign Your Name" now. "I've got a present for you, too," I said, lifting my head.

"You shouldn't have," Brad said.

I rolled off him, rising to my knees by his shoulder. "It's just a little something I threw together," I said with a terrible Aussie accent. I unbuttoned my shirt slowly and tossed it over my shoulder. Brad's eyes enlarged. "Whoa, that's some present."

"Stay where you are," I warned, reaching for the hem of my skirt. "There's more." I lifted my skirt to the tops of my stockings, paused for teasing effect before hoisting it all the way up to my waist, offering a full view of my new undies.

Brad let out a long whistle.

I laughed. "Get your kit off then."

He was naked quicker than you could say didgeridoo.

It was the most powerfully orgasmic sex I'd ever experienced. After making me come with his tongue during foreplay, he flipped me over and slipped into me ... and that was the moment I discovered Brad's banana dick could reach places no other man's dick had touched before. I came immediately – and just kept on coming, warm contractions spreading from my stomach to every part of my body. I felt as though I was levitating in a state of permanent arousal.

We didn't leave the hotel all day. We drank champagne, devoured the strawberries and oysters and washed each other's hair in the marble Jacuzzi bath, where, again, we had sex. Brad was fascinated with my body and eager to learn exactly what turned me on.

That evening we decided to leave our love suite and explore Sydney. "We'll go for dinner and then I'll take you to Luna Park," Brad enthused. "You'll love it – we can catch the ferry there, it's lit up. We can go on the rides ... trust me, it's unreal."

He didn't stop talking about Luna Park. "I can't wait to see your face, Mandy?" he said as we dined alfresco on tapas at the Opera Bar, that rising inflection creeping into his voice again. "You enter the park through a huge, smiling clown's mouth ... it's legendary. There's a magic castle, Ferris wheel ... you like rides, Mandy?"

"I like riding you," I teased.

Brad reached below the table and touched my knee. "Not as much as I enjoy riding you."

"Guess what," I said in a loud whisper.

"What?"

"I'm not wearing any knickers."

Brad grinned and took a quick peek under the table. I crossed and uncrossed my legs, smiling like a naughty schoolgirl. I was wearing the Billabong denim mini skirt Brad had given me earlier.

It was a beautiful Friday night in Sydney – hot, with a gentle, caressing breeze carrying wafts of fresh seaweed off the harbour. After dinner we strolled to Circular Quay to board the ferry to the famous Luna Park. Circular Quay was like an outdoor circus, packed with street performers juggling fire, riding unicycles, and buskers playing didgeridoos.

The ferry journey across the harbour was short – maybe less than ten minutes – but highly romantic. We stood outside on the deck, Brad cocooning me against the breeze with his action-man arms, kissing my neck, whispering sexy thoughts into my ear. But when the ferry chugged beneath the harbour bridge and docked at Luna Park Wharf, Brad suddenly fell silent. I looked up, expecting to see the dazzling illuminations of Luna Park Brad had raved about. But there were no bright lights ... or Mr Moon Face. "Where's the light show?" I asked, as we made our way up the ramp towards the park entrance. The place was in darkness, apart from a gentle glow from a few lamp posts, which made the clown's face look even scarier than I'd imagined. I'd never been a fan of clowns.

"Fuck," said Brad at length, "Looks like it's shut or something. This is normally all lit up, Mandy, honestly – and it's supposed to be open until eleven tonight. I don't understand. I'm sorry."

"It's okay," I said, then, spotting a group of people spilling out of the clown's mouth, added: "Look, it is open – there are people coming out."

There were only shops, restaurants and the games arcade open at Luna Park; for some reason, all the big rides were closed. I could sense Brad's disappointment as we trundled arm in arm through the park, the rides looming over us in darkness, appearing to cackle: "Look what fun you could have had." Inside the games arcade, Brad tried to win me a teddy from a claw crane machine but, despite numerous attempts, it just wasn't happening. "Let's go," I said, circling my arms around his waist as he lowered the claw for what must've been the thirtieth time. This time the open claw fell on the head of a soft green turtle. "Yes," said Brad, his smile a friendly ghost reflecting in the glass. The claw closed, skimmed the turtle's head and lifted once more, leaving the toy on the fluffy pile with its mates. "Fuck," cursed Brad, smacking his palm against the glass, "I can't even win you a teddy bear."

I didn't even want a teddy bear – he'd spoiled me rotten already.

I steered him away from the machine. "Those games are a fix," I said. "Besides, I'm having a great time."

The park was deadly quiet by the time we started making our way to the exit. We stopped at the entrance to the Scenic Railway roller coaster for a kiss. "God, I wish we could do it right here, right now," said Brad, sliding a hand down the back of my skirt.

I rested my head on Brad's shoulder while his fingers mingled with the breeze under my skirt. "What's stopping us?" I said.

"Where will we go?"

"In there," I whispered, nodding sideways at the mock Indian temple facade.

Brad liberated his hand from my skirt. "After you," he beamed.

We hurried into the temple and climbed over the gate into the station, where, against the temple wall, in semi-darkness, we put the Luna back into Luna Park.

Those twenty-four hours in Sydney with Brad were fantastic, and I left feeling sexually rejuvenated and smitten ... albeit somewhat sore. Despite living almost 11,000 miles apart, we managed to meet at least twice a month. I used my flight requests to coincide with his flying schedule and we took our love-fest to Singapore, Hong Kong, LA, New York, London and back Down Under, the sex becoming wilder and more adventurous at each location.

For our one-year anniversary Brad whisked me away to a five-star resort in the Blue Mountains, just outside Sydney. It was a stunning hotel carved into the side of the mountain itself and overlooking a deep canyon skirted by blue eucalyptus forests.

We made love in the minty air in our private terrace hot tub. In fact, that's where most of our shagging took place on this vacation – on the terrace. It was completely secluded so no other guests could see us ... although I'm sure they must have heard us, as we made quite a racket.

After a year together, I thought I knew Brad pretty well. But during this trip to the Blue Mountains I discovered he'd been harbouring a little secret. One evening when Brad was showering I spotted his passport on the bedside table. Out of curiosity I picked it up and flicked to the ID page, expecting no more than to giggle at some ghastly photo booth picture. But my eyes were drawn to the bold black print that told me Brad was born in 1980, which made him twenty-six. I was stunned – he'd told me he was almost thirty-two – the same age as me. I threw his passport onto the bed. Why had he lied to me?

I confronted him when he emerged from the shower. "Why did you lie about your age, Brad?"

"What are you on about, Mandy?" he said, rubbing his head with a fluffy white towel.

"I've seen your passport – you're only twenty six. You said you were thirty-one ... thirty-two, almost."

He looked at me with sheepish eyes. "But I'm nearly twenty-seven."

"That's not the point. I don't understand why you felt the need to lie to me."

He walked towards me, his beautiful naked body glistening with shower dew. "Because I was afraid you wouldn't want me if you knew my real age – and you wouldn't let me near you, at first."

Brad reached for my hands. "It's no biggie, really – what are a few years between lovers, anyway?"

And the next thing I knew I too was naked, lying on the bed with my legs over my head while Brad worked his banana magic.

It was a relationship based entirely on sex. After that trip to the Blue Mountains I began to question whether I actually had a future with Brad. The age gap might not seem a big deal, but I was hoping to settle down with someone closer to my own age. Brad and I hadn't even discussed the possibility of a future together – all we ever talked about was sex. The following week, on a flight back from San Francisco, I shared my concerns with a colleague, Janice, in our usual confession booth: the galley.

"The thing is, the sex is out of this world," I sighed. "I don't know whether I can live without it. If I split up with Brad, I may never have sex like this again."

"That's nonsense," said Janice. "You don't marry your best sex ... you marry your best friend."

Despite Janice's advice, I decided to stick with my best sex for the time being and see how things panned out. But bizarrely, the tipping point for me came when Brad finally brought up the subject of living together. It happened one morning while he was in London on a ten-day stopover. I'd spent a couple of nights with him at the Royal Garden Hotel, Kensington, ahead of flying out to New York. On the morning I was due to leave, as I dashed around our hotel room reclaiming various items of clothing, he sat bolt upright in the bed and said, "Hey Mandy, I've been thinking – why don't we move in together?"

His words didn't register at first; I was running late and still had a pair of jeans to locate.

"What do you reckon?"

"Ah, there they are," I said, spotting my jeans on the floor at the side of the bed.

"Did you hear what I just said, Mandy?"

"Sorry, babe – I'm in a rush. What did you say?"

"I'd like us to move in together. I could ask for a transfer to be based at Heathrow and we could live here ... in London. Imagine waking up together every day? Wouldn't that be awesome?"

I zipped my case and sat on the edge of the bed. "It sounds wonderful," I said. "Can we talk about it when I get back, though? I need to get going or I'll be late."

"Sure babe," he said, "Give me a kiss, then."

I kissed him, I left, and I never saw him again.

I appreciated Brad's gesture, I really did, but I couldn't see how it would work. The thought of introducing him to my family just didn't feel right and made it clear to me that it would feel as though we were forcing the relationship into something it was never meant to be.

As I stood waiting on the platform that morning at High Street Kensington, Brad's words replaying over and over in my mind, a tall, rugged South African guy approached me, asking for directions. He was at least six foot five, and a pair of ice-hockey boots dangled from his rucksack.

"You look like the right person to ask," he said. "I need to get to Heathrow Airport. Could you point me in the right direction, please?"

I smiled. "Sure, you're in the right place – I'm on my way there, too."

"Thanks, I still can't figure out this tube network."

I ended up chatting to this guy with the ice hockey boots – who introduced himself as "Wills" – all the way to Heathrow. He was charming and witty and we seemed to have loads in common – scuba diving and the same taste in music, films and books. He said he'd recently moved to the UK but was flying home to Durban in South Africa for a family wedding. As the conversation flowed, Brad's moving-in idea slipped further to the back of my mind. When Wills and I parted at Heathrow, he scrawled his phone number on a piece of paper. "Let's hook up for coffee sometime," he said, handing me the crumpled note.

"'That'd be nice," I said. I felt an instant attraction towards Wills – both physically and mentally.

"Cool. Have a safe journey," he said, "I'll see you soon."

I watched him disappear into the crowd of passengers thronging the check-in desks, ice-hockey boots swinging from his rucksack. I was already smitten.

I couldn't stop thinking about Wills while I was in New York, which spoke volumes about my relationship with Brad. The fact that I had been so distracted by a complete stranger had really hit me hard on landing back into the UK, and when speaking to Brad on the MSN later that day, I gave him the "It's not you – it's me" speech to end our relationship. I thought it best to remember it for what it was: pure, unadulterated, fantastic sex.

CHAPTER FIFTEEN

SIN CITY

I could hear the tipsy couple's conversation from the back of the Upper Class cabin, where I stood greeting the remainder of our passengers boarding the Las Vegas flight with enthusiastic recitals of "Good morning."

She was young – early twenties – scrawny, perma-tanned and clogging the gangway with her shocking pink case-on-wheels and white plastic garment carrier.

"Oh look, Daz, we even get our own pyjamas," she said, parking her bony white-jeaned bum on the armrest and rifling through her complimentary amenity kit. "And an eye mask ... and spa products ..."

"Never mind the pyjamas," said "Daz", "where's the fucking free booze? I'm gasping."

"'Ere, lads," came another man's voice from the seat behind Daz's, "Who's got the duty-free? Old Daz here is in need of some Dutch courage."

"He'll need it, marrying her," said a further pal.

"Oh fuck off, Gaz," snapped Daz.

"Yeah fuck off, Gaz," echoed the scraggy girl, dropping into her seat, leaving her luggage in the aisle.

Already I could tell it was going to be an arduous flight. In addition to having the rowdy wedding party on board, I was also working with Sharon – the raging alcoholic. Tall and rake-thin, with androgynous features, she had a stern glint in her eye that screamed: "Don't mess with me."

"You can do my PA announcements, as you're up for promotion." she said, heaving the cabin door shut and flinging her PA book in my general direction.

Sharon didn't share the same happy-go-lucky attitude of most cabin crew. All she was interested in was boozing. On trips she'd spend the entire time locked in her room, wouldn't come out and wouldn't let anyone in – just drinking herself into oblivion beneath the duvet.

Even then, as she brushed past me on her way to the galley, I could smell the gin fumes on her breath.

I followed Sharon into the galley. Before starting the safety demo, I needed to sort out Skinny Minnie's luggage, which meant consulting the passenger list; in Upper Class we always addressed passengers by their surnames. I scanned down the list to row four. There they were: Cindy Morris and Darren Smythe.

I walked over to their seats to find Cindy lying on top of Darren, reclining on his chest as he fondled her breasts with his sovereign- and initial-ringed fingers. He had one of those tufty boy-band hairdos – waxed into peaks like little meringues.

"Good afternoon, Miss Morris, Mr Smythe," I said. "I'm Mandy and I'm your attendant for today's flight. What type of flight would you like today?"

Daz winked. "Alright Mandy, any chance of a drink?"

"The full drinks service will begin once we're airborne, but would you like a champagne or soft drink?" I explained. "Now, Miss Morris, would you like me to place your luggage in the overhead locker for you?"

She glowered, orange face framed by masses of frizzy, badly high-lighted blonde hair. "Ain't you supposed to call us by our first names in first class?"

"If you wish, madam," I said.

"Yeah, well, it's Cindy ... Cindi with an 'i'. And he's Darren ... with a 'z' – Daz."

"Okay then, Cindi," I said, lifting the shocking pink case. I picked up the garment carrier. "Shall I hang this in the wardrobe for you?"

Cindi-with-an-i suddenly sprang to life. "That's my wedding dress – don't crease it. We're getting married ... at the Little White Chapel – the one where Britney Spears got married."

"And Joan Collins," added Daz.

"Sounds like a dream wedding to me," I said.

Daz, Gaz and their party of pals with similarly abbreviated names laughed and jeered all the way through the safety demo, singing "Get Me to the Church on Time" interspersed with chants of "'Ere we go, 'ere we go, 'ere we go," while Cindi, outnumbered by lads, pored over photographs of celebrities sporting cellulite in *Heat* magazine.

Cindi and her gang wasted no time getting stuck into the booze at the bar, as soon as the seatbelt signs had gone out. "Remember, one drink in the air is equal to two on the ground," I warned, delivering a third round of champagne to the wedding party.

"Nice one, we'll get drunk quicker," said Gaz, who I'd since learned was Daz's best man.

About two hours into the flight, Cindi and Daz changed into their sleep suits, even though it was still daytime, and paraded back to Economy Class to visit their "poor friends", returning with tales of misery, muttering: "You get what you pay for." Cindi was slurring and Daz sounded as though he'd had one too many, too. I made a mental note not to serve them any more drinks.

"We'll need to keep an eye on that wedding party," I told Sharon as we prepared dinner in the galley. "They're getting pretty rowdy back there."

"Bloody chavs. I'll go and check on them." Sharon pulled the curtain aside and immediately burst out laughing. "For fuck's sake ... that girl's trousers have just fallen down ... oh, and so has she – quick, look."

I put down the packet of prosciutto I was trying to open and turned to check out the scene: Cindi flat on her back, pyjama bottoms ruched around her ankles, legs spread with only a skimpy white G-string to hide her modesty.

"Oh Jesus," I muttered.

"You can see all her breakfast," added Sharon. "Look, her flaps are hanging out."

Gaz and his pals were in fits of laughter. Daz, also laughing, got out of his seat and helped Cindi back on her feet, slapping her bum before he pulled up her trousers.

"I can't work it out," I said.

"Work what out?" said Sharon.

"They've only had a few glasses of champagne."

"Yeah, right, and the rest: they've also been drinking their own duty-free – I saw one of them opening a bottle earlier, and I told them to put it away."

"Mmm, what a bloody pain," I said. "Let's get them fed – maybe that'll help."

Cindi didn't like prosciutto, even though she ordered it from the menu. "I can't eat raw bacon," she complained, eyes rolling. She picked at the fillet of poached salmon and refused to touch her pecan tart and custard, whining, "I'll never get into my dress." Daz insisted on calling me "Treacle" and demanded more champagne. Somewhere between dessert and the cheeseboard, all hell broke loose. I was serving passengers towards the front of the cabin when I heard the commotion.

"Oi, Cindi," hollered a lad called Ad – short for Adrian, apparently. "Why don't you get your minge out again. We could do with a laugh."

"Yeah, go on Cinds," piped Gaz, "Show us your minge."

"Nothing you ain't seen before, eh, Gaz," said Ad.

Daz dropped the piece of Stilton he was about to devour and turned to face his best man. The cabin fell silent. Daz stared Gaz in the eye, nostrils flaring, lips pursed in fury.

"What the fuck is Ad talking about, Gaz?"

Gaz tried to laugh it off. "Don't be daft, mate," he said, "Ad's pulling your leg ... he didn't ..."

"'Nothing you ain't seen before,'" he said. You've been with my bird, haven't you. My best man – how could you?"

"Look, calm down, mate," said Gaz. "It was years ago. It didn't mean anything."

But Daz was already clambering over his seat, raining blows on Gaz's head while Cindi sobbed.

Daz jumped on top of Gaz, dragged him to the floor, where the pair wrestled in a drunken tangle of limbs. Blood spilled from Gaz's mouth, following a blow from Daz's ringed fist. Cindi jumped on top of the fighting pair, trying to prise them apart as the other passengers watched in horror. I dashed back into the galley. "Quick, get the guys from the back galley to bring the restraint kit," I said to Sharon, "We might need the handcuffs."

It took four of us to restrain them. Cindi left the fight of her own accord and returned to her seat – she wasn't achieving anything, anyway. We asked the brawling men a series of routine safety and security questions, and, when they didn't answer, we pounced on them, two of us applying short, sharp shocks to pressure points on their necks to control them, while two stewards cuffed their hands behind their backs. Then we sat them down away from each other, cuffing their tied hands to their seats amid a tirade of foul-mouthed insults. Cindi wept, hiccuped and gurgled. Then she projectile vomited, a fountain of acrid champagne mixed with slithers of partly digested poached salmon splattering the floor and the seat in front of her, soaking her pyjamas and marinating her frizzy hair. "I don't feel well," she moaned, retching again.

"Serves you right, you slag," said Daz.

I gave Cindi a fresh sleep suit and helped her to the bathroom to clean herself up. Fortunately, exhaustion overwhelmed the inebriated mob, and one by one they fell asleep, the bride-no-longer-to-be clutching a sick bag, the cheated groom snoring and the reviled best man sporting a black eye and busted lip. The quickie Vegas wedding was over before it began.

American authorities have a strict policy when it comes to drunken air-rage incidents. So, on landing, police boarded the plane and escorted Daz, Gaz and Cindi into the terminal, where they were grilled by immigration officials and denied entry into the state of Nevada. They were sent back to the UK on the next available flight. We saw them sitting in the glass interrogation room as we walked through customs – Cindi-with-an-i still wearing her sleep suit, looking bedraggled but solemn, Daz and Gaz becoming animated as they argued with the security and immigration officials.

There was no denying that the day's flight had been a tough one, but a five-day trip lay ahead of us in Vegas, which meant only one thing: party time.

We were treated like royalty in Vegas in those days. Nearly every manager of every bar and club on the Strip knew who we were. All we had to do was make a quick call from the hotel, saying, "The Virgin girls are in town," and our names would immediately be added to the top of the most prestigious guest lists. A bevy of pretty air hostesses is always good for business.

On the crew bus I was reunited with my friend Sandra. I hadn't seen her during the flight because she'd been working in Economy.

"Mandy, up here," she shrilled, as I stepped onto the bus. "I've saved you a seat." It was one of those party vehicles, decked out with fairy lights, leather seats and ice-filled mini bars loaded with drinks. The rest of the crew – including Roger the pilot, otherwise known as "Roger the Rogerer" because of his lecherous nature – were already cracking open bottles, chatting excitedly about their plans.

"Squidge-up," I said, sliding into the seat next to Sandra. "How was your flight?"

"Fantastic, thanks. And you?"

"Argh, don't even go there. It was a bloody nightmare."

"Yeah, I heard about the tangerine bride – sounds hellish. Anyway, guess where you're going tonight?"

"Well, it isn't a wedding, that's for sure," I said.

"You're going ..." She said, pausing for effect, "to the VIP marquees in Pure. A supermodel's stag do. He's gorgeous – dated loads of celebs and models. He's over here with Pete and a few of the lads."

Pete was Sandra's fuck buddy: minted and, according to her, a tiger between the sheets with "a cock like a marrow".

"Anyway," she went on, "I think he went out with Kate Moss for a while, and that blonde actress, what's-her-face – the one with the pipe-cleaner legs, always wearing Ugg boots, even in summer ..."

I wanted to share Sandra's enthusiasm, but after the furore I'd just dealt with, I wasn't really in the mood for hanging out with a bunch of smashed stags – or a narcissistic billboard boy whose main mission in life was to shag his way through the entire cast of OK! magazine. And besides, I had my sights on another piece of eye candy – Stephen, a doctor (so he told me when we'd met before the pre-flight briefing at Gatwick), super fit, tall, quite well-to-do and handsome in an early-nineties Hugh Grant kind of way. He was a travelling companion to one of the other dollies, Clare, and though I'd only spoken to him briefly, I sensed he would have had me right then and there over the laminated meeting table, given half the chance. I'd clocked him staring at my breasts, admiring a flash of flesh through a small gape in my shirt – and I'd felt my nipples stiffen and pinch with excitement.

I hadn't had sex for at least four weeks – since I'd split from Brad – and nothing had developed with Wills, the guy I met on the underground. I'd tried calling him, once, but some girl answered the phone and claimed she'd never heard of a "Wills".

"... and apparently he loves brunettes, so you might be in with a chance. Don't know why he's getting married ... he's not the faithful type," concluded Sandra.

"Who's getting married?" I asked.

Sandra sighed.

"The model – the one I just told you about: Jamie or Mark, or something like that – I can't remember his name, but he's gorgeous."

"Sod the model," I said, "Have you seen that doll of a man Clare's brought with her? I wouldn't mind getting my claws into him. It's not her boyfriend, I checked before the flight."

"Well?" asked Sandra, deliberately ignoring my remark.

"Well, what?" I said, craning my head to cop a look at Stephen, who was sitting a few rows ahead. I spied a tanned arm, a firm splayed thigh jutting from the edge of his seat. He looked good enough to eat.

"You are coming, aren't you ... to the stag do?"

"I'm not sure it's really my scene, Sandra," I said.

"Oh, please?" she begged. "There'll be plenty of time for him."

"Okay," I agreed sullenly.

"That's the spirit – we're in Vegas, baby."

It was mid afternoon when we arrived at the Embassy Suites – just in time to squeeze in a quick shower and beautifying session before manager's cocktail hour.

An hour later we emerged from our rooms, glammed-up and raring to hit the town. As usual, the girls looked amazing in tiny dresses and high heels, glossy manes of hair teased to perfection. I'd pulled out all the stops, hoping to attract Stephen's attention, wearing nothing but a pillar-box red halter-neck dress teamed with Brazilian-style knickers and strappy sandals.

In the manager's lounge we joined the rest of the crew, who had already bunched up around a cluster of tables next to potted palm trees, voices drowning out an instrumental version of "The Girl from Ipanema". I scanned the group, looking for Stephen, but there was no sign of him. Sandra sensed my disappointment.

"Don't worry," she said, "You'll have your cock and eat it soon. He'll keep."

"I hope so," I sighed.

"There's always him if you're desperate," said Sandra, darting her cocoa eyes towards Roger the Rogerer, who was sitting opposite us, his tongue virtually hanging out of his rubbery mouth as more and more nubile flesh surrounded him.

"Argh, no – I draw the line there," I said. "I'm no flight deck floozy" – which is what we called the girls who felt the allure of the God complex.

Roger made my flesh crawl. He was in his early fifties, potbellied and balding with a plump, greasy face. He'd dated an air hostess I knew, Lyn, for a while, but she'd told me she dumped him on a Joberg trip when he had asked her to partake in one of his many sexual fetishes: scatting and water sports – and by the latter activity I don't mean jet skiing or wind-surfing. I won't go into detail, but let's just say I won't be eating off any glass tables in Joberg for quite a while!

I watched Roger as he draped an arm over Marsie's shoulder, trying to envelop her in his slimy armpit. "What's the plan for tonight, Marsie?" he said. "Casino, nightclub?" Marsie was a pretty brunette, a bit of a Penelope Cruz lookalike and well out of Roger's league.

"Sorry Roger, I'm going out with the girls," she said. Marsie got up and moved to a seat next to me. Sandra helped herself to a Cosmopolitan, downing it in one. "Ah, that's better," she said, slamming down her glass and picking up another. "I've got an idea," she added, turning towards Marsie and me. "Who's up for playing a little prank on Roger?"

"I'm game for that," Marsie said.

"What type of prank?" I asked.

We huddled together, giggling, as Sandra outlined her plan, which was to trick Roger into believing he was in for a treat that night: a threesome with Marsie and Sandra. They'd entice him up to one of their rooms, get him to undress, then tell him it was all a joke and maybe run off with his clothes. A crowd of us would also be hiding at various locations – the bathroom, wardrobes or under the bed, ready to burst into the room shouting "Surprise!" at the appropriate moment (when Sandra coughed), armed with cameras, of course.

"We're going to have to flirt a little," instructed Sandra. "Otherwise it won't be realistic."

"It'll be funny as fuck, though," said Marsie, pulling her room card out of her handbag. She passed me the card. "Room 111," she said. "Gather a few people."

We downed a couple more cocktails, then Marsie and Sandra went in for the kill, while I surreptitiously gathered a group of spectators.

"Hey Roger, you like a good Rogering, don't you," blurted out Sandra, throwing him a lascivious look across the table.

"Yeah," added Marsie, "What's it like to Roger Roger?"

Roger grinned and licked his rubber-dinghy lips. "There's only one way to find out."

As Sandra and Marsie continued their game plan, the rest of us disappeared, leaving in small groups at a time.

There were at least a dozen of us hiding in Marsie's room. I was crouching in the wardrobe next to John, peeping through the crack in the sliding door. There were two more people in the second wardrobe, a few under the bed and the rest of the crew were hiding in the bathroom. John was holding his nose, snorting. "Be quiet," I said, giving him a gentle nudge, "You'll ruin it."

He snorted again. "I can't help it."

"Shhh," came a voice from under the bed. "They're coming in."

I had a good view. I could see the door and the bed. Marsie came in first, followed by Sandra, then Roger, whose face was flushed molten red.

"Would you like a drink, Roger?" said Marsie, "Or shall we just get down to business?"

Roger sat on the bed and wiped a trickle of sweat from his brow. "No, just come over here and ravish me."

Sandra joined him on the bed, then crossed and uncrossed her velvety legs, Sharon Stone–style. "How about some water sports to get us in the mood? You like that, don't you, Roger?"

Now I was finding it difficult not to laugh. Sandra and Marsie were playing their roles to perfection.

Roger slapped a hand on Sandra's thigh, kneading his podgy fingers into her flesh. "You'll piss on me?"

"Not just yet," teased Marsie, joining them on the bed. "First we need to get you out of those wet clothes. Look how sweaty you are."

"Not a problem," he said, already unbuttoning his shirt, his doughy white gut spilling over his waistband.

Sandra helped him out of his shirt. "I'll take that for you," she said. "Now take off the rest. We're in charge of this threesome."

Roger stood up, shuffled out of his deck shoes and whipped off his chinos, followed by his boxers. Sandra and Marsie stood in front of him, waiting to nick his clothes. I cupped my hand over my mouth. What a sight. Roger's cock was tiny – it looked like a raw cocktail sausage, lost in a mass of greying pubic hair.

"I'll just put these on the chair," said Sandra, picking up Roger's trousers and boxers.

"Wow, what a big boy you are," Marsie remarked, reaching for his shoes.

"Ready when you are," said Roger, throwing his flabby body back onto the bed.

"Come here," Marsie said. "I want you to lie on the floor. We don't want to piss on the bed."

Roger jumped off the bed. "Where do you want me?"

"Right there," said Marsie, pointing to a spot on the other side of the room.

Roger walked across the room, out of view. A couple of seconds later, Sandra coughed.

As planned, we all sprang from our hiding spots to a chorus of "Surprise!" howling with laughter, cameras flashing.

Roger looked as though he was about to have a heart attack. "You fucking ... you little ... you ... you ... bitches," he yelled, cupping his hands over his teeny little willy. Everyone was in hysterics, collapsing on the floor. Roger scrambled to his feet. "Give me my clothes," he demanded. But his sweaty clothes were now being thrown from person to person as he chased them around the room, his pasty bum rippling.

We gave Roger back his clothes ... eventually. He stormed out of the room. You could almost see steam gushing out of his ears. He didn't make a move on anyone during the rest of the trip.

Later that night, as promised, I accompanied Sandra to the model's stag do. As expected, he was a complete tosser – a real pretentious arsehole with floppy hair. His name was Marcus and he spent the entire night trying to fondle my arse, while incessantly gabbing on about his previous celebrity conquests and random aftershave ads he'd appeared in: Armani, Calvin Klein, Bulgari.

"Ever done one for Brut?" I interrupted, "Or Old Spice?" He didn't laugh. On the plus side, the party was an extravagant affair, held in three sprawling marquees along the poolside of the nightclub. We had our own waitress and there was a centre table topped with a gleaming champagne fountain and jugs of every spirit going on ice along the other tables. Pete had come armed with a generous supply of pure cocaine and he and Marcus kept nipping away to the loos for a fix. I was quite happy guzzling the free Cristal champagne and assorted shots being handed out by our waitress, who was dressed as a showgirl. Towards the end of the night I was completely off my face, blabbering incoherently to Sandra about how I was going to give Stephen the ride of his life. "He could be the one, Sandra," I said. "Imagine being a doctor's wife? I could do some charity work in the community."

Alas, the only ride I got that night was the taxi journey back to the hotel.

I awoke the following afternoon, totally parched, teeth coated in fatty clumps of saliva, hair like a scarecrow's, with a slice of pepperoni stuck to my cheek. I rolled over. There was a takeaway box containing a half-eaten pizza on the other pillow. I didn't recall ordering a pizza – or eating one. My heart was thumping; I was still wearing my red dress and the phone was ringing, stinging my temples. I answered. It was Sandra, calling from the lobby.

"Mandy, get your sweet arse down to the bar now," she shrilled.

I sat up and met a ghastly creature in the full-length wall mirror. Christ, I looked rough.

"Bloody hell, Sandra," I said, "What was I doing last night? I've got a *Whatever Happened to Baby Jane* look going on here."

"Never mind last night. Stephen's in the bar – we're having drinks. Get in the shower, give your lady chamber a good old scrub, slip into something sexy and get down here now. He's been asking for you."

It was the best wake-up call ever, obliterating all symptoms of my hangover.

"Give me half an hour," I said.

I showered, doused myself in Angel perfume, slipped into my raciest underwear and scooped my hair up into a loose tumbling twist. A dusting of bronzer, slick of lip gloss, sweep of kohl and mascara, and a change into heels and a little black dress later, I was good to go.

Stephen was the first person I noticed when I sashayed into the bar. He was so hot: mid thirties, at least six-four with ice-blue eyes and tousled fawn hair. He was standing at the bar with Sandra, Clare and a few of the others, laughing riotously at something Sandra was saying. I joined them in time to catch the tail end of Sandra's story.

"So, I had all my weight resting on my forearms on the floor," she giggled. "Butt-naked with him behind me, holding my legs in the air, doing me wheelbarrow fashion. And every time he pounded into me, I was getting pushed further along the carpet. And just as I was coming, the bloody maid walked in."

"Oh my God," Clare piped up. "You must've been mortified. "What did you do?"

Sandra paused and took a sip of her cocktail. "We carried on, of course. I wasn't going to waste an orgasm like that."

We all laughed. Stephen and I exchanged flirtatious glances. I was pleased to see he was staring directly at my cleavage. *So far, so good,* I thought.

"Here Mandy, have a daiquiri," said Sandra, motioning towards the tray of cocktails on the bar. "I was just explaining how I got these carpet burns on my forearms. Look." She rotated her slender limbs to show off her fresh pink grazes.

"Ouch," I said, reaching for a cocktail. "Pete?"

"Yeah, I went back to his hotel after we dropped you off last night. I've been walking like a cowboy all day."

As the drinks flowed I finally found myself alone with Stephen, the others tactfully slipping away to a corner booth where more crew had gathered. The sexual chemistry between us was palpable: we couldn't take our eyes off each other. I loved the way he threw his head back when he laughed, crinkling his eyes shut – genuine, soulful laughter. We talked. He told me he worked in a hospital in Surrey, that he had a brother and a sister and a dog called Blondie. I revealed a few mundane details about myself, but let him do most of the talking. He said he was looking to settle down but had had no luck to date finding a "genuine" girl. I could hear wedding bells chiming in my ears.

A few cocktails later, the conversation turned to sex: our favourite positions, our fantasies, the number of partners we'd both had. Emboldened by daiquiris and Stephen's profuse compliments – apparently I had the sexiest legs he'd ever seen, beautiful eyes and an arse he wanted to bite and slap – I spoke candidly, seductively, all my desires tumbling out of my mouth, words charged with hormones and lust, ending in a breathy: "Do you want to come back to my room?"

It started in the lift: a three-floor ascent filled with passionate, piquant kisses. Stephen slammed me against the mirrored wall, pressing his erection into my stomach, one hand anchored tightly in my hair at the crown of my head, the other sliding beneath the neckline of my dress, firm palm teasing a nipple through the lace of my bra. "Amazing tits ... are they real?" he asked.

"Yeah," I wheezed. He tugged at my hair, forcing my chin skywards, kissed my throat, skin effervescing in the hot, heady current of his breath. My erogenous zones burned and my legs began to buckle at the anticipation of the spicy sex that was about to season the bland hotel room of the Embassy Suites.

We practically fell through the door, hands all over each other, breath fast and fervent.

"Get on the bed," I ordered, breaking free from a daiquiri-flavoured kiss.

Stephen obeyed, took off his shoes and sat on the bed, legs outstretched, torso propped against the headboard.

"Do you want to see me naked?" I asked, thrusting my boobs as I reached for the zip at the back of my dress.

He grinned. "What do you think?"

My dress fell to the floor. I stepped out of the silky circle, enjoying Stephen's reaction.

"Wow," he said.

I knew I looked good. Slim and toned from hours spent in various gyms around the world, I'd often been told I had a "fuck me" body. Still in my heels, I unhooked my bra and slowly peeled it from my chest. Then, teasingly, I tucked my thumbs into the sides of my knickers, hesitating slightly before sliding them down my legs. I stood naked at the foot of the bed in front of the mirror. "Well," I giggled, hands on hips, "What do you reckon?"

Stephen's response was to the point. "Come here, now."

I stepped out of my shoes, climbed onto the bed to meet him. I sat on my knees astride his groin, grinding gently against the stiffness beneath his jeans while he kissed and caressed my breasts. Diana Ross's "Upside Down" played on the cable-TV radio I'd left on and the air con nipped at my flesh. Being fully exposed while he remained dressed felt highly erotic – submissive and forbidden.

Unlatching his mouth from my nipple, Stephen grabbed my hips and, in one deft movement, slid down the bed and pulled me onto his mouth. *Good boy,* I thought, *you understand the meaning of foreplay.*

I leaned forward, palms pressing the wall, unable to stop myself from moaning as contact was made. I writhed like a porn star, arching my back, hips circling, thighs taught, controlling my movements over his face. Diana Ross accompanied Stephen's tongue as it swirled and danced. He knew exactly what he was doing. I relaxed into it and let his mouth claim me, his tongue teasing, lips warm, caressing me until I came – a full-body orgasm, my yelps ricocheting off the wall, trembling round the room, rattling the cups on the tea-making tray.

"Oh my God," I exclaimed, retreating from Stephen's face.

He looked up, eyes sleepy, lustful, hair all ruffled.

"I take it you came," he said.

"No," I joked, unbuttoning his jeans, "I faked it."

I pulled off his jeans, followed by his boxers. He removed his T-shirt to reveal a beautifully toned, sun-blushed chest and abs. Everything about him was neat and ordered. He had the most handsome dick: smooth, well-fashioned and set in a carpet of trimmed curls – he had a full-on bikini line going on. I parted his legs, knelt between them and went down on him, bringing him to the brink of orgasm. At which point he groaned: "Stop, I want to fuck you."

The sexual gymnastics that ensued that night made the *Kama Sutra* look tame. He had me up against the wall, my legs curled around his waist, taking my full body weight while still managing to thrust wildly. We did the cowgirl position, reverse cowgirl, the X position and spoons. He did me over the desk, sideways, back-to-front, upside down and missionary with my legs over my head. I'd never met a man with so much energy – he was turbo-charged. We got through at least six condoms, shagging through the night until we folded beneath the bed sheets, glued together in a damp, pheromonal cocoon.

When I awoke Stephen had gone, vanished like a ghost. The radio was still blaring, an over-enthusiastic DJ gushing about upcoming Fourth-of-July celebrations and glittering casino shows. My inner thighs felt bruised, my stomach raw with hunger. Through all the excitement of the last twenty-four hours, I realised, I'd forgotten to eat.

I didn't get together with Stephen again. I wanted to, but he made it perfectly clear it was just a one-night affair. It was a pity because I really liked him. When we were reunited – at the breakfast buffet that morning – he was standoffish with me.

"Do you fancy doing something later?" I suggested. "I think we're going to Freemont Street."

He didn't reply, so Clare, who was standing beside him, spoke for him. "We have plans for the next few days, Mandy – me and Stephen haven't had a chance to catch up yet." This was an obvious dig at me for stealing her friend for the night.

I ignored her and looked up at Stephen. "Oh … I see … well if you want my number I'll …"

"Look, sorry Mandy," he interrupted. "I like you, but last night was a one-off."

I was really upset – I thought we'd connected. All that stuff he'd come out with about wanting to find a "genuine" girl had clearly been a ploy to get me into bed. I wasn't big on one-night stands; in fact, this was my first. I tried to push Stephen to the back of my mind and enjoy the rest of the trip hanging out with the crew. But it wasn't the same. I kept bumping into

Stephen around the hotel, which was awkward. For once I was pleased to be leaving Vegas.

I cheered up when I discovered I was working in Economy with Sandra on the flight home. At least I didn't have to put up with Sharon's constant whinging. True to form, we hadn't seen Sharon until it was time to leave the hotel, when she'd appeared in the lobby looking pale and drawn with a hotel towel hanging out the side of her case.

"God, I don't know about you but I'm done in," said Sandra, as we welcomed yet another mob of travellers onto the plane.

"I'm not bad, actually," I said. "At least there doesn't seem to be any nutters on board this evening."

"Hmm, I wouldn't be so sure of that," replied Sandra, nodding in the direction of a woman who was striding up the aisle towards us. I had to admit, she did look a bit weird. Her hair was tied back in a bandana and she was wearing a purple hippy-style skirt, mumbling to herself.

"Hey, excuse me, ma'am," she shouted, shoving past people who were still trying to ram their luggage in the overhead lockers. "Hey," she added, clicking her fingers in the air, "You, over here."

"Shall I go?" I asked Sandra. "Seeing as you're feeling a bit rough."

"Yeah, please."

"How can I help you, madam?" I said, walking the hippy-skirted woman back to her seat.

"Water," she said in an American drawl, "I need water."

"If you'd like to sit down, madam," I urged, "I'll get you a glass."

"I need water, get me a whole bottle, goddamn it," she yelled. "I'm pregnant – thirty-six weeks."

"In that case, madam, I'll see what I can do," I said.

"Why is she flying if she's thirty-six weeks pregnant?" asked Sandra, when I returned to the galley. "She needs a doctor's note."

"That's a point, I didn't think of that."

"Does she look thirty-six weeks gone?" added Sandra.

"Well, she's got a bit of a gut," I said, "but maybe she's just fat?"

I made my way back to the woman, who, once again, was out of her seat and standing in the aisle.

"Madam," I said, gently. "It's just been brought to my attention that you need a note to fly if you're as far gone in your pregnancy as you say you are."

She let out a warped laugh, tossing back her bandana-clad head. "I'm not frigging well pregnant. I've got cancer: growths the size of watermelons," she said. "Look, I'll show you."

Then she bent over, grabbed the hem of her hippy skirt and pulled it up – right over her head. And lo and behold, she wasn't wearing any knickers. I was staring at the biggest seventies-style bush I had ever seen. "Look," she continued. "Now you see it?"

"I sure do," I replied.

A quick call to ground staff and she was removed from the plane. She wasn't pregnant, or suffering from cancer – just completely barking mad.

"You seem to attract all the nutters," said Sandra, as we sat in our jump seats ready for take-off. "She was a right fruit loop."

"I know what," I said, "Let's phone the flight deck once we're up, ask Roger if he rogered that."

We giggled like schoolkids as we rose into the Vegas sky, leaving our sins where they belonged: in Sin City.

CHAPTER SIXTEEN

SHORTCOMINGS

"**W**hat's that noise?" said Laura, clawing open the galley curtain and peering down the aisle.

"What noise?"

"It's coming from the wardrobe. I think there's somebody in there, Mandy. Come and listen."

"Maybe it's not locked properly," I said, thumbing through the Upper Class meal presentation book. "Just give it a good slam."

"Oh shit, it's rattling ... I can hear a voice."

I put the book down and peered over Laura's shoulder. The door was pulsating erratically and I too could hear a voice: it sounded like someone blowing high notes on a harmonica. "Yeah, there's somebody in there," I said. "Either that or we've got a poltergeist on board."

"Shit, I locked that door a while ago," Laura said, striding towards the cupboard.

She pushed the door, it burst open and out stomped *Austin Powers* star Verne Troyer, his face flushed, gnarly veins throbbing at his temples, clutching a leather jacket in his tiny fist and yelling: "Goddamn it."

I hid behind the curtain. I couldn't watch – it was too comical. Just the shocked look on Laura's face had made me feel as though I was going to lose control of my bladder. I tried to concentrate on preparing the salmon parcel starters, but I could hear all the commotion from the other side of the curtain and it was sending me into convulsions of laughter.

"Goddamn it, goddamn it," repeated Verne.

"Verne, what were you doing in there? Are you okay?" said Laura.

"Goddamn it, man, I've been locked in that goddamn cupboard for ages. I went in there to get my jacket and, bang, somebody slammed the door and locked it."

I had to hold my nose and cover my mouth. Every time I thought I'd recovered from a fit of giggles, Verne's red face flashed in my mind, setting me off again.

"I'm so sorry. Is there anything we can get you – a drink, perhaps?" There was a tickle in Laura's voice that told me she was on the verge of laughter too.

"I don't want a goddamn drink."

"Is there anything else I can get for you?"

"No ... no I'm fine." He seemed more embarrassed than angry, as he strode off towards his seat.

Laura came back into the galley, took one look at me and burst out laughing. For the next ten minutes or so we couldn't stop, both bent over the counter, shaking, tears rolling down our cheeks.

"How long do you reckon he was in there for?" I said, rubbing my stomach.

"Dunno, I ... locked ... the ..." Laura couldn't even get her words out for giggling. "Twenty minutes or so."

"I'll go and see him in a while," I said. "I'm sure he'll calm down."

Once we'd recovered I headed out to check on Verne. I found him at the Upper Class bar, standing on a stool and joking about the incident with his mates.

"Man, I thought I was never going to get out of there – I was banging on that door for ages." I heard him say.

I left him to it – I didn't want to embarrass him in front of his friends, and it was evident he'd recovered from his drama.

Also travelling with us in Upper Class on this LA-bound flight were members of the indie rock band Kaiser Chiefs. They'd been keeping a low profile – snoozing and watching the in-flight entertainment from their flat bed seats. One of our girls, Cheryl, an ardent celebrity hanger-on, was beside herself with excitement and had insisted that she be the band's personal hostie, which seemed to involve flirting with them for most of the flight. Blonde, petite and busty, with eyes like Prussian-blue ink splodges, Cheryl was always wangling invites to glitzy parties on the back of schmoozing with the rich and famous in Upper Class.

About two hours before touchdown she came breezing into the galley, clapping her hands, "Guess what, guess what?"

"What?" Laura and I said in unison.

"You're going to love me," she enthused.

"Out with it, then," I said.

"I've got us all invited to the Kaiser Chiefs' gig tonight on Hollywood Boulevard."

I thought Cheryl's vocal cords were going to snap with excitement.

"Nice one," said Laura.

"Yeah, and that's not all," added Cheryl. "We're also going to the backstage party afterwards."

It was a top effort on Cheryl's part, and we celebrated her victory with a giggly galley group hug, jumping up and down and squealing.

There was mass excitement on the crew bus – everyone singing Kaiser Chiefs songs en route to our hotel, discussing what to wear to the gig and who'd remembered to pack hair straighteners, tongs, hairspray, serum and a variety of other beauty products necessary to transform ourselves into glamorous rock chicks. "Shall I show off my boobs or my legs?" asked Cheryl. "You should never have both on show."

"Ah, get it all out – if you've got it, flaunt it." was Laura's response.

After checking in at the crew hotel in Torrance, most of the girls – about ten of us – congregated in my room to get ready. Within minutes, the room resembled an explosion in a beauty parlour: the contents of our make-up and toiletry bags tipped out over every surface – the floor, bed, dressing table, bedside tables and chairs – and hair appliances plugged into every available socket. Clothes, shoes and underwear were being tossed around and swapped, and a perfume and hairspray smog hung in the air.

"Does this dress make my thighs look huge?" said Alison, a gregarious Essex girl, whose thighs were as thin as chopsticks. She stood in front of the full-length mirror, pouting at her reflection while backcombing a length of highlighted brown hair.

"Yeah, they look like an elephant's legs," Laura said sarcastically, stepping into a pair of black skinny jeans.

"Oh bugger off, Geordie."

"Anyone fancy a cheeky vodka?" Cheryl said, producing a one-litre bottle from her suitcase, her face caked in mud mask.

Just the mention of the word vodka, and we were downing make-up tools and scrambling around for glasses. Since we were no longer allowed to take miniatures off the aircraft, most of us girls now brought our own bottles with us from home for such an occasion.

Layers of make-up, clouds of perfume and several vodkas later, we were primped and preened to dolly-tastic perfection and ready to unleash ourselves on the mean streets of Hollywood.

Thanks to Cheryl's effortless flirting on the flight out, we skipped the queue outside the Fonda Theatre, where the Kaiser Chiefs were playing; the doorman had a note of Cheryl's name and unclipped the rope barrier with a smile and a wink. The gig was amazing; they'd even reserved seats for us in the front row, although we didn't sit down for long. We danced and jumped around and sang ourselves hoarse – the atmosphere was electrifying.

The backstage party was held on the swish rooftop terrace, which had been beautifully decked out with a fake lawn and hundreds of fairy lights. One section of it was converted into rooms boasting curtains and sofas in Moroccan shades of purple, red and orange. There were bottles of champagne and beer on ice, set on ornate Moroccan tables. Dozens of music biz types, sporting skinny jeans and indie-style vintage outfits, were all milling about trying to look cool. We took over one of the comfy cubicles and helped ourselves to the free champagne – two hours of singing and dancing had left us parched. A few of us left after a short while: Alison wanted to go to another party being thrown by some bloke she'd been seeing called Greg, who played in a rock band none of us had heard of. "I promised him I'd be there an hour ago," she said. "Please come with me. The party's at the Viper Room – it's a great venue and there'll be loads of fit blokes there. Please, please, come. I don't want to lose this one – I think he's a keeper."

How could we refuse? "I'll come," I said.

"I'm in," Laura added.

"Oh fuck it, the Kaiser Chiefs aren't exactly falling over themselves to speak to me ... I may as well join you," said Cheryl.

So the four of us headed to Sunset Boulevard to deliver Alison to her man. And from there the night descended into chaos.

"Sorry ladies, I can't let you in," drawled the imposing doorman when we arrived at the Viper Room. He looked us up and down, plunging his hands deep into the pockets of his knee-length leather coat and puffing out his expansive chest. He looked like a huge leather sofa – even his face was leathery. "Certainly not dressed like that."

What did he mean? We looked great: Cheryl and I in our sexy corset tops, smart jeans and kitten heels, Alison in her little black dress and high-heeled strappy sandals and Laura sporting a short denim skirt and strapless black top – all clutching our little designer evening bags and smelling like a duty-free shop, given the amount of perfume that had been sprayed.

"Well, excuse me," I said, glaring at the inflatable leather man. "That's a bit rude. We've made a big effort tonight, and we've just got off an eleven-hour flight."

"I'm sorry ma'am, but it's a private party ... a grunge party. Man, the girls in there ... they don't dress like this," he said. "Hell, no. I'm sorry, ladies, rules are rules."

"Oi, just you wait a minute, mister," snapped Alison, shifting her weight from one spiky heel to the other, hand on hip, breasts pushed forward. She meant business. "We've just left the Kaiser Chiefs' after party early, to come here. My boyfriend, Greg, is playing here tonight and I'm supposed to be meeting him. I'm already an hour late, I've flown eleven hours to visit him and I just need to get in there."

The doorman recoiled into his leather shroud and sheepishly unclipped the red velvet rope. "In you go then, ladies," he said. "Have a nice evening." His sarcastic tone was only just audible above the noise of the open door.

It was dark and moody inside the club, rather like the Batcave. The floor was sticky and wet in patches from a combination of old and fresh spillages of drinks. The air was humid and saturated with the smell of sweat and stale beer. The walls were filled with graffiti and stickers and it was a fight to even get to the bar through the throng of scruffily dressed clubbers. I could now understand why our leathery friend outside had been hesitant to let us in; not one person in there was dolled-up like us four. Most of the guys were wearing ripped jeans with checked shirts tied messily around hips, the T-shirt of the guy behind the bar read "drink Rye and worship Satan" and the rock chick girls were darting us looks that said, "I'm gonna smack your face in."

"I'm going to find Greg," shouted Alison above the music.

"How the hell are you going to find him in here?" I said, "It's bloody mobbed."

"I will," she insisted. "I have to – I want to get laid tonight." Alison disappeared into the messy crowd, using her slim hips to nudge her way past clubbers.

"Oh my fuckin' God. It's dire in here," shouted Laura. Nirvana's "Smells like Teen Spirit" was now thumping from the speakers and the grunge mob were pogo jumping in all directions.

"Where are all the 'fit' blokes Alison promised us?" Cheryl said. "We should have stayed at the backstage party."

We weaved our way towards the bar, sweaty revellers colliding into us. But before we reached the bar, Alison reappeared, tears streaming down her face. "Mandy," she yelled, holding her Fendi in the air as she dodged past more erratic dancers. I lurched forwards and threw my arms around her. "Get me out of here," she sobbed into my shoulder. I took her hand and led her back through the crowd, Cheryl and Laura hand in hand behind us. The leather man unclipped his velvet rope, unable to disguise a self-satisfied grin. "Have a swell evening, ladies."

As we teetered along Sunset Boulevard, arms linked, Alison relayed her story. "He's a bastard," she sniffed. "A bastard – just like all the others."

"What happened, babe?" I said.

"I found Greg ..." Alison paused to catch her breath. "I found him ... with his tongue down some filthy-looking blonde bird's throat, hands all over her – up her skirt and everything. It was like a live porn show."

"What a prick," Laura said. "I hope you gave him what for."

A light smile played on Alison's glossy lips. "Too right. I grabbed a drink off some random person, slapped Greg hard on the shoulder, and when he turned around I threw the drink in his face ... ice cubes and all."

"Good for you," I said. "Sounds like you're too good for him. You can get any man you want – you're stunning."

Alison shrugged. "And to think I bought him a present. I was going to surprise him with it tonight ... it's a vibrating cock ring."

"Ah, fuck him," Laura said. "Save it for the next fella."

"I'm hungry," Alison added, almost back to her normal self. "Fancy some food?"

We headed back along the boulevard, bursting into choruses of Kaiser Chiefs songs – mainly "Ruby" and "I Predict a Riot", which, in hindsight, was probably a mistake, because we soon discovered Hollywood Boulevard by night isn't the same glitzy, fun promenade it is by day. It's sinister, occupied by street gangs, prostitutes, pimps and kerb-crawlers – and we were attracting attention from some of these unsavoury characters.

"Fuck," said Cheryl, as Alison launched into another rendition of "Ruby", "Don't look now but I think we're being followed." Instinctively, we all whipped our heads around to see two menacing-looking guys in hoodies, jeans hanging low round their arses, advancing in that shifty, limp-style gangster gait.

"Sweet asses," leered one of them.

We quickened our pace, and then ran ... all the way to Popeyes, where, satisfied we'd lost the thugs, stopped off for some well-deserved nosh.

"Bloody hell," said Alison, panting, "That was a close shave."

We thought we were in the clear, but while Alison was ordering her Bonafide Chicken combo meal, the gangster boys appeared again – and made a beeline for us. Their faces were toffee-coloured, probably Hispanic, I thought. One of them had a goatee beard.

"Hey sweet ass," cooed the beardless guy, edging close to Alison. "Fancy making some sweet ass music with me tonight? You are one fine lay-dee. Man, sexy as fuck ..."

Alison ignored him, slipped a fifty-dollar note on the counter for her food and spun round to face me. "Fucking creep," she said, rolling her eyes.

"That'll be five dollars, ma'am," said the man behind the counter.

"I just paid you," snapped Alison. "I put a fifty dollar note ... here," she added, tapping an acrylic pink nail on the counter.

"I didn't see any note, ma'am. That'll be five dollars. No money, no food."

"He took it," said a woman in the queue behind us, pointing at the bearded guy, "I saw him – he put it in his pocket."

Cheryl was already tucking into her food at a table by the window. Laura and I ordered ours and offered to pay for Alison's.

"No," insisted Alison. "I'm telling you. I paid."

She turned to face the bearded guy. "Oi, did you take my money? Give it back. Now."

"You heard the woman," said the man behind the counter in a really weak voice. "Please give her back her money."

A scary silence followed, the gangsters glowering at us. My food arrived, but I didn't dare to pick it up.

"Okay," hissed the thief, "Here's what's gonna happen." Then he raised his right arm, making a gun gesture with his hand. "I'm gonna get my gun, I'm gonna get my car, and I'm gonna drive by this joint and shoot the fucking lot of ya." And after delivering his death threat, the pair limped out of the restaurant.

Alison was handed her food, after I gave over more money, and everybody in the restaurant acted as though nothing had happened.

"Got any ketchup or Daddies sauce?" Alison piped up.

"I'm sorry ma'am ... Daddies who?"

"Oh, never mind," replied Alison and clip-clopped over to join Cheryl at the table. Laura and I exchanged puzzled looks. Two gangsters had just threatened a drive-by shooting at this restaurant and they were sitting in the window eating chicken. Were they nuts?

We grabbed our food and marched over to the table.

"Are you two for real, or what?" I said, tugging Alison's arm. "Do you want to be shot? Did you not hear what that guy just said? Didn't any of it register? Come on, we're going. Take your food, we'll eat it at the hotel."

"But it'll be cold then," whined Alison.

"Now," Laura insisted.

Fortunately, we managed to flag down a taxi on the boulevard and made it back to the hotel unscathed. We weren't the first – or the last – crew members to run into danger in LA. Virgin later cancelled its contract with the hotel in Torrance after two terrifying incidents occurred there – one hostess was attacked and mugged in the lift, and, on the same trip, a steward checked into his room to find a dead prostitute under his bed.

We didn't return to the boulevard on that trip. Instead, we sunbathed by the pool and went on a girly shopping excursion. There was a mall directly opposite our hotel which housed all my favourite shops: Urban Outfitters, Sephora, Jimmy Choo, Bath & Body Works. I went a bit mad on our final day in LA – I think I was still in shock after bumping into those gangsters. I returned from the mall loaded down with bags. I bought stemless wine glasses from Crate & Barrel (a necessary purchase), make-up, a load of products from Bath & Body Works and a pair of wedges from Guess that I'd had my eye on for some time. I wasn't the only one – all the other girls had blown a fortune, too.

It had been a whirlwind two nights in LA and we left feeling exhausted, especially Alison, who spent her second night shagging a KLM steward, Anthony, whom she'd met in the hotel bar (it hadn't taken her long to get over Greg). "I got to use the vibrating cock ring after all," she said as we fell into our seats on the crew bus.

"Anthony any good?" asked Laura.

Alison cocked her head to one side, and in a serious tone said, "He's very good at anal."

It seemed we couldn't escape from celebrities that trip. Courtney Love was on our flight back to London. She had previously been banned from flying Virgin following an air-rage incident that ended with her allegedly flailing around the cabin and branding a stewardess a "fucking bitch". Richard Branson later waived the ban after she apologised to him at a charity concert in London.

Some of the girls felt a bit nervous having Courtney on board, as they were worried she might kick off again. So I volunteered to serve her. For all the bad press surrounding Courtney, I actually liked her. She really opened up to me and we had some interesting conversations. The first time I'd met her, she'd spoken about her late husband, Kurt Cobain – about the legal battles she'd endured over his fortune on behalf of their daughter. I'd perched on the ottoman at the foot of her seat, listening intently. "People have accused me of being a gold-digger," she'd said, "But I honestly didn't know how rich we were until after he was gone."

On this flight, we chatted again. I sat next to her and listened as she spoke about her relationship with comedian Steve Coogan, who had recently moved to the United States. "I hate the man," she said. "I never want to see him again – I don't even want to live on the same planet as him – he's my nemesis."

I nodded. "I can understand why, especially after everything he put you through."

Courtney then delved into her handbag and pulled out a map of the Cotswolds and surrounding areas. "I'm getting out of the States," she explained, unfolding the map across our laps. "I'm not living in the States anymore if Hillary Clinton doesn't get in [as president]. I'm thinking of moving to the UK. What's this area like?"

She pointed at the Cotswolds.

I hesitated. Somehow I couldn't imagine someone as wild as Courtney fitting in amid tranquil rolling hills, or boozing in quaint country pubs. "It's lovely, Courtney, but I'm not sure it'll be your cup of tea. You might find it rather ... quiet and boring. Why don't you move to Hove? It's near Brighton. It's an open-minded city, very bohemian – right up your street."

She nodded her head slowly. "That sounds neat."

Later in the flight I returned to Courtney's seat – only to find her passed out, make-up smudged, the contents of her bag spilled across the seat and little blue Tylenol PMs scattered on the floor by her feet. I put everything back into her bag and tucked her duvet over her. "I take it you don't want that lamb shank dinner, then," I said under my breath.

The next time I saw her she thanked me for recommending Hove, adding that she was seriously considering moving there. She passed out on that flight too, so we never did finish putting the world to rights. I never saw her again, but wherever she's living now, I hope she's happy.

CHAPTER SEVENTEEN

BANKERS, TOGGLES AND TOFFS

"Oh, that bloody Robbie Williams – he's eaten all my favourite chocolates," I cursed, rifling through what was left in the bowl of Lily O'Brien's. "He's had all the raspberry infusions ... and key lime pies ... what a rascal."

Felicity grinned, picked a chocolate out of the bowl and popped it into her mouth. "He fancies you," she said, reaching into the bowl again.

I slapped her hand. "Hey, not the hazelnut torte – that's the only decent one he's left. Who fancies me?"

"Robbie. I can tell."

"Don't be daft – he's a nice guy. I like chatting to him."

"Imagine if you were to date him. You'd be in all those celeb mags. I can just see the headline: 'I'm Loving Mandy Instead,'" added Felicity, laughing at her own joke.

It was 1am and Felicity and I were enjoying a quiet moment in the Upper Class galley while the passengers snoozed and the rest of the crew were on a break. One of the passengers on board this LA-to-London flight was British pop star Robbie Williams. I'd met him on previous flights, and he'd always pop into the galley for a chat and a giggle. I was pleasantly surprised when I first met him; I thought he was going to be one of those demanding diva types, but I found him to be very down to earth and friendly. Occasionally he'd play up to his image – usually when some of the other girls were fawning over him – but I've never been awestruck by famous people and I think Robbie respected that.

Robbie had spent the majority of this flight in the galley talking to me, leaning on the galley surface and scoffing all the chocolates. "Chocolate's one of my worst vices," he'd said, every time his square, nail-bitten fingers spidered into the bowl.

"You'll have to get yourself down the gym tomorrow," I'd replied. "You've demolished about five thousand calories there."

"You look as though you work out a lot, Mandy – you're very well-toned."

"Yeah, I do actually," I said, rolling my eyes and giving him a playful punch. "I bet you say that to all the girls."

Joking aside, we spoke about mundane things – everyday chit chat, really. He talked at length about his dogs settling in after moving to LA. He said he'd named one of his pooches Kenny after the late *Carry On* film actor Kenneth Williams – because his bark sounded just like the comic's raucous laugh. We also discussed spots as he'd walked in on me squeezing mine in the mirror. I was busy dabbing my spots with my tea-tree oil pen when he piped up: "Can I borrow that?"

"No you can't, you cheeky bugger – buy your own," I said.

"I'm always getting spots, Mandy. I draw eyeliner over them to make them look like moles for when I'm on stage."

As I tended to my spot, we leaned on the galley surface and Robbie noticed a note pinned on the oven door that the first officer had left for me. It read: "If Robbie wakes up, can you please get his autograph for my niece, Gemma?"

"Hey, Mandy," he said, pointing at the note, laughing. "What the hell's all this about, 'If Robbie wakes up?' I haven't even been to sleep yet. What the hell have you put in my food?"

"Oh yeah ... that's from the first officer," I said.

He grabbed the piece of paper, picked up my fluffy pink pen and scribbled a message to Gemma. "There, you can tell your first officer I did wake up," he said. "Despite your cooking."

Robbie eventually returned to his flat bed for a kip at around 2am. "Wake me up an hour before we land will you, Mandy?" he said with a wink. "I need at least three espressos before I face the paps."

He returned ten minutes later, peeping his head around the galley curtain, in his Virgin sleep suit, looking rather forlorn.

"I hope you haven't come back for more chocolates," I said. "They're all gone – you've eaten them all."

Robbie pointed to his waist. "It's me toggle, Mandy ... I've lost it – I think it's stuck round the back – look," he said, tugging the waistband of his trousers up over his chest, "they won't stay up."

"My skirt is just as bad," I said. "Look at this." I pulled my red hipster skirt up to my chest too, so that my skirt now resembled a sixties mini dress, and we both pranced about the galley being silly and ever so slightly hypoxic.

"Here, let me," I said, reaching for Robbie's pyjama bottoms.

I bunched up the fabric and slipped my little finger into the sleeve of his waistband and, with my nail, teased out the plastic stopper at the end of the drawstring and pulled out Robbie's toggle. "There you go," I said. "Problem solved."

Robbie glanced down at his toggle. "How did you manage that?" he said. "I've been sitting here for ages trying to get that out."

"You just need a little patience, Robbie." I blurted out, not realising my faux pas.

As he retied his pyjamas he randomly asked, "Do you have a boy-friend, Mandy?"

I shook my head. "What are you like? Yes, I have – we've been together for quite a few years."

"That's a pity," he joked. "Thanks for fixing me toggle, though. I'm off to bed now."

"'Night, Robbie," I said, "Sleep well."

I didn't really have a boyfriend at this point, but I wasn't going to tell Robbie that. Unlike some of the other girls on board that night, I wasn't obsessed with dating celebrities. I couldn't think of anything worse than being stalked by the paparazzi or being known only for my relationship with a famous person. I knew a few hosties who had affairs with celebs – and footballers – and that's all they ever amounted to: brief affairs. One of my colleagues, Christina, a striking six-foot blonde, dated comedian Russell Brand for a while. He pursued her on a New York flight by writing his mobile number on an Upper Class napkin and asking another hostie to pass it to the "Amazonian goddess down the back". They went out for months and, although I don't know the full ins and outs of what went on, Christina described their relationship as being "like a rollercoaster ride".

Another stewardess, Dianne, told us how she'd once shagged a television presenter at a party. A week after the deed he appeared on one of her flights ... with his girlfriend. Dianne made him squirm by constantly going over to his seat and asking, "Is there anything I can get for you, sir?" Later, when he confronted Dianne in the galley, she threatened to tell his girlfriend about their steamy liaison. She didn't carry out her threat – but she did gob in his food.

I met several celebrities working in Upper Class: some nice, some not so nice.

Patrick Swayze was adorable – he once stayed behind on board after the plane had landed to sign autographs and chat to the whole crew – even the pilots loved him.

Of all the male celebrities I met, Robbie was definitely my favourite. We always had a laugh and I wasn't fazed by his flirtatious nature; he was never lecherous or arrogant like some up-their-own-arse stars. I didn't fancy Robbie – although the fib I told him about being in a relationship made me question what the hell was going on with my love life, which, at that point, was virtually non-existent. Since my *highly* embarrassing one-night stand in Vegas, I'd given up on men completely. I'd been on a few dates, but none that led to anything special. Many of the men I did go out with only seemed interested in bedding an air hostess. There were no romantic gestures or efforts to make me feel like a princess. Quite often I ended up paying for most of the drinks. This, however, was all about to change.

In summer 2006, not long after I fixed Robbie's toggle, I started going out more in the UK, hitting bars in the city with my colleague Emma who, at five foot ten, with sweeping blonde hair and a wide smile, could easily have been mistaken for Cameron Diaz. We were always immaculately turned out in our sexy little dresses and heels, so we attracted a lot of attention from super-rich men with money to burn on glamorous air hostesses. Lawyers, bankers, brokers, toffs ... they were all falling over themselves to impress us, and my nights on the town led to a series of thrilling – and bizarre – relationships.

First came Amir, a filthy-rich Malaysian lawyer who, initially, didn't seem like a weirdo at all. Emma introduced me to Amir one night in a swish bar at Canary Wharf where bottles of vodka cost £300 a pop. He was a friend of the hedge fund manager, Richard, who Emma was dating at the time. Amir was good looking, with a buff body, and seemed like a genuinely nice guy: he had a gentlemanly manner that I instantly warmed to. He was extremely interested in me and my job and was an avid traveller himself. We didn't exchange numbers at the end of the night, but I figured I'd probably bump into him again on another night out.

The following evening, just as I was about to set off for a trip to Delhi, my mobile rang.

"Hi Mandy, how're you?"

"Hi, who's this?"

"It's Amir."

I was still confused. "Who?" I asked abruptly.

"Amir ... we met last night. I'm Richard's friend. Canary Wharf, remember."

"Oh, right, yeah, I remember ... how did you get my number?"

"Emma gave it to me."

"Look, Amir," I said, "I'm not being rude but I've got to go – I've got a ten o'clock flight to Delhi and ..."

"Ah, Delhi," Amir butted in, "I love Delhi. Where are you staying?"

"The Hyatt Hotel. I'm sorry, but I really have to go."

"Not at all, Mandy. I just wanted to call to say how charmed I was to meet you last night ... and I wondered whether you'd care to join me for dinner or a coffee sometime."

"That's very kind, but I'm away for five nights."

"Okay, I'll call when you get back," said Amir. "Have a safe flight."

I put down the phone, thinking, *I'll bloody kill Emma*.

The Hyatt Hotel – with its lush spa and pool set in lush tropical gardens – was a great place to chill out on a five-night trip in Delhi.

However, I hadn't anticipated chilling out quite so much as I did on this trip.

As usual, when we arrived at the hotel at lunchtime, we dumped our bags and headed straight for the pool to cool off. It was a baking-hot day –

at least forty degrees Celsius – with a high, blow-dryer hot wind. After a quick dip and an Arabic mezze lunch, I headed back to my room – it was too hot to sunbathe and I needed to catch up on some sleep. I returned to find the voice-mail light flashing on the hotel phone. There were at least ten messages from reception. My heart galloped when I heard the first one. "Miss Smith, please call reception immediately – we have an urgent message for you," said the woman.

Horrid thoughts hurried through my mind. What if something had happened to Mum or Dad, or my brother or my nanna or … anyone? I couldn't bring myself to listen to any of the other messages. I dialled reception straight away. "You're through to reception, how may I help?" came a man's voice.

"Hi, it's Mandy … Mandy Smith. You left me a message on my phone?" I said.

"Ah yes, we've been trying to reach you. We have a very important message from a Mr Amir. He sounds like a very influential man. You must make your way to the Club Olympus spa immediately. He has a gift waiting for you there."

My heart slowed to a regular tempo, and images of a mangled car, flat-lining life-support machine and a grave-faced doctor declaring, "We did everything we could," slipped from my mind, as thoughts of eyebrow threading crept in.

"But I'm going there tomorrow," I said, "to get me eyebrows done. I'm going to sleep now."

"Mr Amir was very insistent. He said you must go."

So I went to the spa, wondering, what the hell is "Mr Amir" playing at? I was in there for five hours. "Mr Amir" – whom I'd only met once – had paid for me to have every treatment going. I was pummelled, cupped, bandaged, covered in hot stones, stroked with banana leaves and scrubbed with lemon sugar over my entire body; one therapist massaged my head and shoulders as another kneaded my feet, while sounds of trickling waterfalls and Indian flute music floated around me. I emerged feeling like I was morphined up to the eyeballs and smelling like a fruit salad, with my face flushed Tandoori red.

I thought it was rather peculiar that Amir had gone to such lengths – I barely knew the guy. But it was a sweet gesture and to show my gratitude

I bought him a bottle of duty-free Issey Miyake aftershave on the flight home.

I was uncertain whether I actually fancied Amir, after meeting him when I was tipsy, so I agreed to go on a dinner date with him: to take him for a test drive, so to speak. We spoke at length on the phone. I told him how I'd been on an almighty spending spree the previous day after returning from Delhi. "They had a sale on in Coast," I gushed. "I bought myself loads of satin corset tops – they're normally over a hundred pounds but they were knocked down to twenty-five. I do love a good bargain, me, like." I then went on to describe in detail a midnight-blue handbag with a diamante clasp I'd wanted to buy but couldn't afford.

"I'll buy it for you," he offered.

"Don't be ridiculous – I'll buy it next time, when it's in the sale," I said.

I'd arranged to meet him at a Thai restaurant on Brewer Street in Soho – a restaurant that appeared to be closed when I arrived. The door was locked and it was dark inside. I tried the door again, peering through the glass. I could see a figure sitting alone at a table in the far corner – a man – but it was too dark to make out whether it was Amir. Then two more figures appeared from the kitchen area at the back of the restaurant – one shuffled towards the man, the other, a Thai woman in a silk dress, towards me. She unlocked the door, opened it and greeted me with the traditional way. "Sawasdee ka, good evening, Mandy," she said, lowering her head to her pressed palms.

"Sawasdee ka," I said, respectfully imitating her bow.

"Please, come in."

I walked in and the waitress locked the door behind me. The man in the corner, now visible in the glow of candle-lit lanterns, rose to his feet. It was Amir.

"What's all this?" I said with a nervous laugh, as I pecked Amir on the cheek.

"I wanted you to feel special, Mandy, so I hired the restaurant for the evening – I hope you don't mind."

I sat down. "Of course I don't mind. It's lovely – and I adore Thai food," I said, although I thought Amir had gone a bit overboard for a first date.

It was the weirdest first date I'd ever been on. I ordered my food – scallops to start, lobster Pad Thai for my main course, accompanied by a glass of Pinot Noir. *May as well push the boat out and have a good feast now I'm here,* I thought. The waitress bowed again and turned to Amir. "I'll have a sparkling water, please," he said.

"Are you not eating?" I asked once the waitress had pattered back to the kitchen.

"No, I don't really eat."

"Oh," I said shifting awkwardly in my seat. "Why don't you have a little glass of wine instead – liquid lunch?"

"I don't drink," he said, resting his hand on mine. "But I want you to enjoy yourself."

This was getting more bizarre by the second. There was I, sitting in a Thai restaurant, on a first date with a teetotaller who didn't even eat. It didn't add up.

"Go on, try a scallop," I said, pushing my plate towards Amir.

He shook his head. "No, thank you."

I knocked back my wine and followed it with two more glasses, while Amir sat there gazing into my eyes and sipping sparkling water. He seemed offended when I gave him the aftershave I bought for him. "You shouldn't have bought me anything. You're not to buy me things," he said.

I should've headed for the nearest tube station after the meal. But it was late and dark, and when Amir insisted on driving me home, I thought it would save all the hassle of trying to navigate my way back to Victoria after three large glasses of Pinot.

But Amir didn't take me home ... he took me to his swanky apartment at Canary Wharf. "I hope you don't mind, Mandy, but I need to go back to my place en route – I've left my phone there and I might get an important work call," he said, as we made our way down the A40. It was a fair excuse, I guess – although I was starting to feel a little uncomfortable.

Amir's apartment was on the fortieth floor of a towering modern development overlooking Canary Wharf. "Do I need to take my shoes off?" I joked as Amir opened the door onto a long white hallway flanked by closed doors. Amir smiled and nodded at a Malaysian-style wicker chair positioned in the corner of the hall by the door. "Sit there for a minute, please," he said.

I sat down, thinking that he was just nipping in to look for his phone. He disappeared into one of the rooms, closing the door behind him. Two minutes later he emerged and went into another room. When he came out of that room, he walked towards the closed door facing me at the opposite end of the hallway and slowly turned round. "I'd like you to go into the two rooms I've just been in and meet me back in this room afterwards," he said pointing with his thumb over his shoulder.

As Amir disappeared into the third room, I went into the first – and did a double take. The room was aglow, with candles on every surface. On the bed were dozens of bags from shops such as Selfridges, Harrods, Radley, Molton Brown, Jo Malone and ... Coast, the shop I'd mentioned to Amir during our telephone conversation. The second bedroom I entered contained even more bags and candles. I could only assume they were meant for me. I walked into the final room – the lounge, thankfully – to find Amir sitting on the sofa holding the handbag I'd described to him from Coast. Resting on the table in front of him was a glass of red wine.

"Come and sit down, Mandy," said Amir, patting the sofa. "I have another gift for you."

"What is all this about, Amir?" I said, perching on the edge of the sofa. "I don't mean to sound ungrateful but ... it's too much. I hardly know you – and how did you know that was the handbag I wanted?"

"I described it to the woman in the shop," he said, then, placing the handbag on the table, added: "Please Mandy, I want you to accept my gifts – I bought them for you – you're my princess."

"Princess?"

"You are beautiful. Your jawline is so prominent, and your cheek-bones are so high and elegant." Amir leaned towards me, hands reaching for my face. "And your eyes are like stars and your ..."

"Sorry, Amir," I interrupted, feeling slightly freaked out. "I can't. I'd like to go home now, please."

A solemn look flooded Amir's face. He flicked his wrist and studied his Rolex. "Well, it's too late for me to drive you home now," he sighed. "You'll have to stay here tonight. I'll take you home in the morning."

"No, I'm not staying, Amir – I'll get a taxi," I said, rising from the sofa. "Thanks for dinner."

"But you haven't even opened all the gifts I bought for you. I've cleared a shelf for all of your things in the bathroom," he persisted.

"Bye, Amir," I said, and made for the exit.

Amir bombarded me with calls for weeks after that first – and only – date. Thankfully, I had call screening so I never picked up. Eventually he stopped calling – until several months later when, stupidly, I forgot to check the number.

"Hi Mandy, it's Amir. I'm just calling to wish you a happy anniversary."

"Anniversary, which anniversary?" I said.

"Our anniversary, Mandy. Today is our one-year anniversary. We got together exactly a year ago today. I can't stop thinking about you."

I hung up.

Then along came the next banker, Andre – a pretty French-Italian, mid twenties, with sapphire eyes, succulent full lips and wavy chin-length brown hair. I nicknamed him my Little Monkey Bum because he had the cutest, hairiest bottom I'd ever seen.

I was dancing with a guy called Xander on the dance floor at a trendy club in Tower Hill when I met Andre. As our dance came to an end, I turned in Xander's arms and continued swaying my hips against him – and that's when I spotted Andre. He was dancing right in front of me, strobe lights intermittently illuminating his face, his sexy grin moving closer and closer with every flash. I threw an imaginary net over his head then lurched forwards into Andre's arms, my lips connecting with his. It was one of those rare moments of instant, mutual sexual attraction.

With hardly any words being exchanged – except for brisk, breathless introductions as we danced closer together – we powered out of the club and flagged down a black cab. "Westminster Bridge Road, Waterloo," Andre blurted at the driver as we fell onto the back seat, hand in hand, our palms glued together with sweat. We kissed all the way to Waterloo, almost biting each other's lips, Andre exploring my body like it was an erotic activity mat, squeezing my breasts through the fabric of my black basque, seeking rapid paths to my waist and inner thighs. Neither of us noticed that the taxi had come to a standstill. Only when the driver switched the interior light on and shouted, "'Ere, d'you two need a bed back there?" did we prise ourselves apart.

Less than ten minutes later I was inside Andre's twentieth-floor apartment, saddled on his lap with my bare tits in his face, as the London Eye watched through the window and Snow Patrol's "Chasing Cars" boomed from the surround-sound speakers.

"Magnifique, magnifique," declared Andre, planting soft, wet kisses on my breasts, one hand pressed into my back, the other unfastening my jeans. I buried my face into his mop of floppy brown waves and inhaled his perfume – he smelt sweet and biscuity. I held onto the back of the sofa, circled my hips and moaned quietly into his hair. He tugged lightly at the waistband of my jeans. "Take these off," he said, lifting his head. I rose to my knees, ready to start a slow striptease – under my jeans I was wearing a tiny red G-string. Biting my lip and flashing Andre my best smouldering eyes look, I teased my jeans down just a little way – then jerked them back up again when I suddenly remembered there was one obstacle in the way here, a particularly large, hairy, rambling obstacle that could kill this moment: I hadn't waxed my bikini line in weeks. My appointment was in San Francisco the next week and I'd been letting it grow, so it was now beginning to resemble one of those novelty stick-on bushy beards. I couldn't let Andre rake through that lot. "Ah, do not tease me, Mandy," said Andre, reaching for my hips.

"Sorry," I squeaked, "I need to pee ... where's the bathroom?"

Andre smiled. "I'll show you."

"It's okay, I'm a big girl, I'll find it – just point me in the right direction."

"Opposite the kitchen," he said, squeezing my hips. "Be quick."

I went into the bathroom, locked the door and took off my jeans and G-string. Glancing around the vast room I couldn't see any products – there wasn't even anything inside the walk-in shower. Everything was white and chrome and gleaming. He must have a cleaner, I decided, opening the wall-mounted mirrored cabinet. I scanned its contents – aftershave, toothpaste, deodorant, dental floss, Nurofen ... condoms – until my eyes fell upon what I'd been searching for: shaving gel and a razor. Placing one foot on the toilet seat, I rinsed Andre's triple-blade razor and shaved off the excess hair, leaving a slim landing strip. Problem solved.

Admittedly, shaving myself with a razor belonging to a man I barely knew was not exactly ladylike or hygienic ... but, boy, it was worth it.

Andre and I went on to have the most rampant, acrobatic sex that night, travelling from room to room, adopting an assortment of positions. We even did it *Fatal Attraction*–style on the edge of the kitchen sink. Andre was very fond of my newly shaved pubic hair. "It's so smooth and soft," he'd remarked when he went down on me.

"I like to keep things in order down there," I'd giggled, wondering how he would react if I'd suddenly blurted: "Yeah, I shaved it off with your razor."

Andre was the perfect fuck buddy and after that night we continued to meet for sporadic sex. He had tremendous stamina and, performance-wise, I'd say he was almost on a par with Brad. Andre was also kind-hearted and chivalrous – the kind of guy who held doors for me – now all I needed was to find someone just like him, only about ten years older.

My relationship with Andre was primarily sexual, and we agreed from the outset that we should both feel free to sleep with other people if we so desired. So I made the most of this opportunity by embracing another category of rich men: toffs – former public schoolboys from rich families, who owned private jets and yachts and spent most of the year abroad, drinking wine and turning leathery in the sun.

I was working behind the bar in Upper Class on an Antigua-to-London flight when I met Tarquin, a rower with hulking arms who counted Kate Middleton, now the Duchess of Cambridge, among his rowing friends. We got chatting and he told me he lived in Clapham and ran his own company, which produced portable oxygen concentrators. He spoke like he had a bag of marbles in his mouth and seemed rather smarmy, but he also had the phwoar factor: tall, with tousled blond hair, sultry looks and a sexy, athletic build. "Are you single?" he asked, between long sips of gin.

"Yeah, free and single," I said. Andre didn't count. "You?"

Tarquin nodded, drained his glass. "Yes, I'm single." Then, after a brief pause, he said, "Would you like go out for a drink – or supper – with me one evening?"

I smiled. "I suppose I could fit that in some time," I said. "Another Tanqueray?"

The following Sunday, Tarquin took me out for drinks and "supper". I translated this to mean, "Let's go out and get pissed and maybe soak up the alcohol at the end of the night with a light bite," so I ate a full roast dinner and apple crumble with custard before I went out. Then I discovered "supper" was a five-course, sit-down meal at an uber-posh French restaurant in Mayfair.

Despite eating so much food, I still managed to get drunk; we sank three bottles of wine over dinner, plus numerous cocktails afterwards in Mahiki.

The next morning I woke up at Tarquin's seven-bedroom Victorian townhouse in Clapham. In bed, naked and enfolded in those sexy rower arms, my mind slowly began piecing the together the sequence of events from the previous night: dinner; Mahiki; me singing "Up the Junction" by Squeeze in the back of the taxi on our way to Clapham (it seemed hilarious at the time); kissing in the taxi; Tarquin carrying me up the stairs to his fourth-floor bedroom; clothes flying off, foreplay, sex – sex that lasted only a few minutes because Tarquin was too drunk to maintain his erection. It was all coming back to me now, as I felt Tarquin stir behind me. He tightened his arms and spooned his body against mine ... there didn't appear to be a problem today.

We had steamy shower sex that morning in Tarquin's en-suite bathroom, which was in the middle of being decorated. It was a fast, frenzied shag and I came almost immediately, standing on one foot with my other leg hoisted over Tarquin's arm, my back leaning against the newly tiled wall as Tarquin powered into me, water filling my mouth, mastic and emulsion fumes wafting up my nose. In his final thrusts towards climax, Tarquin was going at such force I thought I was going to crash through the wall. I felt the Mediterranean-style tiles move against my back, and a few fell into the bath, cracking on landing. Tarquin came with a succession of jolts and heavy grunts to the sound of smashing tiles. "That was magnificent, Mandy," he said afterwards, cupping my face. "Truly sublime."

"What about your lovely tiles? They're all smashed," I said, looking down at the ceramic debris at our feet.

Tarquin shrugged. "It's because they haven't been grouted yet. It's not a problem – I'll buy some more next time I'm in Italy."

I dated Tarquin for almost a year, and again, the relationship was chiefly based on sex. Andre also remained on the scene, although sometimes we'd go weeks without seeing each other. It was hard for me to adjust to this new, no-strings style of dating. Looking back, I think I was a little confused. I'd been so used to long-term relationships, but now, in my thirties, all men seemed interested in was casual sex and having multiple partners.

As the months slipped by, Tarquin grew cold and distant. He cancelled dates and his calls become less frequent. The tipping point came when he announced he was heading off on a rowing expedition across the Atlantic. "I'll come and wave you off, or I could meet you in Antigua, where you finish?" I offered.

"That won't be necessary," Tarquin replied.

So I let him row out of my life ... and shortly after that, I replaced him with another Upper Class toff.

Chapter Eighteen

NEVER BEEN TO ME

A song played over in my mind as England disappeared beneath me. It was that seventies number "I've Never Been to Me", and it'd been bugging me for days. The lyrics seemed to echo my life; *That rueful woman could be me,* I thought. I'd travelled the world and I'd definitely seen plenty of things that a woman wasn't supposed to see. I was now thirty-four, and the novelty of no-strings-attached relationships was beginning to wear thin.

I was still meeting Andre occasionally, while also dating Hugo, whom I met on a flight to Barbados exactly one week after I finished with Tarquin. Hugo was stunning, a real pretty boy who looked as though he'd just walked off the set of *Beverly Hills 90210*: blond, with moonstone eyes and a suave white-teeth grin ... and he was absolutely minted. The only problem was that he'd recently been dumped by his girlfriend, Angelique, and I sensed he was still hankering after her. Her name would continually creep into our conversations, and there was a disingenuous ring in Hugo's voice when he insisted: "Even if she begged me, I wouldn't take her back."

I wanted more than this. I was ready to settle down – get married and have kids, even – and somehow, I couldn't imagine Hugo getting down on one knee and producing a sparkler. And I didn't know what I'd say even if he did.

I peered out of the window and smiled, as the chaos of London dissolved below a veil of wispy clouds. Today I was a passenger – no more pushing trolleys for me for a while. I'd decided to take a few weeks off work to travel ... alone, just me and my backpack, armed with my *Lonely Planet* guide and trekking gear. I was feeling spiritually inspired after reading *The Celestine Prophecy* by James Redfield – a novel charting one man's travels to Peru in search of an ancient manuscript containing nine insights – so I'd booked a trip to South America, where I was about to walk the iconic Inca trail across the Andes to Machu Picchu. I could just picture myself, looking like Lara Croft in my little black shorts and vest top with my long brunette hair tied in a high ponytail, fearlessly scaling perilous paths. I was hoping to find myself, experience some kind of spiritual awakening, exorcise all the negative ghosts lurking within – and Peru had seemed to me like the perfect place for this to happen.

Erasing "I've Never Been to Me" from my mind, I relaxed back in my seat and tried to enjoy the first leg of my journey. I was flying Upper Class to Miami, where I would catch a connecting flight to Lima, then another on to Cusco, where I would spend two days acclimatising to the high altitude before setting off on my trek. Fortunately, I didn't recognise any of the crew on board the Miami flight; I wasn't in the mood for work gossip. This was *my* time. Time to return to me.

My journey to Cusco was relatively straightforward. I managed to get my two connecting flights on standby at the bargain price of twenty dollars each, and there were no delays or traumas. The flight into Cusco was stunning – the plane appeared to skim the tawny peaks of the Andes, which seemed to take on personalities of their own. I could see faces emerging in the numerous crevices and hollows: a bearded laughing man, a forlorn seal with brooding craters for eyes.

The altitude hit me as soon as I stepped off the plane. My head was spinning; I was dehydrated and breathless, and my stomach felt decidedly queasy. It felt similar to a hangover – and I hadn't even been drinking. I thought I was going to keel over after hauling my relatively small thirty-kilo rucksack off the carousel; every physical movement exhausted me. I lumbered through the terminal and outside to the taxi rank, feeling like a centenarian attempting an ironman triathlon. I climbed into the nearest taxi – a dilapidated brown Mercedes with a hanging exhaust pipe – showed the driver the name of my B&B in my trusty *Lonely Planet* and slumped back against the sweaty, ripped leather.

The taxi driver, a cheery guy with a Spanish accent and burly black moustache, talked non-stop. "What you do in Peru?" he asked, glancing at me in the rear-view mirror.

"I'm going trekking in the Andes – walking the Inca trail," I said.

"Ah, I have friend, good friend, who do tours. I put you in touch."

"That's very kind of you, but I'm already booked up," I said. "Can you recommend anything else to do in Cusco?"

I couldn't get a word in edgeways after I asked him this. He was offering to hook me up with friends all over Cusco: a friend who would take me on a tour of the Inca ruins; another pal who would take me to visit a traditional family in Chichubamba; and he knew all the owners of Gringo Alley's bars and restaurants. When we pulled up outside my B&B, he insisted I wait while he jotted down his contacts' details. "Everything you need is here," he said, passing the piece of paper over his seat. I thanked him and slipped the list between the pages of my *Lonely Planet*.

"You might want to get this car serviced," I joked when he got my rucksack out of the boot. He was ages trying to open the boot, pushing the car up and down, exhaust knocking the pavement, until it finally sprang open.

He winked, his bushy moustache rising at one side. "I have friend."

Compared to the five-star hotels I was used to staying in, the Hostal Incawasi was very basic, but comfortable. Considering it was only costing me twenty dollars a night and was situated on the main square, Plaza de Armas, it was a complete bargain. The receptionist showed me around and kindly made me a cup of coca-leaf tea to ease my altitude sickness, which worked a treat. After two cups I was almost back to my normal self again – and rather giggly.

I spent my first afternoon and evening in Cusco resting in my room, reading up on the Inca trail and indulging in a spot of meditation. It was nice to just sit in a quiet room for once and think of nothing – to clear my head of all thoughts of men and work.

The following day, feeling rejuvenated, I went along Gringo Alley and booked a white-water rafting excursion on the Urubamba River, which was a brilliant laugh. I also met two lovely Dutch guys, Rick and Max, and I ended up going out with them in Cusco after the excursion. We went for dinner at a charming hole-in-the-wall restaurant, Chez Maggy, down Gringo Alley, where Max ordered the national dish of Peru, *cuy* ... otherwise known as deep-fried or roasted guinea pig.

He tried to convince me to order it too. "It's delicious," he said. "It tastes a bit like bacon."

I'm not a fussy eater and certainly not adverse to sampling new and unusual dishes, but guinea pig? I couldn't do it. "I'll stick to pizza today," I said. "I'm still acclimatising and my stomach's been a bit iffy."

Max's guinea pig was served up whole, sprawled over a mountain of potatoes with a wedge of orange stuffed in its mouth and a herb-garnished tomato resting on its head like a party hat. Its leaping pose made it look as though it had jumped into the oil of its own accord.

I woke early the next morning, my stomach fluttering with nervous excitement. I downed another cup of coca tea, ate a humungous breakfast and made my way to the meeting point in Cusco. From there we boarded a coach to the starting point of the Inca trail in the village of Mollepata. There were about twenty of us on the tour, including a Norwegian girl called Kristen, who spoke with a lovely sing-song accent and gasped every time she said *"Ja"*, meaning "Yes". She was tall with fifties-movie-star black hair, spoke near-perfect English and had a brilliant sense of humour. As soon as I got chatting to her on the way to the starting point, I knew she'd be my friend for the trek.

I gasped when I stepped off the coach and saw the view before me. The mountains were so vast, and embroidered with green forests stretching up to pale blue peaks engulfed in hazy clouds. Although the air was thin, it felt remarkably fresh and invigorating. The atmosphere was still and silent, except for the distant harmony of singing birds. It was like stepping into a dream landscape.

We stopped at a nearby farming area called Marco Casa, at the start of the trail. There was a little market stall where we could buy coca leaves for the trek, and I stocked up – I was growing fond of the stuff. We met up with the *arrieros* (wranglers) and their mules and horses, who would carry our gear during the trip. One of our guides, Mike, outlined the first leg of our trek, which would take us on a gentle hike into the Cordillera Vilcabamba: above the green river valley, we hiked steadily along the plateau, where we would camp beneath the icy peaks of the Vilcabamba range ready for our 6am start the next morning. "Go at your own pace," Mike warned. "The altitude here is just over 12,000 feet. If you feel faint or need to rest, just shout. Welcome to the Inca trail."

We filed slowly along the well-worn path, dust pluming up over our hefty boots. I was on my way.

Although the first day of the trek was not overly strenuous, it was long and flat, as we headed alongside the mountain range to our base camp. I chatted to Kristen along the way – when we could find the breath. I discovered she was a teacher from Oslo and had been with her boyfriend, Anders, for five years. Like me, she was taking some time out from work to do something she'd always dreamed of doing.

"Did your boyfriend not fancy coming?" I asked her.

"No, he has to work. To be honest, I think he's pleased to have some peace and quiet."

As we continued along the narrow paths, Mike stopped to point out an Inca ruins site, which reminded me of crumbly, chunky biscuits, and some of the flora and fauna. There were pink and white orchids blooming out of the slopes and we also saw an angel's trumpet plant, its flowers resembling upside-down trumpets and, according to Mike, containing hallucinogenic toxins. The paths were extremely narrow and crumbling, and you really had to watch your step.

The next night we set up camp in a cloud forest near the town of Soraypampa, where we met two American lads, Sam and Ted, whom we nicknamed the Whisky Twins – because all they did was drink whisky. They had decided to trek the Inca trail alone, as opposed to joining an organised tour. They weren't really twins, but they did have similar chiselled features, Californian tans and beach-buff bodies. They stayed for dinner with us at camp that night, swigging whisky and recounting tales of forgetting their crampons and trying to scale glaciers while half-cut. They were mad. Good fun, but completely bonkers.

I got along with everyone on our tour. They were all really down to earth and genuine. We had a good laugh – the funniest moments at the camp coming every time someone needed to go to the loo, which meant hovering over a hole in the ground enclosed with a few sheets of tarpaulin, while holding a torch in one hand and loo roll in the other.

On the second day I had an accident. It happened towards the end of the day, as we hiked down a glacier towards our base camp. I was feeling weary and my feet were slipping on the moss. In the distance I could see the porters unpacking our gear from the donkeys' backs, and I began to think about food, rest and pulling off my pinching boots. My concentration slipped ... and so did I. My right foot twisted and I fell to the ground, landing on my back with my right leg bent beneath me. I had to hobble down to the camp resting on Kristen's shoulder.

Determined to carry on – I hadn't come all this way for nothing – I bandaged my swollen, sprained ankle and carried on hiking the following day. I couldn't see Lara Croft turning down a mission due to a swollen ankle, so it was onwards and upwards for me. A lovely Scottish couple, Stuart and Jude, kindly lent me their hiking sticks, which was a huge help. They were really sweet: just married and on a year's holiday exploring the world.

I hobbled along on my two crutches and I seemed to be doing fine – until it came to crossing a steep waterfall ravine. The only way to cross the gorge was to walk across two tree trunks pushed together. I handed my sticks to Kristen and let her and the others go first, watching them stroll effortlessly across the tree trunks. But when it came to my turn, I froze. I stood at the edge of the ravine and looked down – there was at least a 250-foot drop, and the waterfall was cascading from about the same height above the makeshift bridge. I'd never suffered from vertigo in my life, yet this was making me feel physically sick. I stood there for at least ten minutes, contemplating the logs, which were no wider than three feet placed together, while the rest of the group shouted from the other side for me to make the crossing. The incessant roar of the tumbling water added to my fear. But I had no choice – I had to get to the other side. Taking a deep breath I knelt down and crawled onto the logs on all fours. After a few tentative movements I froze again. My heart was skipping beats, my knees trembling, and I couldn't take my eyes off the moist wood separating me from the rocks below. The rest of the group were chanting, "Come on Mandy, you can do it," and, "Don't look down – keep on crawling." I felt like such an idiot. *Bang goes my Lara Croft moment,* I thought. The chants continued, "Go Mandy, go Mandy – you can do it."

I had to do it; I couldn't keep everyone waiting any longer. So I started crawling again, slowly, edging forwards inch by inch, "I can do this," I said out loud. My fellow trekkers began to cheer and clap. I could see the finishing line. I was almost there. I blew out my cheeks, counted to five, then crawled, without stopping, to the end of the logs, where I was helped back onto my feet and into a group hug.

We had a further scare later that day. We were hiking up a mountain path with a sheer drop on the right-hand side when a group of Peruvians dressed in colourful ponchos came running up towards us, hollering in Quechua, and pushed us into the bushes that hugged the left-hand side of the path. I thought they were going to attack us – we couldn't understand a word they were saying. Seconds later, a bull steamed past us and veered into the bushes further along the path. The Peruvians had effectively saved our lives; if the bull had charged into us we probably would have fallen over the edge. We thanked them in Spanish and continued on our way.

By day seven – the final day of hiking – I was exhausted. We'd been getting up at 5.30am and walking for twelve hours every day. My ankle was still killing me and I'd developed huge purple sun blisters on my bottom lip, forehead and across my shoulders – due to the changing climates through the mountains. Our last trek took us into Machu Picchu, the mysterious "Lost City of the Incas". The golden ruins were stunning: bathed in sunlight and folded in clouds. Some people in our group sobbed at the sight, but for me it felt a bit too touristy. There was a snack bar by the gates to the ruins and the Machu Picchu Sanctuary Lodge (where we could use a proper toilet for the first time in days), and scores of tourists taking photographs, including the Whisky Twins. After the tour of the ruins, I broke away from the group, found a quiet spot near the edge of the mountain and meditated for a while. It was blissful, and I finally experienced my moment of inner peace: I opened my eyes to see a butterfly landing on my muddy hiking boot – I paused for a moment, everything went silent, and I had tunnel vision, focusing only on him in his worry-free little life. Then I sighed as he fluttered off, and I became aware of everything else around me again.

Back in Cusco, we celebrated our Inca trail triumph with a night out at Mama Africa nightclub. It was heaving with tourists dancing on tables to cheesy Euro pop hits. The Whisky Twins were there, and Ted tried to snog me on the dance floor, but I pushed him away – I couldn't kiss him with that huge blister on my mouth, no matter how handsome he was.

Despite spraining my ankle and my two near-death experiences, I thoroughly enjoyed my trek through the Andes. I'd made some great friends – people I'm still in touch with today – and discovered a lot about myself. I hadn't thought about Hugo once over the last few weeks, and I was filled with positive energy that I never knew existed in me.

My next stop was Lake Titicaca. I took the night bus there. It was a relaxing journey, as the bus had seats that reclined into flat beds. I spent a day in Lake Titicaca, where I then booked a trip to La Paz, Bolivia, at the tourist information centre. And from there, things took a turn for the worse.

I'd paid fifty US dollars for my bus ticket to Bolivia, only to be told when I boarded the bus that there were no spare seats available. I was then forced to spend the six-hour journey perched on a box in the aisle at the front of the bus. It was so humiliating. I subsequently discovered, after speaking to a New Zealand couple sitting above me in their comfy seats, that the bus tickets only cost ten dollars. The woman in the tourist information centre had ripped me off big time.

I arrived in La Paz, Bolivia, at night, with a dull ache in my bum. At the bus station I jumped in a taxi, which, in hindsight, was a stupid thing to do. The driver – a gloomy-looking character with greasy black hair, barnacled nose and honking body odour – took me to a dark back street, pulled over and snapped: "Eight."

I looked around but couldn't see any hotels – only ramshackle houses and tipped-over rubbish carts. I did spot streetlights at the end of the road and assumed my hotel must be in that direction. I leaned forwards in the cab to count out eight bolivianos, and as I did so, the driver stretched over the seat and snatched my purse out of my hand. I thought he was trying to help – that he'd take the fare money from my purse and then hand it back. How naive was I? He emptied the contents of my purse into his lap then chucked it out of the window. I couldn't confront him – for all I knew, he could have been armed with a knife or a gun. I flew out of the cab and pegged it down the road, retrieving my purse on the way. Fortunately,

I had spare stashes of money tucked in my socks and money belt. I ran towards the streetlights, choking on the stench of strewn rubbish, and flagged down another cab.

I seemed to be heading from one disaster to the next. When I arrived at the hotel the receptionist had no note of my booking or payment – that bloody tourist information officer had mugged me again – so I had to pay for another room. It was a shitty little room with no lock on the door, bare-bulb lighting and an easily accessible balcony. I barricaded the door with a chair and my rucksack, and blocked the balcony doors with an ironing board – I wasn't taking any chances now. I couldn't sleep: I'd heard too many stories of tourists being raped by intruders in Bolivian hotels. I sat on the bed and turned on my mobile phone. There was a text from Dad: "Hello pet, how're you getting on? Keep safe. Love you, Dad."

Dad always seemed to know when something was wrong. I replied to Dad's message, saying that I was safe, well and having a wonderful time. Of course, this was a lie, but I couldn't exactly send him a message saying, "I've been mugged once, ripped off twice and Bolivia is the arsehole of the world."

I stayed awake until the early hours, then I checked out of the hotel and took a taxi (this time with a bone fide transport police–registered firm) to the airport. I flew back to Miami, then Upper Class back to the UK.

Even though I'd experienced a few hiccups, I did feel spiritually fulfilled after my adventure. I was calmer and more confident; I'd lost loads of weight and all that trekking had left me in the best shape I'd been in for years. My legs were toned, my tummy flat and I couldn't wait to show off my Inca-honed curves to Hugo.

I called him two days after I returned home. It was Friday afternoon, and I had no plans for the evening – I wasn't due back at work until the following week. Hugo was surprised to hear from me.

"I thought you were still in Peru," he said.

"I came back early – thought I'd give the salt flats a miss, long story. What are you doing tonight? Fancy meeting up?"

"Yes. I'd like to see you, actually," Hugo replied. "I can come to your place about 7pm, if that suits?"

"Sure, I thought we could go out for dinner. I'm in need of a good feed."

"Great, I'll see you then."

Three hours I spent getting dolled up for Hugo: I waxed, exfoliated, moisturised, put on a mud mask, painted my nails, styled my hair into a Bridget Bardot–inspired do and paid meticulous attention to my make-up. I put on a sexy black bodice (I was still into my bodices), a pair of black skinny jeans and three-inch heels, and when the doorbell rang at 7pm, I was still adding final touches to my make-up and deciding which jewellery to wear.

"You look beautiful," Hugo said, when I opened the door. "Simply ravishing."

I pecked him on the cheek. "Thanks, babe."

I directed Hugo into the lounge. "I'll be two minutes," I said. "I just have to run upstairs for my bag. I thought we could maybe go for Thai? Or Indian, or ..."

Hugo stopped me there. "I need to talk to you about something," he said, staring down at his polo boots.

"I'll literally just be two minutes."

"It's important, Mandy," he added.

"Okay, I'm listening."

We didn't even sit down. We stood in the lounge doorway, Hugo holding my shoulders with a contrite expression on his face, as he blurted out: "While you were away, I rekindled my romance with Angelique. We're back together, so I'm terribly sorry, but I won't be able to see you again."

"What do you mean?" I said, shaking his hands off my shoulders.

"She came to me. She apologised and told me she wanted to get back together. I love her, Mandy."

"Well good for you," I said. "I've just wasted three hours of my life getting ready for you – just to hear you say, 'You're beautiful ... and dumped'? You could at least have broken it to me gently over dinner, or told me over the phone."

"I'm sorry Mandy – I didn't mean to hurt you."

"Oh, just go," I snapped.

Hugo apologised again and disappeared, closing the front door behind him with a soft, apologetic click.

I sat in the lounge for a few minutes, cursing Hugo and his daft polo boots and his posh-bugger ways and his tragic dumping speech. I was all dressed up with nowhere to go. I wandered upstairs, determined not to cry, walked into the bedroom and grabbed my mobile phone off the dressing table. *There's got to be someone who wants to go out tonight,* I thought, knowing full well that all my girls were away on trips, as I'd just seen them the day before. I went to my address book – the first name was Andre's. I called him, and five minutes later I was in a cab on my way to Waterloo. A girl doesn't spend three hours getting done up for nothing.

CHAPTER NINETEEN

THE HIGH LIFE

"**Y**ou should get yourself a rich man, Mands," said Ania. "Never mind all those toy boys and pilots, you need a proper *man* – someone who's going to treat you like a princess."

We were in Vegas, drinking cocktails and basking in the early evening sun by our private infinity pool at the ridiculously posh Wynn resort – courtesy of one of Ania's many high roller "man friends".

"That's easy for you to say," I said, "You've only ever dated wealthy men."

"Yeah, and I wouldn't have it any other way," she added, massaging suncream into her two perfect mounds of silicone. "I'm living the dream. You need to cast your net a little further, honey."

"But I've already been through the rich men," I said. "I've dated a few bankers and toffs, and look where that got me."

Ania shook her head slowly. "They were just kids, Mandy. I'm talking super-wealthy men: millionaires, billionaires, Arabs, business tycoons – there's loads of them out there all dying to snap up a beautiful woman like you."

Ania, a fellow Virgin dolly, was stunning: Swedish, tall, leggy and the spitting image of Bridget Bardot – albeit slightly enhanced. I'd met her on a few Vegas jaunts and we'd become firm friends. She spent most of her time in Vegas or Dubai, where she led a lavish life funded by filthy rich men. She'd been dating a Saudi prince for over a year now and was convinced he was on the brink of proposing.

Ania reclined in her sun lounger and adjusted her Brazilian-style white bikini bottoms. "You're picking the wrong men, Mands," she said.

Maybe Ania had a point. Two hours ago I'd arrived at her apartment in floods of tears after a disastrous date in Death Valley with a first officer called Mike. I'd met Mike on an Orlando trip, and we'd really hit it off. He had a great sense of humour: on our night out in Orlando, he pushed me all the way from the restaurant to the hotel lobby in a shopping trolley; during the flight home he taught me how to fly the plane – a Boeing 747-400 – while the captain was on a loo break. He had a quirky nature that appealed to me, and I thought he had potential. Tall and muscular with army-boy looks, he seemed just my type. We'd kissed, once, in Orlando: a hard, passionate kiss up against the wall in the hotel corridor. He'd then invited me back to his room, but I'd declined – I didn't want to appear too eager.

I'd rearranged my roster to come on this five-night trip to Vegas with Mike. It had caused a lot of hassle – Vegas trips were popular, and I practically had to beg one of the girls to swap flights with me. Now I wished I hadn't bothered. Our date to Death Valley was as successful as its name.

Mike had made our little road trip sound so romantic: "We'll have a picnic in the grounds of Scotty's Castle and hike to the Darwin Falls." But two hours into our drive, his mobile phone rang, and he pulled over on the desolate Badwater Road. "I'll be two minutes," he said, and got out of the car to take the call. I wound the window down to eavesdrop. There was something unnerving about his demeanour: he was pacing back and forth, his free hand clamped to the back of his head, his voice becoming louder, agitated. I was catching fragments, the occasional "for fuck's sake" and "get a grip". But it was when I heard him bellow, "Of course I still love you," that I knew he was a lying, cheating bastard.

"Sorry about that," Mike said when he got back into the car. "Sisters, eh."

"Take me back to Vegas," I demanded.

He slapped his hand on my thigh. "Don't say that, we're going to Scotty's Castle – surely you don't want to turn back yet?"

I pushed his hand off my leg. "Don't touch me," I said, "Do you think I'm an imbecile? Sister? More like your girlfriend."

"I don't have a girlfriend."

I let out a sarcastic laugh. "I heard you. 'Of course I still love you,'" I said in a melodramatic voice.

Mike tugged at the steering wheel, lost for words.

"Well?

"Okay," he relented. "Yes, I do have a girlfriend ... but not for long. It's run its course – she doesn't understand me ... my needs."

"Ah, that old chestnut," I scoffed.

"No, really, Mandy, I'm into stuff, you know – stuff she's not willing to do. Whereas you're different. You're open, up for doing things other women are too scared to try."

"What do you mean, 'stuff'?"

Mike's "stuff" tumbled out of his mouth. He was into S&M and "Nazi torture games" and loved being bound, blindfolded, spanked and whipped with an assortment of instruments: paddles, riding crops, cat-o'-nine-tails whips and belts. I gazed ahead of me, eyes lost in the rainbow-coloured rock formations, thinking, *Shall I just get out of the car now?*

"The thrill of being flogged – or even just spanked – is out of this world. I can't even begin to explain how exhilarating it is," he continued.

"Well, I think you've done a pretty good job of explaining it," I mocked.

Mike reached out and touched my face. I recoiled.

"You'd make a great dominatrix, Mandy," he said. "I'd love to see you in a female Nazi guard's outfit ... would you be up for it?"

I couldn't believe what I was hearing. Was I offended? A little, per-haps, but part of me just felt sorry for Mike, as he was obviously barking up the wrong tree.

I decided to adopt a diplomatic approach to the situation. "Look, Mike," I said firmly. "If that kind of thing floats your boat, then good for you – I'm not going to judge you. But it's really not for me. So if you don't mind, I'd like you to turn the car around and take me back to Vegas, please."

Sheepishly, Mike started the engine and U-turned back to Vegas.

I didn't cry in front of Mike – I waited until I got to Ania's villa, when I let it all out. They weren't tears of sorrow as such. They were angry, frus-trated, why-do-I-attract-all-the-nutters tears. Ania had thrown her arms around me, rubbed my back and cooed, "It's okay darling, I'm here. I'll call the butler; it sounds like you're in need of a daiquiri."

I was now on my fourth daiquiri – and beginning to find the whole Mike scenario quite amusing. I vacuumed the pink liquid up through the straw and rolled over onto my front on the lounger, which was more like a bed. "Nazi sex games," I exclaimed. "Why on earth would he think I'd be into that shit? Do I look like a Nazi guard?"

Ania laughed. "Maybe you could get yourself a little stick-on Hitler moustache?"

I burst out laughing, daiquiri spraying out of my nose.

"Another daiquiri?" slurred Ania. "Or shall we move onto something a little more exotic?"

"Whatever you fancy – I'll drink anything, me."

Ania swung her Bond girl legs off the lounger and looped her bikini top over her head. "I'll call the butler," she said, and disappeared into the villa.

She returned with the suntanned butler, who was balancing a tray topped with two Pina Coladas above his head. He placed the drinks on the table. "Is there anything else I can get for you ladies?" he said, with a cheesy Vegas grin.

"Maybe another two of these in half an hour?" replied Ania, reaching for her glass.

"Certainly, ma'am. Enjoy the sunshine, ladies," he drawled, then turned on his heels and tapped back through the villa.

I raised my glass. "Here's to no more psycho men," I said loudly.

"And here's to millionaires and billionaires," declared Ania, grabbing her Gucci crocodile-leather tote bag from a chair by the table. "I've got a present for you," she added, pulling a book out of her bag and handing it to me.

"*The Rules: How to Capture the Heart of Mr Right?*" I mused, squinting one eye to read the book's title out loud. "What's this?"

"It's a guide to dating," explained Ania, dropping her tiny, toned bum onto the lounger. "You can have it. I've read it cover to cover a million times. It's full of great advice – it worked for me."

I scanned the contents page. "Rule Thirty: Next! And Other Rules for Dealing with Rejection. I think I'll read that one first," I said.

"Read it and learn," Ania said, unleashing her 30DDs from her white bikini top. "It's worked for me."

We sat there sinking cocktails until the sun went down, getting deliriously drunk. I felt better already.

I read *The Rules* in one sitting – I couldn't put it down. Ania was right; it was full of insightful tips – although some of them seemed to date back to the fifties' dutiful housewife era.

I was also beginning to think that Ania's suggestion that I find myself a "rich man" may not be such a bad idea after all. Why be miserable with a poor man when I could be happy with a wealthy one? I deluded myself into thinking that maybe I could just marry someone for their money … even if I didn't fancy them, I could maybe just sleep with them now and then and just enjoy the lifestyle. I was looking for husband material, after all.

I was sitting by the pool with the girls at the Marriott Harbour Hotel in Dubai when my first opportunity arose to test *The Rules* on a rich man. A random Bluetooth message appeared on my mobile: "Hello, Cloud Angel [my phone name], you seem really nice. Are you interested in dinner tonight?"

I looked across the pool through my Jackie O–style Dior sunglasses, scanning the restaurant and bar area – where a group of suited businessmen were lunching – but I couldn't see anyone holding a mobile phone or waving. This was weird. I felt a bit intimidated; whoever had sent this message could see me but I couldn't see them. I messaged him back. "Who are you?"

An immediate reply flashed up on the screen. "I like your style; lovely hat."

"Tell me your name?" I typed.

"Mahir Asker. I have to go, I'll be in touch."

I turned to Stacey, the girl I'd worked with during the engine fire on the Miami-bound flight.

"Here, babe," I said, handing her my phone. "Check this out. Some weirdo is sending me messages, but I can't see him."

Stacey flicked through the messages. "Hmm, weird. Are you going to take him up on his offer?"

"I don't even know what he looks like. He could be a psychopath for all I know. It's a bit stalker-ish, don't you think?

"Just get yourself out there and enjoy a free meal," piped up Christine, another dolly, spritzing her face with Evian mist. "Jesus, it's too hot here. Anyone for a dip?"

Meanwhile, as my phone was getting passed around the girls, one of the poolside waiters came over and presented me with a bottle of Dom Perignon on ice.

"I didn't order champagne," I said, as he popped the cork.

He filled a champagne flute. "Courtesy of the gentleman at the bar, madam," he said, turning his head towards the table where the businessmen were sitting about 300 yards away.

I followed his gaze to the table. One of the suited men – who from this distance appeared to be in his early thirties with black hair and designer stubble – dipped his head and waved in my direction. I waved back. "Alright?" I said, even though he couldn't hear me. The girls also started waving, shouting, "Hello, Mahir."

I turned to the waiter. "Here, would you mind fetching some extra glasses for the girls, please?"

"Certainly, madam."

Stacey burst out laughing. "Mandy, what are you like? He obviously wants you to share that champagne with him. You should go over there and join him – he looks like a nice bloke."

I took a generous gulp. "Are you kidding me? No way, that's not in *The Rules*. Rule number two says you shouldn't talk to a man first. And besides, he can come and speak to me if he's so keen. He's got legs."

"And he's using them now," said Stacey, nodding in the direction of the restaurant.

I turned round to see Mahir walking towards me, smiling broadly, dressed in a crisp white shirt, cerise silk tie and charcoal suit trousers, designer shades to match his black designer stubble. He was quite tasty, really.

"I'm delighted to make your acquaintance, Cloud Angel," said Mahir, walking right up to my sun bed.

I lifted the brim of my oversized hat. "It's Mandy, actually," I said. "What are you up to? Randomly sending me messages – it's a bit strange, don't you think? And how did you know you were messaging me?"

He took off his shades. For somebody so dark-skinned, I was expecting him to have brown eyes, but they were blue-grey in colour, almond-shaped and trimmed with long, black lashes. "Because you were the only one I could see using a mobile phone." He bowed his head again, adding, "It's a pleasure to meet you, Mandy."

Just then, the waiter appeared on his shoulder – with a tray full of champagne glasses.

I giggled. "I was going to have a little drink with the girls ... you can join us if you want."

Before Mahir could reply, Stacey butted in. "I think I'll join Christine for that swim."

Exchanging conspiratorial winks, all six girls got off their sun beds, picked their bikinis out of their bums and headed for the pool, leaving me alone with Mahir ... and the bottle of champagne.

Mahir was polite, well-mannered and easy to talk to. We chatted for the next hour, while the girls played noisily in the pool. He spoke with a sexy Omar Sharif accent and told me he worked in the "oil business", was thirty-four, and still had a nanny. "A nanny," I said, giggling. "Does she burp you?"

"More or less," he said. "It's our culture – she'll be with me until I'm married ... and then she no longer has to look after me."

I told Mahir about my job and my family. "We don't have nannies where I was brought up, in Hartlepool," I joked. "You've just got to get out there and stand on your own two feet, fend for yourselves. Although I do have a lovely family who I'm very close to."

He looked at me through his long lashes. "Yes I think I might have liked that ... to know my family a little better."

I decided that Mahir wasn't a psycho or a stalker after all, so I agreed to go for dinner with him that evening. "My driver will pick you up at seven," he said.

As a precautionary measure, I called Ania to check out Mahir's credentials.

"I know that name, Mandy," she said, "I think his dad is a billionaire oil tycoon. Oh my God, you have to stick with him – we'll be able to double date."

"It's just a dinner date," I said, "I don't even know where he's taking me ... what shall I wear?"

"Something sophisticated, Mandy. You'll be going somewhere uber-posh."

Wearing a knee-length black dress and three-inch-heel silver sandals, I went down to the lobby at seven to meet Mahir's white-gloved chauffeur, who led me outside to a sparkling magnolia Bentley. "Your journey this evening will be approximately ten minutes," said the driver, as he opened the back door of the Bentley. "Do relax and enjoy a glass of champagne," he added, motioning towards the champagne-filled lead crystal glass nestling in a chrome holder. "Thank you," I said, thinking, *I could get used to this*.

The drive seemed to take less than ten minutes. I'd only drunk half a glass of champagne when we pulled up at the marina. I was half-tempted to ask the chauffeur to run me round the block a few times so I could sink a couple more glasses – it was by far the most delicious champagne I'd ever tasted, and I loved the little angel wings on the bottle.

I climbed out of the car, clutching my half-glass of champagne (I don't like waste), onto a red carpet that stretched out to the back deck of a luxury yacht decorated with white fairy lights. Mahir was waiting on the deck, holding two more glasses of champagne and flanked by two men dressed in dinner suits. Mahir had gone for more of a casual look: khaki shorts, short-sleeved open neck black shirt and flip-flops. I teetered along the red carpet, necking the half-glass of bubbly in two gulps.

"I thought we were going to a restaurant," I said, stepping onto the yacht. "If I'd known, I would have worn more sensible heels."

Mahir handed me a glass. I offered my empty one. "Shall we do swapsies?"

He passed the empty glass to one of the other men and reached for my hand.

"Mandy" he said, lifting my hand to his lips and lightly kissing my knuckles, "welcome aboard. You look magnificent."

Mahir treated me like a princess. He was the perfect gentleman – unassuming, kind and not too forward. We sailed around the Persian Gulf, watching the sun set behind the dramatic skyline of space-age skyscrapers, while feasting on an array of delicious dishes served at our candle-lit table on the deck by Mahir's servants. It seemed like a never-ending meal, with at least eight courses, including salmon tartare, steak, lobster and caviar – all accompanied by champagne and palate-cleansing sorbets.

I was surprised by how much Mahir and I had in common. We had similar tastes in music; he too was a big fan of the French house-music producer David Guetta, and he knew almost all of the DJs I liked. When I told him the line-up from our weekend trip to the dance event Sensation White in Amsterdam the previous month, he almost burst at the seams, he was so envious. Mahir had it all – looks, loads of money and personality – but I didn't feel any sexual attraction towards him. He ended our date by kissing my hand again. "I'm enchanted," he said. "Let's do this again next time you're in Dubai."

Our paths never crossed again. I didn't think it would be fair to string Mahir along, even though I'd thoroughly enjoyed a little slice of the Dubai high life. So my hunt for a more suitable rich man continued.

My travels led me to David, a millionaire I met on a New York flight who made his living selling designer handbags and shoes. We went on a date in London, where he wined and dined me at Claridge's. I told him about all the knock-off handbags I'd bought in New York and Hong Kong, and he laughed and said, "I can get you genuine designer bags – and shoes – for free." He was in his mid forties and had gone completely bald, but there was a gentlemanly handsomeness about him that appealed to me. Following *The Rules*, I didn't sleep with him, but I did give him a peck on the cheek at the end of the night and agreed to see him again.

My next date with David happened sooner than I'd expected. Less than forty-eight hours after we'd kissed goodnight, he appeared on my flight to San Francisco. I was preparing the meal service in the Upper Class galley when one of the call lights flashed. I headed out to the seat in the twelfth row and there he was. "Surprise," he sang, smiling and waving his hands by his face like Broadway star.

"What are you doing here?" I said.

"You mentioned you were flying to San Francisco today, so I thought I'd surprise you. I'm going to take you out for dinner tonight."

"But I've already got plans – I'm going to the Cheesecake Factory with the crew."

David looked up, his eyebrows lifting into the frown folds on his bald forehead. "But I'll take you somewhere nice," he said. "Come on Mandy,

I've gone to all this effort. I've got no friends in San Francisco. I'll be lonely ... please?"

I took one look at his pleading face and relented. After all, he had splashed out two grand on a flight just to see me – it would be rude of me to decline his generous offer.

"Okay," I said, bopping my head, "you can take me to that garlic restaurant – the Stinking Rose – I've always wanted to go there."

"That's the spirit," he beamed. Where are you staying?"

"The Marriott Hotel, near Union Square ... but don't you go thinking you're staying with me tonight."

"The thought never even crossed my mind," said David. "I'll pick you up at eight."

It was awkward. As soon as we sat down to eat at Little Italy's Stinking Rose, I was wishing I'd gone to the Cheesecake Factory instead. There were lots of uncomfortable silences and the conversation was jagged and clumsy. We didn't seem to have much to talk about other than the fact that he'd turned up unannounced on my flight. "I must admit, David," I said, pushing the garlic ice cream around my bowl, "it was quite a weird thing to do. What if I'd changed flights with someone? You would have wasted two grand."

"Two grand is nothing to me, Mandy," he said. "I'm sorry, I didn't mean to make you feel uncomfortable."

On the drive back to my hotel David came out with a bizarre request. "Will you write to me, Mandy?" he asked, as we headed along Columbus Avenue. "Send me some emails?"

"Sure," I said, "I've got your email address."

"I mean real writing, Mandy. I want you to tell me about all your past experiences."

"Okay," I said, after a lengthy pause. "What do you mean by that?"

"Erotic stories. I can send you some that past girlfriends have written for me – it'll give you a feel for the kind of thing I'm looking for."

"I'll think about it," I said. I didn't want to insult him.

When we pulled up outside the hotel, I kissed him goodnight. It was a very garlicky kiss, David forcing his tongue into my mouth. "Thanks for a lovely evening," I said, getting out of the car. "See you soon." Although I think I'd already decided I wouldn't be seeing David again.

Out of curiosity, I read some of the erotic musings from David's ex-girlfriends when he emailed them to me that very night – they were filthy.

After David, I had a brief fling with a billionaire called Robert, who owned a football team. Again, I met him in Upper Class, at the bar, and he showered me with expensive gifts and took me for fancy meals. But he was always cancelling dates due to his hectic work schedule. I was supposed to meet him in Orlando once for a romantic weekend at the Ritz-Carlton Hotel at Grande Lakes, but he texted me – just after I'd landed at Orlando International Airport – to say he couldn't make it, because he was too busy at work. "The Ritz is booked," he said in his message. "You should still go there – enjoy the suite." I didn't bother; I stayed at the crew hotel instead. I was starting to think dating billionaires was a bad idea, as you never knew where they bloody were, and they were always so unpredictable.

While I was in Orlando, I called Ania. I was disappointed that Robert had stood me up and figured some advice from my dating guru would lift my spirits. She answered the phone with a soft, croaky, "Yes?"

"Oh, sorry babes, did I wake you up?" I said.

The line went silent.

"Ania, are you okay? Speak to me. It's me, Mandy."

"I'm fine," she said, and then burst into tears.

"The prince dumped me," she sobbed. "His family have set him up with an arranged bloody marriage. He said he'd never be able to marry me, anyway – because of his religion."

"What a bastard. He should have let you know sooner, instead of stringing you along."

Ania sniffed. "He was the richest one so far, Mandy."

I didn't tell Ania about Robert – she had enough on her plate coming to terms with her own loss, but I'd decided not to be messed about by anyone anymore, so Robert was now history.

On New Year's Eve, 2007 – just when I was losing all hope of ever finding Mr Right – Emma set me up on a blind date with a divorced millionaire security firm boss called Colin. "He's a fair bit older than you, Mandy, but he's a real gentleman, and he's minted. He's a lovely guy – got totally done over by his wife. She screwed him for £4 million."

"I don't know if I want to get involved with someone with baggage, Em. How old is he, anyway?"

"Early fifties, late forties possibly. At least meet him. I've got a ticket for you to a party at a mansion in Surrey this evening. He's going to be there."

I thought about Emma's invite for a moment. She was being rather vague, but I wasn't working, and I'd made no plans for the evening's celebrations. I had no boyfriend, and most of my friends were either working or had already booked tickets for New Year's parties. Maybe a blind date was not such a bad idea after all.

"Okay," I said, "but if he turns out to be a nutter, you'll have to rescue me."

"Brilliant. I think you'll really like him, Mandy."

At fifty-five, Colin was old enough to be my father, but he had charisma and was quite fit for an older guy: trim, with silver hair and pistachio-green eyes. We hit it off immediately. He was witty, chatty and didn't strike me as being a jaded divorcee. There was no need for Emma to rescue me – I enjoyed his company, and the more I spoke to him, the more I liked him. We danced all night at the party and, at midnight, as "Auld Lang Syne" played, we kissed beneath the disco ball. It was nice to feel wanted again – to be held and kissed. I'd been so lonely after being messed around for so long by Robert.

My blind date with Colin merged into a four-month relationship. But as I got to know him better, I noticed how insecure he was. If he thought another man was eyeing me off, he'd protectively grab my bum as if to say, "Eyes off, she's mine." Once, when we were in the Punch & Judy pub in London's Covent Garden, he asked me to kiss him simply because he thought a group of lads were leering at me. "Quick, kiss me, Mandy," he begged. "Kiss me while those guys are looking. I want them to know that you're mine – they probably think I'm your dad."

It was as though Colin's wife had kicked all the confidence out of him. I felt sorry for him, so I did my best to boost him up and make him feel special. "Why are you so down on yourself?" I said after I'd put on a show for the lads he thought were ogling me. "You're a great-looking man. You're kind, generous ... successful. You've got everything going for you."

He took hold of my hand and dropped his chin to his chest. "I can't believe that someone as young and beautiful as you would want to be with an old man like me," he said.

I reached out and lightly lifted his chin. "Look at me," I said. "You're not old. I think you're wonderful – there're plenty of years left in you yet, boy."

I honestly didn't notice the age gap initially. I didn't even consider what would happen if I settled down with Colin and decided I wanted to have children with him. This only became an issue after I'd had sex with him. It was the blandest, quietest, most mechanical sex I'd ever encountered. It happened one weekend when I stayed over at his mansion in Suffolk. There was no fore-play Colin just slipped on a condom, rolled on top of me and started thrusting away. He didn't even make a noise when he came. He just stopped, pulled out and rolled back over to his side of the bed. For a lass who'd graduated from the swing-from-the-chandelier school of sex, this was a shock to the system. I turned onto my side to face him. "Did you enjoy that?" I asked.

Colin smiled. "That was amazing, Mandy ... fancy a cuppa?"

While Colin made the coffee I switched on the television – I needed some noise.

"I just had a thought," Colin said when he returned to the bedroom. He handed me a mug and slipped back under the duvet.

"What?"

"I don't need to wear a condom – I've had a vasectomy. My ex-wife made me have one after we had our second son."

He'd already told me he had two sons, both in their late twenties, but he'd never mentioned his vasectomy up until now. I stared at the television, suddenly engrossed in an episode of *Saturday Morning Kitchen*.

"I've never really liked using condoms, anyway."

I couldn't conjure up a response other than: "They're making hollandaise sauce."

"Is it a problem that I've had a vasectomy?" Colin added.

It was a huge problem. "Well, kind of ... I'm not sure what you can bring to this relationship, Colin," I said. "I'd like to have children one day and ..."

"That's okay," Colin interrupted, "I can get the vasectomy reversed. I'll speak to my doctor – it's a straightforward procedure."

I let him down gently, thanked him for his kind offer, but told him I wanted to be on my own for a while. After that, I'd look for opportunities to meet single men closer to my own age – if there were any decent ones left out there – with or without baggage.

"I understand," he sighed. "But if you ever change your mind I'm always here for you, Mandy."

I kissed his cheek. "I'm sure you'll find someone soon."

The question was: would I?

CHAPTER TWENTY

GOODBYE, DOLLY

It was summer 2007 and I was single ... again. Single yet hopeful. I was certain my Mr Right was out there somewhere, and I just hadn't found him yet. I was in great shape – the slimmest I'd ever been – and going on scores of dates with some lovely men, but none of them seemed to fit the bill.

I wasn't alone; Laura and Felicity were also single and searching for love.

There was a moment – a drunken moment – when Felicity and I actually wondered whether we might be gay. It was a Friday night and we were on our third bottle of wine, sitting on Felicity's sofa, eating pizza and moaning about men. "Maybe we're lesbians, Mands," said Felicity, filling my glass. "Maybe that's why we're not attracting the right fellas – because we're giving off the wrong vibes."

"Oh, I'd never thought of that," I said, "That would explain everything. Mind you, I've never really had any lesbian inclinations."

"Me neither ... but maybe that's just because I've never experienced being with another woman."

"Do you think we're missing out on something?" I joked.

Felicity shot me a mock worried look. "Yes, I think this is the answer, Mands. I'm a lesbian ... I must be."

"Me too ... I think."

The doorbell rang. "Hold that thought, Mands," Felicity said.

Felicity answered the door and came back into the lounge with Nick, one of our work friends. "Get your glad rags on, girls," he said, waving two bottles of champagne in the air.

"Me and Mands think we might be lesbians, Nick," said Felicity.

Nick cocked his head and fluttered his eyelids. "Well there's only one way to find out, sweetie."

Two hours later Felicity, Nick and I were in the Candy Box – the dullest gay bar in Kemptown, Brighton's gay village – dolled up as though we were going to the Oscars and surrounded by lesbians. We tried to act normal as possible, by strutting in confidently – even though we looked completely out of place. The atmosphere was tense and miserable. Most of the other girls in the bar were wearing jeans, and some had shaven heads and facial piercings. "I thought you said tonight was ladies night, Nick" said Felicity, as we teetered towards the bar. "This lot don't look as though they've gone to any effort."

"I think ladies night just means lesbian-only night, right?" I said, looking at Nick for back up.

He didn't speak, just shrugged in agreement – half pushing us through the doors by linking our arms.

We sat at the bar – me in my cobalt-blue silk dress, Felicity wearing a coral chiffon number – observing the girls. "I can't really spot any good-looking ones, can you?" said Felicity sitting down on a bar stool, then, adjusting the top of her low-plunging dress to reveal more cleavage, added: "Do I look alright – am I giving out the right vibes?"

"You look great, babes. Do I?"

Felicity nodded. "Superb."

All was fine until I went to the toilet and left Nick and Felicity at the bar ordering drinks. I was reapplying my lippy when Fliss came bursting into the toilets. "Shit, Mands, we've got to get out of here," she said, tugging at my arm. "But we've only just got here," I slurred. "How will we know if we're lesbians or not if we leave now?"

"I've changed my mind, I'm not a lesbian ... and neither are you. Quick, let's go."

She grabbed my arm and hurried me out of the bar. As we staggered along the road, Felicity explained why we had made such a hasty exit. After I'd disappeared to the loo, she'd been hit on by a very butch older lady. "She was all over me, Mands," she said, "She was touching my leg and was really aggressive. She wasn't wearing any make-up, and she had a ring through her nose. Then she started a fight with Nick, saying he was standing too close to her."

"Sounds like she's not the one for you, hon," I tittered. We linked arms as we teetered up the road into a more friendly little pub where Nick was meeting some friends, and a beautiful blonde drag queen was on stage, flanked by two seven-foot girlies in sequinned Union Jack dresses. "Thank God for that," I said, brushing the rain off my jacket and reaching for a glass of champagne. "Back to a bit of normality."

So, I'd established I wasn't a lesbian. But this didn't solve my dilemma. I was thirty-four, an age that had sounded ancient to me ten years ago. If anyone had asked me then, "Where do you see yourself in ten years?" my answer would have been, "Happily married with kids." I had to get a move on.

I decided to cast my net wider and try online dating. Laura had recently signed up to match.com and had already lined up two dates. "It's fucking brilliant, man," she'd said. "There's loads of fellas out there – get yourself signed up."

Describing myself as "fun, tactile and sporty", I uploaded my profile, adding my height, five foot ten (this was important because I didn't do short men), and a nice photograph. There appeared to be some nice-looking men on the site – all looking for love and companionship, or so they claimed.

My first match.com date was with an ex-paratrooper called Luke – a six-foot-seven, hulking rugby player whose hobbies included salsa dancing and travelling. He ticked most of the boxes: tall, muscular and obviously well-travelled. The only problem was there didn't seem to be much going on upstairs. As we chatted over drinks at the Shakespeare Tavern, near Victoria Station, I told him I was interested in popular science and admired the work of Brian Cox, and also Stephen Hawking, as I'd just started to read his book *A Brief History of Time*.

"Oh yeah," Luke said, wiping away a frothy lager moustache with his tattooed hand. "That's the bloke in the wheelchair, ain't it."

Instant turn-off.

After Luke came James, a plumber from East London. Stupidly, I gave him my home address. He picked me up from my house in his Porsche

911, and from the moment I climbed into the car I knew he wasn't the man for me. "I call this car my Dyson," he said, revving the engine.

"Oh yeah, why is that?" I asked.

He grinned. "Because I use it to pick up bits of fluff."

"Oh really ... is that what you think I am, a bit of fluff?" I said, rolling my eyes.

"Of course not – I was only joking."

James looked the same in the flesh as he did in his online photograph: late twenties, with clipped brown hair and a cheeky grin. But I got a shock when we got out of the car. He was about a foot shorter than me. I was wearing my heels, which made me about six foot three. We looked like Little and Large walking into the pub. If he'd been any shorter, he'd have fit in my bloody handbag. Why hadn't he mentioned his height in his profile?

James was a chancer. It was obvious he was only after one thing: sex. We'd only been in the pub ten minutes, and he was trying to slide his hand up my skirt. "What do you think you're doing?" I said, grabbing his hand and pushing it away.

He looked taken aback. "You said you were tactile in your profile."

"I am a very tactile person," I said, "but that doesn't mean you can shove your hand up my skirt on our first date."

"Oops, sorry, I won't do it again," he said.

After that we got along fine. James was actually a good conversationalist and we had a laugh, but by no means was he husband material. I left it an hour after he'd dropped me home before I texted him. I thanked him for the date and explained that I didn't think we were compatible. Then I called Laura to fill her in on the details.

"Well, how did it go?" she said in a hopeful voice.

"Put it this way, I won't be seeing him again. He's only about five foot six ... and he shoved his hand up my skirt in the pub."

Laura snorted. "Cheeky twat. Mind you, he doesn't sound as bad as the one I've just binned. I went on a date with someone from 'match' last night ... Jesus. He didn't even bother telling me he only had one arm and one leg, and I'd been chatting to him on the phone for a week. He was sat down when I went into the pub to meet him, so I got a bit of a shock when, half an hour into the conversation, I noticed they were missing."

I shouldn't have laughed, but I couldn't help myself. "You're joking? Why hadn't he bloody told you?"

"God knows – he was sweet about it when I asked him, and he said he'd been in some kind of motorbike accident. But he'd never even mentioned it beforehand, and all his profile pics were from before the accident. My profile clearly states that I'm into rock climbing, white-water rafting and kayaking. What kind of match dot com is that?"

"Maybe we'll both have more luck next time, babe," I said.

"I bloody well hope so."

James texted me every day for a week after our date, demanding to know why I didn't want to see him again. "I thought we had chemistry," he wrote. "Who do you think you are, bitch?" Some of his messages were like essays – psychotic essays.

He finally got the hint when I sent all his messages back to him and wrote, "Do me a favour: read these and then come back to me and tell me why we're not going on another date."

Juggling the task of finding a suitor in the UK with work was difficult, and flying over 700 hours a year was beginning to take its toll. My health was suffering: breathing in all that germ-laden cabin air meant I was forever catching colds and suffering from sinus problems. The long trips had become few and far between, and we were expected to work entire sectors, which could be anything up to sixteen hours, with no proper break. I felt as though I'd lost all control over my life, and I was missing out on all the important family events. I couldn't go to my nanna's eightieth-birthday celebration in Keldy Forest, because I was in Barbados. I was gutted – she'd rented a cabin for the weekend and invited the whole family along. I missed my favourite cousin's farewell party before he moved to Perth, Australia, and countless weddings and christenings. Some of my friends outside the airline industry couldn't understand why this upset me. "Oh, poor you," they'd say. "Can't go to the party because you're in the Caribbean. What a tough, deprived life you lead."

One important celebration I did manage to be home for, however, was Felicity's thirtieth birthday. It was a night that changed my life. For years my married friends had been chanting that old dating cliché to me: "You'll meet the person of your dreams when you least expect it," and I'd longed for this to be true. After Felicity's party, Nick had dragged me to visit his boyfriend, who was the manager of the Koba cocktail bar in Brighton. They were arguing, as usual, so I was sat at the bar pretending to look at my phone. I hadn't been expecting to meet anyone ... I'd given up all hope of bumping into the man of my dreams in a crowded bar long ago, hence I'd turned to internet dating. But strangely enough, it did happen.

I was waiting at the bar to be served when he sidled up beside me. "It takes forever to get served in here, doesn't it," he said.

My eyes met his. "Nightmare."

"I'm Glenn, by the way," he added.

"Mandy."

He was strikingly handsome, with public schoolboy looks, soft hazel-green eyes, ruffled short brown hair, a coy smile – and he was huge, not just taller than me (at least six foot four), but with the widest shoulders I had ever seen. I also noticed he had massive yet soft hands, which looked like they'd never seen a day's work in their lovely manicured life.

I spent the next half-hour or so chatting to Glenn. The conversation was comfortable – no awkward moments – and he wasn't trying to impress me with cheesy one-liners. We sparked; the chemistry was amazing and he made me laugh with his sparkly personality, which seemed to light up the room. When I asked him what he did for a living, he said, "I play Xbox – earn a fortune. I'm really climbing up the Xbox career ladder."

"Shut up," I teased. "What do you really do?"

"It's boring, really – I sell corporate gym memberships ... and play rugby. I'm captain for Hove."

When we parted company, we exchanged phone numbers. "I'll call you," he said.

I was asleep when he called at 2am the following morning, drunk and hyper. "Mandy, I won, I won," he shrieked down the phone.

"Who is this?" I whispered.

"Glenn ... I won a thousand pounds. I went to the casino with my mates after I met you and won a thousand pounds on roulette. I won a thousand pounds ... at the casino. You must be my lucky charm."

"I'm really happy for you," I said, smothering a yawn. "Call me in the morning. I'm really tired."

"What time?"

"About ten or eleven."

"I won a thousand pounds." I could hear him still celebrating with his friends as the phone clicked into silence.

"Goodnight, Glenn."

At 10am, on the dot, he called again. I recognised his number from the night before and answered it. "You must have a stinking hangover."

"I woke up to find a washing machine in my bedroom – haven't got a clue how it got there," he said.

"Maybe you bought it on the way home with your winnings?"

"So," he said, changing the subject. "Will you let me take you out? I need to spend some of this money I've won."

"Okay," I said casually.

April 7, 2008. The date is still engraved in my mind. It was a Monday: the day I went on my first official date with Glenn. He took me to Brighton for the day, where we had lunch in Yo! Sushi and ambled through the cobbled lanes. We bought lots of little trinkets and tried on silly hats displayed on stalls outside hippy shops. In the late afternoon, as we strolled along the pier, Glenn kissed me for the first time. I was leaning against the railing at the end of the pier, inhaling the fresh sea air infused with the sugary scents of popcorn and candy floss, enfolded in Glenn's arms, my head resting back against his chest. We stood there for a moment, gazing at the sun-glazed sea. It was a clear day, but there was a crisp nip in the air. "I love this view," I said. "It's funny – I've travelled the world and seen some spectacular beaches, but I absolutely adore Brighton."

"It's stunning," agreed Glenn, kissing the crown of my head. I was wearing a cashmere cap, but I could feel the heat of his mouth through the wool. I turned to face him, tilting my head, and our lips connected. It was a gentle, warm kiss that tasted like the banana and chocolate crepe we'd just shared.

From that day onwards, Glenn and I were inseparable. There was a real chemistry between us, both physically and mentally. He was super intelligent – he beat me at Trivial Pursuit, which I wasn't too chuffed about – and we shared the same interests. We didn't stop talking: some nights we'd chat into the early hours, curled up on Glenn's sofa, or mine. We'd discuss politics, the universe and, most importantly, our future together. For the first time in years, I felt content and secure.

I waited eight weeks before I slept with Glenn. But when it happened, it was the most wonderful feeling in the world. It was tender and spiritual – I felt so close to him, so loved.

A month later, I moved into his flat in Brighton and rented my house out to Virgin colleagues. Finally, I was in a relationship that was working. Glenn was my lover and friend, and I missed him terribly when I was away on trips. The novelty of travelling the world and partying twenty-four seven was beginning to wane. As my love for Glenn grew deeper and stronger, I also started to think about my own mortality, which I had never done before.

In July 2009 Virgin Atlantic announced plans to cull 600 jobs amid reduced winter services. The airline's chief executive, Steve Ridgway, warned the industry was "as bleak as ever" but vowed to keep job losses to a minimum. As a manager I was offered voluntary redundancy, which after much consideration, I accepted. It wasn't an easy decision to make; I'd had a fantastic career and met some amazing friends along the way – friends who had become my family. But my new life belonged here, in England, with the love of my life, Glenn. It was time for me to hang up that red skirt and move on.

My final trip as a Virgin trolley dolly was to New York – the same dream city where my crazy career began. The outbound flight was a nightmare; I'd caught a nasty stomach bug and spent most of time running to the toilet. The good news, though, was that Laura was on this trip, and we planned to relive all the fun we'd had when we'd first met in New York ten years earlier – visit all the old haunts and reminisce over the good old days.

This time we were staying at the Helmsley Hotel on East Forty-Second Street. "Right," Laura said as we picked up our room cards, "Three S's and I'll meet you in the lobby in thirty."

"I reckon – seeing as this is my last trip – we should share a room," I suggested. "Have a proper girly weekend."

"Sounds good to me," Laura giggled. Standing there in the lobby, Laura looked no different to ten years ago: she still had the same impish grin and flawless skin, and there wasn't one wrinkle visible around those vivid green eyes that had captivated me from the moment we met. "I can't believe this is the last time we'll ever do this," I sighed, surveying the chaos in the lobby. It was the usual scene: cases strewn across the floor, lots of excitable chatter and room numbers being exchanged.

"Ah, for fuck's sake, don't you start getting all sentimental on me – we're here to have fun, remember," Laura said, nudging me in the ribs. "Now let's get upstairs and crack open the vodka."

It was the best New York trip ever. On our first evening, we returned to the W Bar with the rest of the crew and reminisced over all the outrageous stories from bygone years. Laura recounted the tale of when we'd skinny dipped in Barbados with "flowers shoved up our arses", and our escapade in New York in the cop car, among a string of embarrassing stories and details of my chequered love life. "Do you remember that bloke who asked you to dress up as a Nazi officer?" she blurted out after her fifth Manhattan. "And what about that sexy pilot you shagged all over the world – God, he was hot. And what about that ..."

"Enough," I interrupted. "That was years ago. You have to kiss a few frogs before you meet your prince."

It was just like old times.

I took lots of photographs on that trip. Laura and I spent our second day wandering the streets of New York as though we were tourists visiting for the first time. She took photos of me at the LOVE sculpture on Sixth Avenue, adopting a variety of poses: peering through the gap between the V and the E, kissing the E and leaning against the side of the V, my body angled forwards as if I was about to fall. We went to Central Park, the Empire State Building, Fifth Avenue, and, of course, our beauty mecca, Sephora ... where I spent a fortune. I was chucking everything into my basket – moisturisers, every Bare Minerals product I could lay my hands on (Bare Minerals is my must-have brand), perfume, nail varnishes and face packs. "Bloody hell, Mands, have you got enough there?" Laura said. "You'll need to take out a mortgage to buy that lot."

"But what if I never come here again?" I said, my eyes falling on a product called Glam Glow.

"Don't be soft – you'll be back – you can come on trips with me. Or I can always bring shit back for you. Some of us still have to work."

I hugged her. "Okay, I'll put back the Marc Jacobs perfume and a couple of nail varnishes ... but the Bare Minerals is staying."

Leaving New York was sad. It had always felt like a second home to me, and I'd miss its energetic charm and comforting smells: the waft of freshly brewed coffee and cinnamon bagels from the delis; the smell of warm pretzels in Central Park and honey-coated peanuts along Fifth Avenue; the meaty and herby scents of Chinatown. But as I boarded the crew bus outside the Helmsley Hotel for the final time, I realised it was the people I'd shared all my happy moments in New York with that I'd miss the most: the crew. I cried when I hugged them all goodbye at Heathrow. Glenn had come to meet me, so there was no need to catch the crew bus back to Gatwick. Some of the crew I'd only just met on this last trip, but to me, they were still family. My chosen family.

The following week I returned my uniform: it was strange walking into the tailoress's room again. Seeing a girl twirling in front of the mirror as the tailoress pinned the hem of her skirt, I was transported back to the day of my fitting. I remembered the giddy excitement I'd felt when I emerged from the changing room. I walked over to the tailoress. "Hi," I said, "I'm here to return my uniform."

"Just hang it on that rail," she mumbled, speaking through pin-clenched lips.

It was as though I didn't belong in her world anymore. She didn't even look at my uniform – I could have kept it and she wouldn't have known any different. I hung my uniform on the rail and turned towards the girl. She was young, early twenties, with blonde hair and a freckled face. "You look fantastic," I said. "It really suits you."

She smiled. "Thanks, I'm so excited – I never thought I'd make it through the course ... then I thought I was going to lose my job, because I was one of the last people recruited before the redundancies. I've lost so much weight with all the stress that I need a refit."

"Ah, the good old Ab Initio diet," I said. "I remember being on that ten years ago."

She laughed and straightened her neck scarf. "What's it been like to be a Virgin hostie?"

I had to think for a moment – it wasn't something I could sum up in one sentence. "I can't begin to describe it," I said. "But trust me, there're lots of fun times ahead for you. Just remember to smile ... and enjoy." I turned and walked out of the room with a broad smile on my face – the smile that had been the tool of my trade for so long.

I was still enjoying the perks of the job after I left Virgin Atlantic. I had some free staff flights to use up, so I took Glenn to New York for his birthday, and for our eighteen-month anniversary, we jetted out to Grenada in the Caribbean. On our second night there, as we took a romantic stroll along the beach beneath a canopy of stars, something amazing happened.

Glenn had been acting strange all evening. I thought maybe the heat was getting to him. He was nervy and sweating a lot, and he barely ate any of his dinner. We were drinking cocktails on the hotel's terrace bar overlooking St George's beach, listening to a live Caribbean steel band play Bob Marley tunes, when he suggested going for a walk.

"Let me finish my Sex on the Beach first," I said, "I've still got half a glass here."

"I'll get you another one when we get back," he said, taking the glass from my hand and hurrying me out of my seat. "Come on – the stars are out, it'll be romantic."

The beach was deserted and calm. I slipped off my shoes and took Glenn's hand. I loved the way my entire hand disappeared inside his when he held it. The sand was still warm. "Fancy a paddle?" I said, veering us towards the sea playfully.

"No, let's sit over here for a while and watch the stars," said Glenn, leading me away from the water into a perfumed mini forest of palm and bougainvillea trees.

After a few leisurely steps, Glenn let go of my hand and crouched down in the sand. I thought maybe he'd dropped something, so I crouched down too, searching the dark ground.

"What's up, have you lost something?" I said, raking my fingers through the sand. He looked at me, moonlight sculpting his face. "I'm fine. Stand up, Mandy."

"What are you doing?" I said, rising to my feet. I was confused.

Then he knelt in the sand (on one knee) and reached for my left hand. His voice was jagged, his fingers damp with sweat. I looked into his eyes; he seemed about to cry. "Mandy," he said.

"Yeah?" I was still slightly puzzled.

Glenn cleared his throat. "Mandy, you're the girl of my dreams. Will you make me the happiest man in the world and marry me?"

I burst into tears. "Yes ... yes, of course I'll marry you."

"It's a good job I brought this, then," Glenn said, producing a diamond ring, which he'd kept hidden in his shoe. He slipped the ring onto my third finger – It was beautiful, an oval one-carat diamond set on a platinum band.

"It's stunning," I said, tears streaming down my face. "I would have chosen the same one myself."

I fell to my knees and threw my arms around him, smothering his face with kisses and tears. In the distance I could hear the mellow beats of Bob Marley's "Three Little Birds" reverberating from the steel drums, and I smiled, knowing I didn't need to worry about a thing anymore, either.

I sat back on my heels, folded Glenn's hands in mine and whispered: "Thank you."

Epilogue

There are times when I look back at my career and wonder: did all that really happen to me? At the time everything flashed past me in a blur: the parties, relationships, juggling life on the ground with life in the air, dotting from country to country. It was a crazy existence, but I wouldn't change a single day.

Being an air hostess isn't a job for just anyone; it takes stamina, commitment, patience and a level-headed attitude to cope with the pressures we dollies are up against on a daily basis. In addition to serving tea and coffee, you're also expected to be a first-rate nurse, therapist, policewoman and negotiator – and to smile throughout every trauma and mishap.

Not every day was a party for me; there were some dark times too. The events of 9/11 shook the airline industry to its very core, both economically and emotionally. Some people lost their jobs; others left, too fearful to fly again; and, of course, we felt for the crew who had lost their lives doing the same job we did day in, day out. Those were tough times.

However, I like to think that the good times far outweighed the bad. The comradeship among cabin crew is like nothing I've experienced in any other workplace. Your colleagues really do become your family when you're flying, and I've made some amazing friends for life. I still meet up regularly with the girls – some of whom are still flying – and whenever we get together, it's as though no time has passed. We meet for cocktails and talk about the good old days – reliving the stories, remembering the laughs we had, the mischief we got up to and the beautiful countries we explored. They keep me up to date with all the latest Galley FM gossip so, in a way, it's as though I never left Virgin Atlantic.

Laura, Suzy and Felicity are still flying, still returning from trips with more hilarious tales – and Sephora products for me. Those girls have kept me in Bare Minerals cosmetics for the last four years. They're all in happy relationships now. Laura recently moved in with her long-term boyfriend, an architect called Alan. Suzy has just got engaged to her man, Phil. He bought her an emerald-cut sapphire engagement ring, flanked by two solitaires. It's similar to the engagement ring Chandler gave to Monica in *Friends*. Of course, I helped him choose it. Suzy was over the moon.

Felicity met an air-traffic controller, Liam, and they got hitched in August 2013. She's thoroughly enjoying married life ... although she's still quite partial to a spot of skinny dipping down-route. She even tried to get me in the sea during my hens weekend in Brighton.

In comparison to my flying days, I live pretty quietly now. Although, with Glenn being a male version of me, and a rugby captain, our social life is still a little crazy and very busy at weekends.

I married Glenn in June 2010 at our village church in Poynings, just north of Brighton, and our reception was held in a marquee in the grounds of a seventeenth-century manor house: Great Ote Hall, in East Sussex. Laura, Felicity and Suzy were bridesmaids and the majority of my guests were Virgin cabin crew. It was the perfect dream wedding. A year later our daughter was born. She's just adorable but, like anything worth having, bloody hard work at times.

There are days when I miss flying, when I long to be back in the galley, hearing all the gossip, or down-route partying. But then I look at my little family and I realise I've made the right choice. Finally, I'm home.